CUSHING'S COUP

CUSHING'S COUP

*The True Story of How
Lt. Col. James M. Cushing
and His Filipino Guerrillas
Captured Japan's* Plan Z
*and Changed the Course
of the Pacific War*

DIRK JAN BARREVELD

CASEMATE
Philadelphia & Oxford

Published in the United States of America and Great Britain in 2015 by
CASEMATE PUBLISHERS
908 Darby Road, Havertown, PA 19083
and
10 Hythe Bridge Street, Oxford, OX1 2EW

ISBN 978-1-61200-307-8
Digital Edition: ISBN 978-1-61200-308-5

Cataloging-in-publication data is available from the Library of Congress and
the British Library.

10 9 8 7 6 5 4 3 2 1

Printed and bound in the United States of America.

For a complete list of Casemate titles please contact:

CASEMATE PUBLISHERS (US)
Telephone (610) 853-9131, Fax (610) 853-9146
E-mail: casemate@casematepublishing.com

CASEMATE PUBLISHERS (UK)
Telephone (01865) 241249, Fax (01865) 794449
E-mail: casemate-uk@casematepublishing.co.uk

CONTENTS

PREFACE

WORLD WAR II ended 70 years ago, after resulting in somewhere between 50 and 70 million fatalities. Many millions more people were displaced or lost friends and relatives. Certainly, in hindsight, it is unimaginable what the world did to itself. Thousands and thousands of books have been written about the war, the horrors, the successes and failures, and of course about the heroes. Notwithstanding the vast literature there are still important stories that have never been told. The story of Lt. Colonel James M. Cushing is one of those untold sagas. It is a story about a simple American mining engineer on the Philippine Island of Cebu during World War II after the Japanese Empire had ridden roughshod across the Pacific.

James Cushing, Jim to his friends, became a feared and highly successful guerrilla leader on his island. He and his guerrillas managed to stand up for more than four years against an overwhelming force of 10,000 Japanese soldiers and managed to capture not only the Chief of Staff of the Imperial Japanese Navy, but also the complete 1944 Naval Battle Strategy of Japan (the so called "Plan Z"). Knowledge gained from these plans was subsequently instrumental in the Allied victory in the Battle of the Philippine Sea (June 1944) and the Battle of Leyte Gulf (October 1944). Because of Jim Cushing's actions, General Douglas MacArthur managed to shorten the war in the Pacific by at least two months, thus saving the lives of thousands of Allied soldiers and sailors as well as civilians on both sides. Jim's forces were confirmed to have killed 10,400 Japanese soldiers during their four and a half year struggle.

On the special orders of General MacArthur, the capture of Admiral

Fukudome, Chief Staff of the Japanese Imperial Navy, and Japan's Naval Battle Strategy were kept under extreme secrecy. That is why the story was never told.

In the midst of all the death and destruction, the misery and sorrow, of World War II, Colonel James M. Cushing was a shining example of what a human being under extreme circumstances could do and achieve. And not only achieve, but be able to survive all the odds that were against him. He could have told his story after the war, like so many war heroes did. However, that was not the way James Cushing was. He shrugged his shoulders, took a beer, and went on with his life. The war was over, that was it.

General Douglas McArthur calls Cushing's capture of Admiral Shigeru Fukudome in his auto-biography *Reminiscences*: "one of the most dramatic incidents of the war." Actually MacArthur pays more attention in his book to Colonel James Cushing than to all the other Filipino guerrilla commanders together.[1]

Of course Cushing's activities were not completely forgotten. In the 1970s Col. Manuel F. Segura, a former World War II guerillero himself, and a comrade in arms of Cushing, paid attention to his deeds in several of his books. Steven Trent Smith, in his *The Rescue*, also mentions Cushing. But never, until now, has Cushing taken his place as the central figure in the story. It is, in my view, high time to put Col. James M. Cushing full in the floodlights. It is certainly not exaggerated to nominate Col. James M. Cushing as one of the greatestest heroes of World War II in the Pacific.

ACKNOWLEDGMENTS

THERE ARE VERY few eyewitnesses left from the guerrilla movement on Cebu Island from World War II. By now they are all in their nineties, and most no longer have a clear memory of what happened in those days. There was one exception: Retired Philippine Colonel Manuel F. Segura. Segura, born in 1919, became one of the cornerstones of the Cebu guerrilla movement. His memory, as I found out, was still crystal clear. Unfortunately he passed away in November 2013 at the age of 94. I had no other choice than to base this book mainly on the numerous written sources that can be found in the archives of many libraries and archives worldwide. I am deeply indebted to the many librarians who helped me in selecting the material.

Dirk J. Barreveld
Manila, February 2015

PART ONE

THE PACIFIC ON FIRE

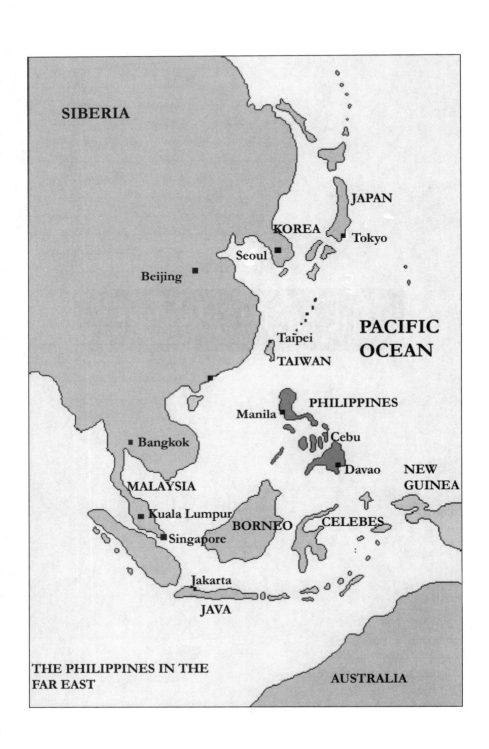

SIBERIA

JAPAN

KOREA
Seoul ■   ■ Tokyo

Beijing ■

Taipei
TAIWAN

PACIFIC
OCEAN

PHILIPPINES
Manila ■

■ Bangkok   Cebu

Davao ■   NEW
GUINEA

MALAYSIA

■ Kuala Lumpur
Singapore ■   BORNEO   CELEBES

Jakarta ■

JAVA

THE PHILIPPINES IN THE
FAR EAST   AUSTRALIA

PROLOGUE: THE ORIGINS OF THE SECOND WORLD WAR

WARS DO NOT erupt suddenly like volcanoes. They are usually the result of a long process of frustration, deliberate or coincidental misunderstanding, and different interpretation of certain facts or events. People and politicians often do not like to listen to arguments which they do not like. Often political decisions are not based on logical thinking, but on fear or misinterpretation of possibilities. Furthermore, winners often cannot resist humiliating losers. Then there is the media that plays its own role. World War II was a war between Germany, Italy and Japan on one side, against the rest of the world.

The origin of Germany's move to war lay in its late unification in the 19th century, which caused it to largely miss the great era of colonial expansion. The country's latent dynamism burst into the Great War in Europe, which Germany narrowly lost, and which resulted in the treaties of Versailles and Saint Germain, both concluded in 1919. The peace treaties were, first and foremost, designed to humiliate the supposed instigator of the conflict. Germany lost not only a considerable part of its territory, but also had to pay enormous amounts of reparations. It was also limited in having an army, navy and air force. The Germans felt they had been degraded to a second-class state, which for the former Holy Roman Empire was a disgrace. The Treaty of Versailles was signed in a railway car in the Compiègne Forest near Paris.

From the very beginning it was clear that Germany could not pay the reparations, and combined with the economic depression of the late 1920s and 1930s, the country became a showcase of poverty and misery. The situation gave rise to Adolf Hitler, who resurrected German strength, and promptly launched a reprise of the Great War in order to re-establish German power once and for all. The mindset of the Germans can easily be judged on the fact that when France surrendered in 1940 Hitler demanded that the surrender had to be signed in the same place and in the same railway car as the Treaty of Versailles was signed in 1919.

With Japan it was not much different. Japan was isolated for more than 300 years from the rest of the world, and the only Western country allowed to trade with it was the Netherlands. The opening up of Japan by US Commodore Perry, over the barrel of a gun, in 1854 was felt by most Japanese as a huge loss of face. Asians have extremely long memories. This loss of face had to be corrected one time. Gradually Japan modernized, but it never became a democratic nation such as Europe or the USA. In its build-up to a modern industrialized country it became more and more hindered by the lack of raw materials. In 1910 it annexed Korea. In 1931 it took Manchuria. In 1937 it invaded China. In these times it started to promote the *Greater Asian Co-Prosperity Sphere* and an "Asia for Asians" philosophy in a clear attempt to wrestle European and American colonies from their colonial masters. Japanese policies were threatened by trade restrictions by the USA, the Netherlands, France and Britain. It created the feeling of being humiliated and ended with the attack on Pearl Harbor on 7 December, 1941.

Following the attack on Pearl Harbor, the Japanese launched offensives against Allies in South East Asia, with simultaneous attacks on Hong Kong, British Malaya, the Dutch East Indies and the Philippines. Hong Kong surrendered to the Japanese on 25 December 1941. Malaya followed soon. The Allied forces were forced to retreat to Singapore. Lack of proper equipment made holding Singapore impossible. The city surrendered to the Japanese on 15 February 1942. The Japanese then sized the key oil production zones of Borneo, Central Java, Malang, Cepu, Sumatra and Dutch New Guinea of the late Dutch East Indies. The Japanese then consolidated their lines of supply through capturing key islands of the Pacific, including Guadalcanal.

The Philippines had nothing to do with the quarrel between the USA and its Allies and Japan. The country was pulled into this war because it was a colony of the USA. The Filipinos in general had no real appetite for the Japanese Greater Asian Co-Prosperity Sphere and the "Asia for Asians" idea but it was forced upon them.

Once the war started General Douglas MacArthur, commander of USAFFE, the Philippine-American Army, decided to pull back to the Bataan

Pensinsula. His USAFFE "under construction" was simply not ready for a war on a massive scale.

The fight for Bataan proved for the Japanese more difficult than was expected. In April 1942 Bataan finally fell, followed in May by the surrender of the island fortress of Corregidor. The island of Cebu was occupied in April 1942. Soon everywhere in the country guerrilla forces were created to fight the ruthless Japanese invaders.

CHAPTER 1

THE OTSU INCIDENT

T HE NIGHT OF 31 March / 1 April 1944 appeared beautiful and serene. The sky was clear and as long as the moon was shining you could see miles away over Bohol Strait. Around 0130 the moon went under and it became much darker. Around two o'clock in the morning on 1 April 1944, Ricardo Bolo, a lieutenant of Barrio Balud, municipality of San Fernando, on the Philippine Island of Cebu woke up because of the sound of a very low flying airplane. Ricardo secretly worked for the guerrilla movement in the mountains. His main job was the collection and procurement of food for the guerrillas. But why was a plane flying so low? There must be more to it. He went quickly outside his house and looked in the direction of the sound of the engines. At first he saw nothing, and suddenly the engine sound stopped. Then he saw far in the distance, in the direction of Bohol, some kind of flash and a golden glow over the horizon. It was not the moon; it must have been the plane. It crossed his mind that it had probably crashed. He decided to inform the guerrillas as soon as the sun was up.[1]

About a kilometer away, Volunteer Guard (VG) Commander Cornelio "Nene" Manugas in Barrio Sangat, San Fernando, also heard the sound of airplane engines. He also went outside and was just in time to see a giant seaplane plunge into the sea and explode. It was followed by smaller explosions and flashes of orange light. Meanwhile Bolo, accompanied by his younger brother Edilberto, and a neighbor named Valeriano Paradero decided to go out to sea and investigate. Manugas and some of his friends also got into their small *barotos* (outrigger canoes) and paddled to the crash site. There was no wind; the sea was flat like a mirror.

The exact site was off the coast of Barrio Sangat, San Fernando between

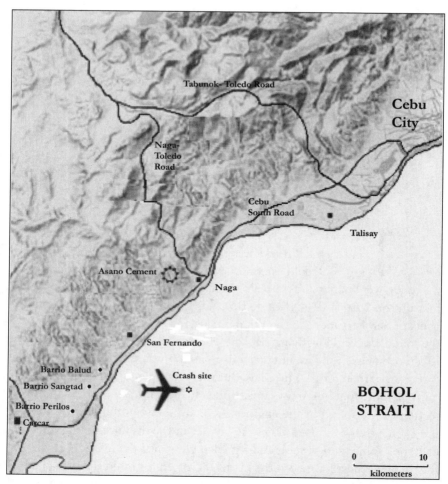

THE CRASH SITE

Sitio Magtalisay of Barrio Balud, San Fernando and Sitio Bas of Barrio Per-
ilos, Carcar, some 33 kilometers south of Cebu City. Approximately three
kilometers meters from the shore line they encountered a group of ten swimming men. They were towing a body and chanting in a strange language "*hon
cha, hon cha, hon cha.*" Manugas believed that this was a count to coordinate
their swimming strokes for more power and speed in towing their uncon-
scious companion. As Bolo and his companions approached the swimmers
they counted a dozen men, they called for help.[2]

VG Feliciano Hermosa, a fisherman under Manugas, was watching on the beach at Barrio Sangat when he spotted in the upcoming sun two persons on the reef, about one-third of a kilometer from the shore. It was low tide but there were places where the water was deep. He took out his baroto and paddled to the reef. Upon nearing the two men he recognized them to be the feared and hated Japanese. He reacted in a very strange way. In his fear for the Japanese he jumped out of his canoe, pushed it towards the two Japanese and swam in a hurry as fast as he could back to the beach. The two Japanese managed to reach in the semi-darkness the beach in Barrio Sangat. From there they made it to the *"Malacañang Palace"* of Vicente Rabor, the puppet Mayor of San Fernando, who took them to the nearby Japanese garrison at Tina-an, Naga. In this way the Japanese were warned at a very early stage that one of their planes had crashed nearby. And not only that, they knew that a very important Japanese admiral, with vital secret war plans, was on board.

By seven o'clock the ten were pulled out of the sea. Behind the group of ten the Filipino fishermen had spotted another swimmer. He was much older than the ten and apparently he was seriously wounded but initially he refused to be picked up. He continued swimming toward shore, two or three canoes came out to rescue him, but he still hesitated because he was not sure whether they were friends or enemies. Near the limit of his physical strength, he finally decided to take a chance and be rescued. Upon reaching shore, he was quickly seized by five or six Filipinos.[3] He feared, or actually hoped, that he would be killed quickly, it would save him from the embarrassment being a prisoner of war. But once his captors realized the plane had not come to attack the island or the natives, they offered medical treatment. At this point, the older man realized that he was not only a prisoner of war, but he was first flag-rank officer in Japanese history who had allowed himself to be captured by an enemy. This was an unimaginable loss of face for him, and for the entire Japanese Imperial Navy.

Japanese soldiers never surrender and never were to be taken prisoner. This was against all rules and customs. It was his duty to commit *seppuku* or *harakiri*, the ritual suicide by disembowelment. But how could he do that here as a prisoner? He had no *tanto*, or *wakizashi*, the short sword to plunge into his abdomen. He had no *kaishakunin*, or helper to perform *kaishaku*, the decapitation that followed the disembowelment.[4] And for sure these Filipinos, once they found out who he was, would guard him day and night as a precious object. It bothered him much that he had to forsake his duty.

If he ever survived this ordeal he would have to appear before the Naval

Board of Inquiry in Tokyo to defend himself on the issue why he did not commit seppuku. Such an appearance before the Board for an issue such as this could be the most shameful and dishonoring thing that could happen to a Japanese officer, and the shame would extend far beyond him. His family, his relatives, would all have to suffer from his misfortune.[5]

In the meantime a large crowd of Filipinos had gathered on the beach. The news about the plane crash and the survivors had quickly spread. A total of eleven survivors were recovered by Filipinos at the Magtalisay beach. Not all went smoothly. One of the Japanese tried to resist capture, which forced the Filipinos to bind the wrists of all the survivors. Then there was the dead body the Japanese had dragged along for hours. It was lying on the beach and was badly burned. The Japanese had laid out the body ceremoniously on the beach and they kept repeating the word "Koga." This led the Filipinos to think about the identity of the dead man. Was Koga the name of this person? Was he the most senior officer in the group? Was there an admiral in the group? Some of the more educated Volunteer Guards had heard about an Admiral Koga.

Since it was already light, the Filipinos and their captives moved rapidly inland. The Japanese prisoners wanted to carry the dead man along but Lieutenant Bolo and the VG's did not allow them to do so. It would delay the withdrawal into the mountains and that carried the risk that the Japanese army might catch up with them. They left the body on the beach. The unburied corpse was soon eaten by dogs and the bones were recovered two weeks later by Japanese soldiers.

While the prisoners were being walked inland, one of them attacked Roque Bacla-an, one of the Filipino guards. This was the same prisoner who had tried to resist capture at the beach. The Filipino, who had been mercilessly maltreated days before by other Japanese soldiers, became so angry that he beat the Japanese to death.

Around ten o' clock in the morning the Filipinos saw a Japanese search plane apparently looking for them. It kept on circling over the greater San Fernando area. The two Japanese who had paddled off had made their way to the Japanese army garrison at a nearby town and told officials of the crash and survivors.

The Volunteer Guards and their prisoners quickly hid in the brush. Shortly Teniente Bolo turned the prisoners over to Teopisto Tangub, the Volunteer Guard Commander of Barrio Sangat. He convinced the apparent leader of the prisoners to change clothes with him. The Japanese had no problem with that and took off his uniform. The Japanese clothes, partly made of silk, fit Tangub perfectly. All the other prisoners changed their clothes with those of the guerrillas. In civilian clothes the prisoners were not so easy to single out and Tangub thought it would reduce the risk of escape. He let his brother Gregorio carry the wounded leader on his back because the leg-wounds of the man made walking practically impossible.[6,7]

The Japanese launched a massive air and land search for the crashed plane and survivors as well as "important documents" that may have drifted ashore. Day and night the Japanese conducted search operations. Many people were picked up, beaten and tortured in the hope of finding news of the prisoners. There was a report that an infant was impaled with a bayonet and held aloft in front of its terrified parents. The Kempeitai, or Japanese military police, took more civilians to the Sangad Elementary School and the Sangad Chapel for interrogation. The Japanese also offered incentives for those who would volunteer information. A young girl, who had given the survivors bananas and coconuts when they passed through Sangat, was rewarded with rice for her kindness. Aside from the survivors, the Japanese were also demanding the whereabouts of certain documents which were in the crashed plane. The Kempeitai occupied the house of a civilian named Onyong Abendan and killed his wife on the suspicion that she had some knowledge about the papers.[8,9]

In the meantime the guerrillas and their prisoners moved slowly over the steep mountains and deep valleys of Cebu's interior in the direction of their headquarters in Tabunan. They were tremendously hindered by the condition of the wounded Japanese leader. He had to be carried all the way. The way the other Japanese treated this leader made them think they might have caught a very important person. They carefully avoided main roads. Their progress was very slow. Tired and hungry, the prisoners ate what the resistance people did, often no more than bananas, coconuts and relish.

In Barrio Mac-arco, Tangub and his group were joined by more guerrillas under Captain Jose Ponce. By this time the guerrillas had learned something about their prisoners. They tried to scare them by pointing a revolver at them; however, this did not draw any reaction. But when Cayetano "Kaing" Enad drew his *pinoti*, a sword-like fighting bolo with a 21-inch razor sharp blade, the Japanese drew back in fear. When a pinoti was pointed threateningly at their leader, they cried and bowed low.

Some of the Japanese spoke a little English; one man, a slightly built

Japanese officer, spoke it well. He continuously stressed that he wanted to be brought to Cebu City. They found a picture of Emperor Hirohito in his pocket.

After a short break the party pressed on. They made a huge detour to avoid contact with Japanese patrols. At nightfall they arrived in Binabag, Pinamungajan, a few kilometers east of the west coast of Cebu Island, in the camp of Captain Marcelino Eridiano. The next morning, 3 April 1944, they continued their journey. In the afternoon they arrived at the Command Post of Company "A," 87th Infantry at Calapayan.[10] They did not stay long because of a Japanese attack on the headquarters. They finally crossed the Talisay-Toledo road and reached the guerrilla aid station at Caloctogan, Sabon, where the wounded were treated by Major Ramon Torralba. Some of the Japanese prisoners were in bad shape, the leader being especially weak with festering wounds and a fever of about 104°F. From here on the road to the guerrilla headquarters in Tabunan became even worse. For a few months the guerrillas had been back in Tabunan and had rebuilt the place, after it was taken and ransacked in March 1943 by the Japanese.[11]

News about an approaching column of Japanese prisoners had already filtered through to Tabunan. There were also reports indicating that a massive seven-pronged Japanese drive into the interior was taking place. The Japanese units were identified as belonging to the *Ohnisi Butai*, a highly trained and well-equipped Japanese regiment named after its commander, Col. Seiiti Ohnisi. Most of its members were veterans of the campaigns in Manchuria. The Ohnisi Butai and other units attacked simultaneously and overran all guerrilla defenses, razed villages to the ground and tortured and killed numerous civilians. At the same time Japanese planes dropped leaflets demanding the return of the Japanese prisoners and documents. The Japanese conditionally released a Filipino prisoner to deliver a letter, signed by the Japanese Island Commander, to Lieutenant Colonel James M. Cushing, the overall commander of the *Cebu Area Command*, Cebu's guerrilla organization, ordering him to surrender the prisoners immediately.[12, 13]

The pressure on Jim Cushing and his men was mounting. Jim had not seen the prisoners yet; actually they had not even arrived in his camp. The way the Japanese acted, with such ruthless violence, was for Jim the clear proof that something out of the ordinary was going on. Either the prisoners or the documents, or maybe both, must be of extreme importance to the Japanese, he thought.[14]

On 8 April, 1944 it was clear to Jim that it was time to inform head-quarters in Australia what was going on. The following coded radio message was sent to SWPA (Headquarters, Southwest Pacific Area) in Australia:

SECRET
TO: GENERAL MACARTHUR
FROM: CUSHING
NR 7:8 APRIL
WE HAVE 10 JAPANESE PRISONERS NOW EN ROUTE TO OUR
HEADQUARTERS PLEASE ADVISE ACTION TO BE TAKEN.
CONSTANT ENEMY PRESSURE MAKE THIS SITUATION VERY
PRECARIOUS. FURTHER INFORMATION FROM PRISONERS
WILL FOLLOW.
SECRET[15]

This message reached General MacArthur's staff on 9 April. Reaction in Australia was subdued when the dispatch was delivered. Ten prisoners, probably only privates and corporals, was no big deal. This happened all the time. Colonel Courtney Whitney, who knew Jim Cushing personally very well, clearly had a different view when he received Jim's message NR 7. He wrote a memo for the high command:

Any of our other guerrilla leaders would have decided this problem with 10 bullets without reference to this Headquarters. CUSHING has, however, before demonstrated a more disciplined regard for the will of higher authority. I believe you will find in CUSHING an able but still subordinate fighter and leader in whom you can fully depend to discharge his mission. At the crucial time this is what you will require.

In action on the question raised I believe it should be assumed that the message of the C-in-C may reach the hands of the enemy and precautions in its phraseology taken accordingly.[16]

Whitney then sent a message back to Cebu, telling the guerrilla com-mander that the "disposition of prisoners must be in accord with our rules of land warfare, if their removal to the area of another command in better posi-tion to secure the prisoners is possible I will issue the necessary instruction to the commander thereof to facilitate such action." He also offered to facilitate the removal of the captives to another island if necessary.[17]

It was not the answer Jim had expected and hoped for. Actually it did not help him at all. In practice Whitney no more or no less suggested that he send the prisoners to Colonel Abcede, the guerrilla commander on neighboring island of Negros, or Colonel Fertig in Mindanao. That was certainly the last thing he would do.

In the meantime Jim received reports from various resistance units all over Cebu Island about the continuous attacks from Japanese units. Two columns seemed to be on their way to Tabunan headquarters. Another column was heading for the Tupas Range, just behind the headquarters. Jim decided to move out of Tabunan and make his headquarters mobile for the time being. He initially moved to Sitio Kamungayan.

After settling down in Kamungayan and establishing the necessary communications Jim left with a small party of officers. They crossed the ravine on the east of Tupas Range to warn the staff of the Base Hospital to evacuate the area and to make arrangements for his wife Felisa, "Fritzi," who was living nearby. It was on Tupas Range, on the trail to Cantipla, after seven long and hard days that the prisoners' march had come, at least for the time being, to an end. They were locked up in a palm-thatched building which normally housed the commandos. Guards took position outside the hut.

When, a little later, Jim and his staff entered the hut the captured Japanese immediately realized that these were guerrilla commanders. They automatically lined up according to rank, with the highest-ranking officers on the left. Two of the prisoners were so badly wounded they could not stand.

The leader of the group was a fairly tall, rather fat man; he had a somewhat Buddha-like appearance. The way he behaved made him different from the other Japanese. The second in command, who identified himself as Commander Yamamoto, spoke reasonable English and was the one who did the talking in the beginning. Once Jim came into the room things changed. He hated Japanese. He knew what they were doing to the civilian population and the horrible things they were doing in the Cebu Normal School, headquarters of the dreaded Kempeitai. Notwithstanding his hatred he kept cool and polite. Jim talked to the leader and the Japanese answered directly, commander to commander, in fluent English. The Japanese identified himself as General Twani Furomei, Commander of Land and Sea Forces of Macassar. For the guerrillas it was a mystery, since Macassar was an Indonesian city on the southern tip of the island of Celebes that was very far from there.[18] Also the names and ranks of the other Japanese prisoners were collected. Jim sent the following radio message in code to General MacArthur:

TO: GENERAL MACARTHUR
FROM: CUSHING
NR 8: 9TH APRIL
REFERENCE TEN JAP PRISONERS—THEY CAME FROM FOUR MOTORED PLANE WHICH CRASHED OFF SAN FERNANDO AT TWO O'CLOCK IN THE MORNING THIS 1ST APRIL THEIR NAMES:
    GENERAL TWANI FUROMEI, COMMANDING OFFICER OF LAND AND SEA FORCES IN MACASSAR
    YOJI YAMAMOTO, MARINE OFFICER BOUND FOR MACASSAR
    YASUKICHI YAMAGATA
    MATSUTARE OKANURA, AVIATOR
    USHIKISA INANISHI
    KEIS OKUJESIMI, AERONAUTICAL ENGINEER
    TOMIDO OLASOGI, OPERATOR
    TUSHIDO OKADA, ENGINEER
    NASA TUSI YUSITO, OPERATOR
    TAKASHI TANIKA, ENGINEER
THEIR PERSONL EFFECTS: A PAIR OF SHOULDER STRAPS FROM MARINE OFFICER YAMAMOTO, ONE MEMORANDUM NOTEBOOK WITH JAPANESE SCRIPTS, ONE WRAPPED PACKAGE OF JAPANESE RELICS. THREE HOSPITAL CASES, INCLUDING GENERAL FUROMEI AND MARINE OFFICER YAMAMOTO, RUMORS THAT PLANE SHOT DOWN BY ANTIAIRCRAFT FIRE FROM SUBMARINE, HOWEVER WE ARE CHECKING. DUE TO GENERAL CONDITION OF PRISONERS AND SITUATION AS IT IS, FURTHER INFO MAY BE SOMEWHAT DELAYED.[19]

Jim's message NR 8 was received by SWPA at six o'clock on the morning of 10 April. They were shocked with excitement—capturing a Japanese general was very rare. GHQ decided that it must act quickly to get the prisoners off Cebu and down to Australia. In their excitement they forgot to check if there was any general Twani Furomei in Macassar or anywhere else in the Japanese military. They did check the listening stations for any unusual Japanese message. If a general was taken prisoner he must be missing somewhere. There was nothing this time.

The navy was ordered to check if there was any ship, possibly a submarine, in the area to pick up the Japanese prisoners. The first reaction of the navy was that Cebu did not have any place on the coast that could be used for a pick-up. There were simply too many navigational hazards. The only possibility was a pick-up from neighboring Bohol. The closest submarine was the USS *Haddo*, by coincidence commanded by Lt. Commander Chester Nimitz Jr., son of the Commander in Chief, United States Pacific Fleet. The *Haddo* was on patrol near the Japanese-held Philippine island of Tawi-Tawi, only a few hundred miles away from Bohol and Cebu. Late on 11 April Admiral Ralph Waldo Christie, commander of submarines, sent Nimitz Jr. an order to head north toward the Visayas, there to stand by for a special mission.[20,21]

In the meantime Cushing's position became precarious. Kamungayan offered only partial security. Late in the afternoon of 9 April he received a runner with an urgent message. Two Japanese columns were rapidly approaching, and one was suspected to be heading for Tupas Ridge. Japanese troops always took to the high ground, and Tupas Ridge offered a commanding height opposite Kamungayan. Before closing down into radio silence, to avoid detection by the enemy, Jim sent out the following coded message:

TO: GENERAL MACARTHUR
FROM: CUSHING (VIA WAT)
NR 11: 9 APRIL
JAP CAPTIVES FROM PALAO. ENEMY AWARE THEIR PRESENCE HERE. WE ARE CATCHING HELL. WE ARE STAGING A FAKE REMOVAL FROM THIS ISLAND TO WITHDRAW PRESSURE WHILE AWAITING YOUR FURTHER ORDERS PD SOUTHEAST COAST CEBU IMPOSSIBLE NOW. WILL MAKE EVERY ATTEMPT TO HOLD THE JAPANESE GENERAL AND NEXT RANKING OFFICER. PLEASE RUSH ADVICE. NORTHEAST COAST STILL CLEAR FOR SUBMARINE.[22]

The radio operator was not able to contact Australia directly; this was not unusual, and so it went out via station WAT at Negros Oriental. Unfortunately station WAT was also not able to send it directly to SWPA, and the message went via Col. Fertig's station on Mindanao. Fertig's station, however, did not handle the message with the priority it deserved. Whether or not this delay had to do with the animosity between Fertig and Cushing was never really sorted out, but it cannot be excluded. It meant that Whitney in Australia only received the message on 12 April.

After reading the message that was already two days old, Whitney realized that the situation on Cebu was rapidly deteriorating. He worked at top speed to send a reply to Cushing's message NR 11. At two o'clock in the afternoon he wired:

SWPA NR 5
11 APRIL 1944

DESIRE IF POSSIBLE EVACUATION TO THIS HEAD QUARTERS AT EARLIEST OPPORTUNITY OF THE SENIOR PRISONERS, SELECTED IN ACCORD WITH RELATIVE IMPORTANCE. NORTHEAST COAST OF CEBU IS NAVIGATIONALLY IMPOSSIBLE. CAN YOU SEND THEM UNDER SAFE CONDUCT TO A RENDEZVOUS
SITE SOUTHERN BOHOL OR SOUTHERN NEGROS. HOW SOON COULD PARTY BE AT SITE. PARTY BELIEVED OF UTMOST IMPORTANCE BE ALERT TO USE OF ASSUMED NAMES AND RANKS UNDER WHICH SENIOR PRISONER MAY POSE AS JUNIOR. DO ALL POSSIBLE TO KEEP THEM SAFE FOR EVACUATION AND PREVENT RECAPTURE [underscoring in original].[23]

In Tokyo, the Japanese High Command was becoming greatly concerned about what had happened in the Philippines. It sent out a message to commanding officers in the Pacific stating that two aircraft, one carrying Admiral Mineichi Koga, Commander in Chief of the Japanese Imperial Navy, and the other his Chief of Staff, Admiral Shigeru Fukudome, were missing. The airplanes of the type Kawanishi H8K were on their way from the Pacific island of Palau to the City of Davao in the Southern Philippines. The Navy was investigating the situation, but the addressees were told to keep the affair top secret and minimize the number of people who knew about it. Future messages would refer to the affair as the *"Otsu incident."*[24]

Americans intercepted and decoded the message. Within hours, it was at the Far East desk of naval intelligence in Washington, D.C. However, it would take a while for the information to find its way back to Gen. Douglas MacArthur's Southwest Pacific Area (SWPA) headquarters in Brisbane, Australia. Strangely enough, the Americans never had picked up any message concerning the trip of Admiral Koga.

Meanwhile, the Japanese in the Philippines began a ruthless campaign to uncover information about the missing aircraft. Lt. Col. Seiiti Ohnisi, Japanese commander at Cebu City, went with his men on a rampage that Cebu had not seen before; he had his soldiers burn villages and ravage and kill hundreds of innocent civilians in an attempt to find the missing admiral and the documents.

But aside from the missing Japanese admirals, what of the man who now sat at the epicenter of the epicenter of the drama? Incongruously, an American civilian transformed by war into a renowned guerrilla and commander of the Filipino resistance on Cebu island?

CHAPTER 2

JOINING THE GOLD RUSH

I T WAS A sunny morning in 1936, with a cloudless sky, the sea as flat as a mirror, and visibility more than 30 miles. James M. Cushing, or Jim as his friends called him, stared in amazement at the green hills that dotted the shoreline of the Bataan Peninsula. Small columns of smoke rose up from between what he thought to be coconut palms. The tall, slim American with dark rimmed glasses was standing at the upper deck, on the port side, of the elegant SS *President Hoover* of the Dollar Line. Finally he was about to arrive in what his brothers called the Promised Country, the land of milk and honey.

Born in 1908, Jim was the youngest son of George Cushing, an Irishman who left his country in 1887 at age fifteen for Canada. Ireland, in those times, was ravaged by hunger, disease and lack of prospects so that millions emigrated to Canada and the United States. George could not make it in Canada as there was little work or opportunity. Instead he headed for the gold and silver fields of the United States and finally became a successful mining engineer in northern Mexico. Here he met Simona, a beautiful Mexican lady. They were married and settled down in El Paso, on the Mexican-American border.[1]

The couple had nine children, with George Jr. the first and James the last. It was the time of the Mexican Revolution, when more than 95% of Mexican lands were in the hands of less than 5% of the population, and General Porfirio Diaz ran the country with an iron fist. It was a matter of time before Diaz was challenged by several revolutionary generals. The most prominent was José Doroteo Arango Arámbula, better known by his pseudonym Francisco Villa, or his nickname *Pancho Villa*. As commander of the División del

Norte, he was the veritable *caudillo* of the Northern Mexican State of Chihuahua, which, given its size, mineral wealth, and proximity to the United
States, provided him with extensive resources. Villa was seen as a sort of Mexican Robin Hood. He robbed trains, confiscated lands from the rich, and distributed the wealth among the poor. As a boy of five Jimmy watched Villa
lay siege to the town of Juarez. A few years later he found himself riding on
a train, together with his brother Walter, near Chihuahua in the middle of a
battle between Mexican government troops and Pancho Villa's *banditos*. The
Mexican struggle between rich and poor left a lasting impression on the
young Jimmy.[2]

After World War I business in the El Paso area slowed down considerably. George Sr. decided on a last big step and moved to booming California.
It proved to be a good decision and the Cushing family did very well. Eldest
son George Jr. finished his studies to be a mining engineer. Attracted by the
colorful stories of life and prospects in the Philippines, America's new colony,
in 1927 George followed many of his friends to the Far East. Two years later,
when the effects of the collapse of Wall Street and the American economy
became clear, Charles Cushing followed in the footsteps of his elder brother.
In 1932 another brother, Walter, could not resist the dream of becoming rich
in the Philippines, and followed his two siblings. With the help of Charles
and Walter (George had died suddenly in 1934) Jim was the next to follow
the call of gold and adventure.

The Philippine Gold Rush
After a short war, in 1898 the Philippine Islands were ceded by Spain to the
United States for the amount of US$20 million. Although some gold was
mined in the archipelago, for instance in Bicol and in Southern Mindanao,
there was little organized prospecting going on. It didn't take long, however,
before American prospectors flooded the country. Copper, which is often
found together with gold, was sporadically mined in the Suyoc-Mankayan
area of North Luzon. It was the American John W. Haussermann, originating
from Richmond, Ohio, who became convinced of the gold riches of Benguet
in Luzon. Haussermann was a former army officer who fought in 1898 in
the Philippines during the Spanish-American war. He was convinced that
there was lots of gold there, and after being discharged from the army he
went back to the islands and in 1903 became one of the founders of the
Benguet Mining Company.[3] By the late 1920s it looked as if Haussermann

was indeed successful, but most mining experts still considered his finds a fluke. Even in the 1920s most geologists and mining engineers were convinced that the Philippines "was not a mineral country."

The world economic disaster of 1929–33 put the potential mineral riches of the Philippines in a different light. This was encouraged by articles in, among others, *Fortune* magazine in 1935 that stated for instance that "mining increases at times of depression."[4] Charles Hardy's 1936 study, "Is There Enough Gold"[5] was another shot in the same direction. The underlying issue in those times was whether or not to continue with the gold standard as the basis for currency. With the gold standard the value of money was based on a fixed amount of gold, and such a system required banks to hold large gold deposits. The metal was in demand, doubtless to say, and in 1933 the price of gold rose in a single year from $20.67 to $35.00 a troy ounce.[6]

Haussermann, whose mines at Benguet and Balatoc had been storing their gold in San Francisco, managed to arrange a settlement with the government. The firms had been told that all gold mined before 28 April 1932 must sell at the $20.67 price. Haussermann argued, successfully, that the Philippines was not part of the United States and should obtain world prices for its product. These legal issues led to a lot of publicity and a drastic escalation in the Philippines, as mining fever hit the Manila stock exchange and hundreds of companies were formed. For example, in 1932, a total of 16,566 mining claims had been filed. The next year, when the price of gold was allowed to float, 42,737 claims were filed. Haussermann's operations at Benguet, Balatoc and Ipo in the following years uncovered huge amounts of gold, and John Marsman's empire around Paracale was more than successful. In 1935 another commercial giant, Andres Soriano, incorporated Atlas Mining, a copper mine on Cebu Island that would at one point become the world's largest. Soriano also owned several gold mines at Paracale (Camarinas Norte) and on Masbate. The boom was on. By 1939, the Philippines was one of the world's leading gold producers. Among United States gold producers, the islands ranked second only to California.[7,8] And almost to a man the mining personnel at the management level were American.

In 1936 while approaching Manila Bay, Jim Cushing noticed far ahead the emergence of a rather small but elevated island. That must be Corregidor, he thought, the Gibraltar of the Far East. He had read many stories about this island fortress. If ever war with Japan broke out the enemy would be stopped here. The 12-inch, 50-ton mortars on the island were real monsters.

Looking backwards, at the wake of the beautiful liner, he noticed that the ship was slowly turning to port and they were entering Manila Bay. A little while later he saw on the starboard side a small rocky island emerging. He walked to the other side of the upper deck to get a better view.

"That's Fort Drum, you're looking at," his neighbor, apparently an American first lieutenant, pointed to the small rock in the distance.

"I have been there once," he continued. "It's constructed like a concrete battleship. You're American?"

"Yeah, but I'm half Mexican."

"Thought so, you could easily pass for a Filipino, although you're a little tall for that.

You're also in the service?"

"No, I'm in mining. Actually, I was in mining in California. Today nothing much is going on. Because of the crisis many mines closed down. I got two brothers in the Philippines who are in mining. I'd like to try the same. You never know, maybe I'll hit a pot of gold."

"I'm stationed over there, on Corregidor, an artillery officer with the 60th Coastal Artillery Regiment. My unit takes care of the antiaircraft batteries. The island is really a formidable fort; you wouldn't believe how many guns we have there. They call it the Gibraltar of the Far East. You got any relatives here?"

"As I said, I have two brothers here, they are also in mining. Actually I had three, my eldest brother died last year, we still don't know why. He died somewhere in the north, in a place by the name of Benguet or so."

"Yeah, that is the problem in this country. It is the tropics and the jungle. You never know what hits you. Whether it's malaria, dysentery, dengue fever, snakes or rabid dogs, leprosy or hepatitis, you have to be careful every step you take. We in the in the artillery are rather lucky, we seldom have to suffer in the jungle. Besides we have medics and medicines, you miners are all on your own. By the way, my name is John McDermott, First lieutenant."

"Nice to meet you John, I'm James Cushing, my friends call me Jim."

The SS *President Hoover* continued adjusting its course slowly to port. Corregidor Island was now clearly on the port side and Fort Drum almost on starboard. Far in the distance, some 30 sea miles ahead, Jim could see the first buildings of Manila on the horizon.

The bay serves the Port of Manila, and is considered one of the best natural typhoon-free harbors in Southeast Asia and one of the finest in the world. Strategically located around the capital city of the Philippines, Manila Bay is crucial for commerce and trade between the Philippines and its neighbors. With an area of 1,994 km² (769.9 sq. miles), and a coastline of 190 km (118 miles), Manila Bay is situated in the western part of Luzon, the Philippines' main-island, and is bounded by Cavite and Metro Manila on the east, Bulacan and Pampanga on the north, and the Bataan Peninsula on the west and northwest. The town of Mariveles, in the province of Bataan, is an anchorage just inside the northern entrance and Sangley Point is the location of Cavite Naval Base. On either side of the bay there are volcanic peaks topped with tropical foliage.

Across the entrance to Manila Bay are several islands, the largest of which is Corregidor, located three kilometers from the Bataan Peninsula and, along with the island of Caballo, separates the mouth of the bay into the North and South Channel. In the South Channel is El Fraile Island and outside the entrance is Carabao Island. El Fraile, a rocky island some four acres in area, supports the massive concrete and steel construction of Fort Drum, constructed by the United States Army to defend the southern entrance of the bay. To the immediate north and south are additional harbors, upon which both local and international ports are situated. A large number of ships at the northern and southern harbors facilitate maritime activities in the bay. The North Harbor, the smaller of the two, is used for inter-island shipping. The South Harbor is used for large ocean-going vessels.

This was the setting for the Battle of Manila Bay in 1898 in which the American Asiatic Fleet led by Commodore George Dewey seized the area and, by destroying the Spanish Pacific Fleet, sealed the fate of the Philippines for the next fifty years. Manila Bay, together with the Port of Manila, is the main access to the country. Who controls the entrance, controls the Philippines.

"You going straight up north or you staying first for a while in Manila to acclimatize?" McDermott asked.

"I don't know really, I assume my brothers will arrange these things. At any rate they are supposed to pick me up."

"If you look for a nice place to stay take the Admiral Hotel on Dewey Boulevard,[9] they have a nice bar and a good restaurant. It's a hotel for people like you and me, junior officers, businessmen and the like. The top brass goes to the Manila Hotel, that's where General MacArthur stays; he occupies the penthouse on the top floor. There aren't many high-rises in Manila. The

Manila Hotel is one of the first buildings you see if you come from this direction."

With a good chat time goes fast, Jim noticed. He saw the skyline of Manila coming closer and closer. Indeed, the Manila Hotel stood out at the left side of the skyline. Jim saw it clearly. From the entrance of Manila Bay to the Port of Manila took almost two hours. Just outside the harbor the pilot, an American, boarded the luxury liner to guide the ship into the port. The ship moored at Pier 1, just in front of the massive Manila Hotel.

The pier was overcrowded. Porters, vendors, relatives, longshoremen, were all running around. It was difficult to see whether Walter or Charles was there. After a while Jim thought he spotted his two brothers. Once the mooring lines were secured it took another 20 minutes before the gangway was lowered and customs and immigration came on board. An hour later passengers were allowed to disembark. Porters raced up the gangway, against the stream of disembarking passengers, to get a piece of the pie.

"Sir, how many pieces of luggage you have? One dollar a piece," a young porter shouted at him. Jim had no idea about prices. In the US he wouldn't even think about it for one dollar. He felt he had no choice and followed the porter with his two suitcases down the gangway.

At the foot of the gangway Walter and Charles waited for him. Jim had not seen his brothers for years so it was a happy reunion. There were only a few taxis around and all were occupied. They boarded a *calesa*, a horse-drawn carriage, and turned at the end of Pier 1 to the right in the direction of Dewey Boulevard.

"We'll stay for a few days at the Admiral Hotel," Walter explained. You need time to get used to this country."

It was really a nice hotel, Jim thought. Not too big, a small swimming pool, a nice bar and a spacious restaurant. Most of the guests were military men, lieutenants, captains and a single major. He did not see anyone colonel or higher. John McDermott was right.

They went sightseeing the rest of the day. They visited Intramuros, the oldest district and historic core of Manila. Known as the Walled City, the original fortified city of Manila was the seat of the government during the Spanish colonial period. Intramuros is Latin for "within the walls"; districts beyond the walls were referred as the extramuros of Manila, meaning "outside the walls." Inside the walls was the San Agustin Church, the oldest Roman Catholic church of Manila, built by the Augustinians in 1607. They strolled through Luneta Park, Mabini Street and M.H. del Pilar, smiling at the numerous beautiful girls, followed by "Hi Joe, how are you today?" or "Hi Joe, where do you stay?"

The streets were full of vendors of sunglasses, newspapers and magazines, barbecue sticks and cooked eggs.

"Jimmy you try one of those eggs," Walter said with a suspicious smile. "They are really good, a little bit salty, but that is the specialty here."

Jim paid a few centavos to the smiling vendor, peeled of the skin of the egg and took a hefty bite. His brothers were looking at him with a kind of grin. They burst out in laughter when they saw the sudden change on Jimmy's face. He almost choked on the egg, spitting it out in disgust. "What the hell is that?" He looked at what he spit out; it looked like the half of a baby chicken.

His brothers couldn't stop laughing.

"That is *balut*," Walter explained, "one of the Filipino delicacies, brooded eggs. You can get them according to taste, brooded for a few days up to eighteen or nineteen days. The longer they are brooded the more chicken and the more feathers inside the egg shell."

Walter went back to the surprised vendor and bought a balut himself. "If you're used to it it tastes delicious. For sure you ate worms in Mexico."

Walter was right. Jim remembered his days in northern Mexico, there in the mining camps where life was sometimes hard with nothing much to eat. He really did eat worms there. So why not eat balut? Why not try it again? He bought another one, and after all it was not that bad.

They continued their walk along M.H. del Pilar Street. The street was a mixture of old Spanish mansions and here and there an exclusive bar or restaurant. At the end of the street, on the righthand side, was the Admiral Hotel. They had dinner at the hotel. Walter ordered typical Filipino food such as *lechon*, barbecued pork, *pansit*, rice-noodles and a San Miguel beer.

After dinner they had a beer at the hotel bar, which was full of American officers and civilians and, Jim noticed, there were many beautiful girls. Walter and Charles introduced Jim to some of their friends and colleagues. Later that night he met Courtney Whitney, the vice president of Southern Cross Mines, a company located near Benguet in the northern Philippines. Walter was the mine's manager.[10] Charles Cushing also worked for Southern Cross. It was agreed that James would join his two brothers in the company.

Courtney Whitney was born in Washington, DC in 1897; he enlisted in the U.S. Army in 1917 and became a pursuit pilot. He received his law degree from George Washington University in 1927 and left the Army to open a private practice in Manila. George Malcolm of the Philippine Supreme Court[11] recalled that Whitney was only a so-so lawyer, but he had a sharp mind, nimble wit, and "gentlemanly appearance." He developed a close friendship with the MacArthur family during his years in Manila. Then the mining boom of the 1930s enticed Whitney, and he became a leading investor and board member of a dozen or so gold operations in Northern Luzon.

The next five days were used to buy equipment for Southern Cross and to continue Jim's familiarization with the Philippines. He easily adjusted. He noticed, however, marked differences with things he was used to in California.[12] The American colonization of the Philippines had prompted the flocking of many Filipinos to America, who worked as laborers or on farms or as domestic helpers in California households. The 1924 Immigration Act dictated that Filipinos were neither American citizens nor foreigners but were *colonized people*. Technically they were American nationals.[13] Nevertheless, racial discrimination toward Filipinos in America was evident during the colonial period. Filipinos were often labeled as half-civilized or half-savage, worthless, uneducated and unscrupulous. They were perceived to be taking the jobs of Caucasian Americans.[14, 15] They were also accused of attracting Caucasian women which was against anti-miscegenation laws[16] which were in force in many American states. Such laws had been introduced long before the Civil War and remained in many states until 1967. After the Second World War, an increasing number of states repealed their anti-miscegenation laws, and in 1967 the remaining ones were held to be unconstitutional by the Supreme Court.[17]

In the US crime and violence was likely to be associated with Filipinos and they were shunned for their substandard living conditions, where in some instances there could be as many as twenty people sleeping in a room. These were just racial prejudices and Filipinos in America were affected by various socio-economic factors. The majority of Filipinos were men, with a gender ratio to Filipino females in California of approximately 14 to 1. Filipino workers were forced to live in poor conditions since they were poorly waged.

Filipinos were discriminated against primarily due to economic reasons. Caucasian Americans disliked Filipinos for their willingness to work for low wages, thus they perceived a loss of job opportunities and a downward trend in pay. Anti-Filipino sentiment was further fueled by the preference for hiring

Filipinos because their build was thought to be ideal for "stoop labor," or bent over kind of work.[18]

Notwithstanding the antagonism against inter-racial familiarity, which was so common in California, in the Philippines there was not much of that noticeable. Jim did not see any signs such as "colored people only" or "we trade to white people only," but there was certainly a more subtle form of racism around. American army units did not have any Filipino soldiers, and the Filipino army units had American officers. There were bars and restaurants where only Americans were seen, and in the typical Filipino establishments you saw hardly any Americans.

As far as anti-miscegenation laws were concerned, they seemed not to be in existence. Sex between Filipino women and American men was common, and many resident American men had either live-in Filipino partners or married their girlfriends. But that bringing these women home to the States would be a problem for the Filipina partners was seldom taken into account. Jim absorbed all of this and more, and admired the way the Filipinos coped with the American occupation.

World War II would become a significant turning point in American views towards Filipinos. During the early period of the war, Filipinos were prohibited to join the army. However in 1942 President Franklin Roosevelt, after pressure from General Douglas MacArthur, allowed them to serve in the armed forces. Many Filipinos fought with the Americans in Asia and Europe while some opted to be civilians involved in the mobilization effort. Filipinos earned the acceptance and admiration of Americans by the end of the war. Meantime the United States recognized and affirmed the Filipinos' right to citizenship with the amended Nationality Act of 1940. Through the amendment, non-citizens who joined the military were given opportunity to attain citizenship. About ten thousand Filipinos became American citizens through the amendment.[19]

Less than a week after his arrival Jim, together with his two brothers, was on his way to Benguet province. Southern Cross Mines was located some 15 kilometers past Baguio, the most important town in the mountains of the Northern Philippines.

After a few years in Benguet Jim moved on to another location. He worked for several mining outfits in other parts of the country. Mindanao especially attracted him. Benguet could be rather cold and rainy in the winter months while Mindanao was tropical in the extreme. It was an extremely hot and humid island, and full of dangerous diseases, poisonous snakes and croc-odiles.[20]

His favorite relaxation spot was Cebu, an island more or less halfway between Manila and Mindanao. Cebu was part of the Visayas Region in the middle part of the Philippines. Cebu City, the island's capital, was much smaller than Manila and less congested. There were also few foreigners in Cebu City and the city enjoyed an attractive nightlife.

It was here in Cebu that Jim met Felisa Tabando, a beautiful Filipina from Baybay on the neighboring island of Leyte. She was nicknamed "Fritzi," and she and Jim got married in 1940 in Cebu City.[21] Life was looking good for Jim. He loved the Philippines, the people, the way of life and especially in the Visayas he felt at home. He worked at that time as a master mechanic for Mambulao Consolidated in South Luzon.[22] He also bought his own mine in Surigao, on the northeastern corner of Mindanao. Soon he would settle down in Surigao.

CHAPTER 3

THE MAGIC OF CEBU[1]

T HE PHILIPPINES IS the northernmost island group of the Malay Archipelago, situated between Taiwan in the north and Borneo in the south. On the west is the Asian continent; on the east is the Pacific Ocean.

After a long and hazardous voyage the Spanish sailor Ferdinand Magellan landed on 7 April 1521 on the Philippine Island of Cebu. From the very beginning Magellan was fascinated by Cebu. The friendly people, the abundance of food, the excellent climate and the beautiful beaches were a welcome change after the horrors of the Magellan Straits and the long journey across the Pacific. He claimed the country for Spain and made Cebu City the capital of the new colony. The Spanish would remain for almost 350 years in the Philippines and would leave an everlasting mark on the country. They made it the only Christian country in Asia and introduced European administration and legislature.

When I came in Cebu for the first time, more than 300 years later, it was still the favorite destination of sailors. I still remember the smiling faces of our crew when our captain told us the next port was going to be Cebu.

The Americans
As a result of a dispute over Cuba, in 1898, war erupted between the USA and Spain. The Philippines, as a Spanish colony, was pulled into the conflict. When the American fleet under Admiral Dewey defeated the Spanish fleet in Manila Bay, the Filipinos, seizing their chance to strike against the Spanish, fought on the side of the US. As soon as the hostilities were over the Filipinos, under General Emilio Aguinaldo, declared themselves independent.

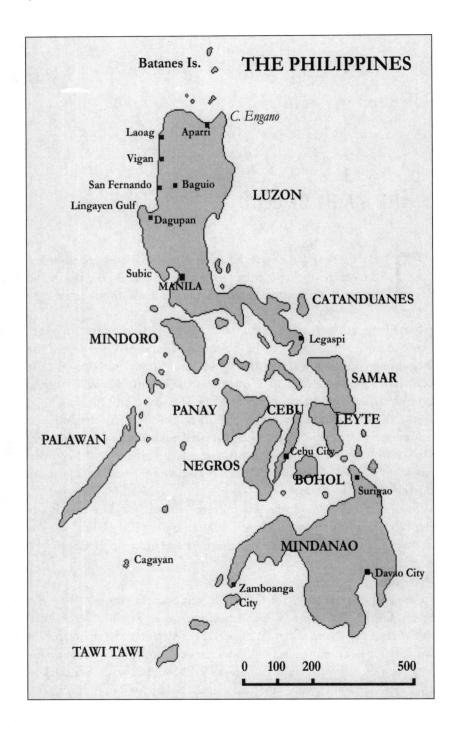

Batanes Is.

THE PHILIPPINES

C. Engano

Laoag
Aparri

Vigan

San Fernando ■ Baguio

Lingayen Gulf

Dagupan

LUZON

Subic

MANILA

CATANDUANES

MINDORO

Legaspi

SAMAR

PANAY CEBU LEYTE

PALAWAN

NEGROS

Cebu City

BOHOL

Surigao

Cagayan

MINDANAO

Davao City

Zamboanga
City

TAWI TAWI

0   100   200   500

The US, however, ignored the role the Filipinos had played in the war and the Filipinos had to begin their struggle again, this time against the US. The main insurrection lasted until 1902.

For the Americans the Philippines was their first large colony, and they intended to Americanize the country as soon as possible. An American-style school system was created, and the occupiers also established a judicial system, drew up a legal code to replace antiquated Spanish ordinances, and organized an (American-style) civil service. What they did *not* do was change the political administrative division of the Philippines. This system is based on the "barangay" (or Barrio). A barangay is the smallest administrative division in the Philippines and is the native Filipino term for a village, district or ward. The barangay is headed by elected officials, the topmost being the *Punong Barangay* (addressed as Kapitan; also known as the Barangay Captain).

In 1934 the Tydings-McDuffie Bill granted the Philippines absolute and complete independence by 1946. The Philippine commonwealth was established on 15 November 1935, with Manuel L. Quezon as the first president. He was reelected in 1941.

At the beginning of World War II the capital Manila was by far the largest urban area of the country. Cebu City was the second largest. Manila was also the largest port in the country, with Cebu City in second place. Other important ports were Davao, Zamboanga, in Southern Mindanao, Cagayan de Oro and Surigao in Northern Mindanao, Ilo-Ilo in Western Visayas and Legaspi at the southern tip of Luzon Island.

Manila had an international airport just south of the city. Cebu had a small airport, Lahug Airport, on the northern side of the city. The largest air force base in 1941 in the Philippines was Fort Stotsenburg (today Clark Airbase), some 80 kilometers north of Manila. The second largest was Nichols Airbase, near Manila.

Philippine Pre-War Economics
Before the American occupation the Philippines was predominately an agricultural country that produced rice, coconut and fishing products. Exports were limited to some fruits (mainly mango), lumber and frozen fish (tuna).

Prior to the 1930s the Philippines was not considered a promising mining country. The influx of American adventurers and prospectors, such as Haussermann, changed the situation dramatically. Initially it was gold they were after; however, base metals also profited from the interest in gold mining. The new roads in Mountain Province led to the discovery of one of the world's largest copper deposits, operated by the Lepanto Mining Company. By 1940 the huge Lepanto copper output was all being shipped to Japan.[2,3,4] Even iron ore, chromite, manganese and lead were found and mined during this era. In 1938 the Philippines was ranked sixth in the world in base metal production.[5]

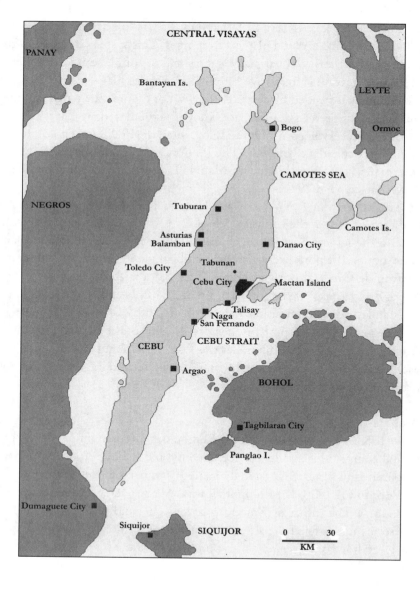

By the outbreak of World War II the Philippines was one of the new world leaders in mineral production. The United States and Japan absorbed most of her base metals. The administrators and managers of the businesses were Americans; the bulk of the employees at the mines were Filipinos. They were the laborers, bearers, cooks, guards, guides, and in some cases the foremen.[6,7]

Philippine mining and mineral resources at the brink of World War II were an important issue for the Philippines itself, but also for Japan as importer of the bulk of the mined products. Not only the volume of mining products was important to Japan, but above all the kind of minerals. Japan was a country with hardly any minerals at all, and for its war industry it needed above all minerals like copper, iron, gold, nickel and chromite. Occupying the Philippines was for Japan a strategic issue with a very high priority.[8]

Cebu Island[9] is the ninth largest island of the Philippine archipelago. The island-province is located in the Central Philippines, between the islands of Bohol and Leyte in the east and Negros in the west. The province, part of the Visayan Region, also includes several small islands adjacent to Cebu, such as Bantayan in the north, Camotes in thenortheast and Mactan and Olango in the east. Cebu is a long and narrow island; from north to south approximately 217 km, and about 32 km across at its greatest width. The island is mountainous with several mountains higher than 700 meters and a highest peak (Mount Cabalasan) of 1,013 meters. The coasts are steep and offer only few sheltered places for ships. The island is almost completely deforested; mountain slopes are partly bare, partly covered by scrub vegetation. The valleys, however, are fertile and yield valuable crops of tobacco, sugar, cotton, coffee, hemp and maize. Contrary to most other islands of the archipelago little rice is grown. The staple food in the province is maize. The population of the province in 1940 was about one million; half living in Cebu City, the capital.

History

When the Spanish conquistador Ferdinand Magellan arrived in Cebu in 1521 he found a kind of kingdom that was ruled by Rajah (king) Humabon.[10] This Rajahnate was a Philippine state founded somewhere in the 13th century then known as Zubu (or Sugbo).[11]

The arrival of Magellan changed everything. From now on the Spanish would rule the islands for almost 400 years. The real colonizer of the new Spanish colony was Miguel Lopez de Legazpi. In 1565 he founded Cebu

City and made it the capital of the new colony. Colon Street in Cebu City became the oldest street in the Philippines and the Santo Niño Cathedral the oldest church in the country.

Through the ages Cebu City and the Island of Cebu did fairly well. At the start of World War II Cebu City was a thriving place that made its money mainly with inter-island and international trade. Copper and gold was discovered in the 1930s near Toledo on the west coast of the island, while coal took care of most of the island's energy needs. The Cebu port was well equipped, and the Lahug airport functioned reasonably well. An airstrip on neighboring Mactan Island was used by the military only. A narrow gauge railway connected Argao in the south with Danao, Cebu's sugar centre, in the north. In Cebu, more than anywhere else in the Philippines, James Cushing felt at home.[12]

CHAPTER 4

SITUATION UNTENABLE

A

FTER HE DISPATCHED message NR 11 to MacArthur's headquarters on the afternoon of 9 April, Jim ordered his men to
prepare the evacuation of the Base Hospital on short notice and
to be ready to move the prisoners to a safer location. The next morning, before
it was completely light, they woke up to start their evacuation. Jim had sent
his wife Fritzi to a cave hideout in the forested area between Tupas Ridge
and Cantipla. A barely visible trail led past this hideout. When the ladder
used to climb to the hideout was pulled up nobody would ever realize there
was a refuge there. He kept his beautiful dog Senta, a Great Dane, with him.

In the middle of the preparations to leave, suddenly shots were heard
from the sentries posted around the camp. Jim did not think a split second,
but ordered: "Drop everything and get out and follow me." He led the way
down a hidden trail towards the bottom of the ravine that separated Tupas
Ridge from Kamungayan. Looking back he saw the Japanese already searching the camp he had left; they were no more than 100 meters away.

At the first shot Sergeant Alfredo Marigomen, with the help of Sergeant
Meliton Endagan and a few other commandos, rushed the prisoners along
the pre-selected trail to Kamungayan and from there to the rendezvous at
Maurela, a high point on the north end of the Sunog Ridge.

Upon reaching the bottom of the ravine Jim's group started on a trail
that went diagonally up the face of the slope towards Kamungayan. This trail
was at certain places in full view of the Tupas Ridge, particularly from a high
hill at Tap-tap, but the Old Man (as Jim Cushing was often called by his
men) confidently and briskly led the group. Ahead of the guerrilla leader
trotted Senta, the Great Dane. Behind Cushing came Captain Montayre,

followed by Lieutenant Titang Cabras, Colonel Baura, Lieutenant Gloria Sena and Major Manuel Segura.[1]

Suddenly a hail of bullets hit the group and moments later they heard the unmistakable chatter of a heavy Japanese machinegun at Tap-tap. It was accurate fire from a distance of at least 1,000 meters. Within seconds Captain Montayre and Lieutenant Sena were hit. A bullet also slammed into Corporal Garido. He had been hit in the head and was immediately dead. Jim tried to return fire, but his Thompson submachinegun was not suitable for fire at that range. In order to present a dispersed target, Jim distributed his people as much as possible. After a while a Japanese seaplane arrived on the scene; it looked like a Yokosuka E14Y. It acted not only as observer for the Japanese, but also fired its machinegun if it noticed something move.

Once the seaplane was gone each little group of guerrillas found its way to the rendezvous at Odlum below the white cliffs of Met-ol where the Base Hospital was temporarily relocated. It was tucked under an overhang of the cliff where a hidden waterfall cascaded down into a pool of clear water. Finally the group could take a rest.

Jim checked his men: Captain Montayre and Lieutenant Sena were seriously wounded, and Corporal Garido was dead. Jim was mad and wanted revenge. During their retreat they had picked up two Japanese soldiers. Jim ordered their summary execution. Lieutenant Pedro "Pete" Villareal was given the task and he led the two doomed men to a large *batang*, an old wooden log, covered with moss and undergrowth. The lieutenant spoke some Nippongo and explained to the men what was going to happen. With stoic calm they heard their verdict. Because of the nearness of Japanese patrols a firing squad was impossible since the noise would give away their position. Instead Lieutenant Villareal selected a large *bolo* and started sharpening it. A bolo was actually not very suitable to behead someone he thought, these sword-like knives were actually used to cut sugar cane. He wished he had a Japanese *katana*,[2] which he had seen many times in Japan. With a katana you could behead someone in a split-second. In the meantime the Japanese prisoners, aware of the preparations and the fate that awaited them, started to sing a classic Japanese song: *"Miyo! Tokai no sora akete!"* (*Look! Dawn is breaking over the eastern sea!*).[3] When Villareal thought his blade was sharp enough he told the younger of the two Japanese to lie down on the batang. Jim and some of his men watched the execution with stone faces. Although Villareal tried with one blow to cut off the head of the soldier, he was not lucky. Blood spouted everywhere; it was a messy affair. Villareal needed three blows before finally the head dropped of the batang. The beheading of the second Japanese did not go much better. They did not bother to bury the bodies. "Let it be a warning for their friends if they pass by," Jim said. "We can be just as brutal as they are."

After the execution of the two Japanese and a short rest, the group's resistance fighters moved on to a guerrilla camp at Masurela. Beside the camp stood the round peak of *Ma-oyog* where Major Eulogio "Ehoy" Bonsukan kept his radios. From Masurela Jim led the men through the deserted GHQ site at Tabunan up to the top of the ridge and down the other side back to Kamungayan. Not long afterward the 10 Japanese prisoners were also brought back to Kamungayan and were locked up in a Nipa-hut.

There was still no answer from MacArthur's headquarters in Brisbane. Jim called his top officers to a conference in order to discuss what to do next. Their situation was difficult, their movements were restricted, and from all sides they were informed that numerous innocent civilians were being rounded up and might be killed. They wondered who the captured senior officer Furomei really was. He had at one time said he was a general but later identified himself as an admiral. Was he the cause of the Ohnisi Butai's fury unleashed upon the hapless civilians? And how many men and women had been rounded up?[4]

Other questions were why it took General MacArthur so long to answer their radio messages? Was the admiral who seemed so important to the Japanese in Cebu City of no importance to the top brass at SWPA Headquarters? They remembered that the Japanese often had used the name "Koga" in connection with the dead body they had left on the beach. What if that really was Admiral Koga? Were the lives of ten Japanese prisoners worth the lives of maybe hundreds of Filipino civilians? Jim wondered. They all looked to him for answers, answers he did not have.

During the meeting disturbing messages from field commanders trickled in. Five other Japanese columns were bulldozing their way through the guerrilla lines from the north and northwest, from the west, southwest and south. Two other columns had converged upon Tupas Ridge. All these enemy columns left in their wake burning houses and executed civilians. They were slowly but surely being surrounded by the Ohnisi Butai.

They could not go on like this, all agreed. If they waited too long they would be overrun and the prisoners liberated. They would have fought for nothing. In the end there seemed to be no other solution then to try to negotiate with the enemy for the possibility of exchanging the ten Japanese prisoners for the civilians and their livestock which had been captured by the invaders.[5]

Jim sent for Admiral or General Furomei and had a long talk with him. As a result of this it was decided to send a message to Colonel Ohnisi proposing that he refrain from further attacks on the guerrillas and the civilians in exchange for the prisoners. It was also decided to send four men—two guerrillas and two Japanese prisoners—across to some 500 Japanese troops now camping on the Tupas Ridge. Jim drafted a message in English which was translated into Japanese characters by Captain Yamamoto:

1. For your information we have in custody from a fallen plane Marine General FUROMEI, Lt. YAMAMOTO, Lt. OKAMRA, Lt. YAMANATA, and six sailors.
2. It is our desire to return to you General FUROMEI on condition that your soldiers will stop killing of innocent civilians. Our civilian population is innocent of any crime and must be given consideration.

> JAMES M. CUSHING
> Lieut-Colonel, Inf., Commanding[6]

Jim asked for two volunteers. Corporals Herminio Cerna and Numeriano Padayao Teves stepped forward. Carrying a white flag and accompanied by two of the Japanese prisoners they went on their way to the other side of the ravine. Their order was to deliver the message to Col. Ohnisi.

Around four in the afternoon the four returned with "Akibuno" cigarettes, some Japanese liquor, and an answer from Col. Ohnisi. The Japanese commander demanded the immediate release of all the prisoners:

I understand what you meant in your letter. Our purpose of operation this time is to rescue the Japanese Navy Officers that had crashed.

I hereby promise you that our Japanese Forces will guarantee without fail that lives and properities of your men and civilians in case you will set them free to our hand.

> Sincerely yours,
> Seiiti Ohnisi, Lt. Col. Japanese Forces[7]

Desperately stalling for time, hoping that an answer from Australia would come, Jim made an answer offering to release four of the prisoners initially. In about four days time he would release the remaining six wounded prisoners at the gates of Cebu City.

Col. Ohnisi did not agree to this, his answer was: *"All or no one at all."*[8] Jim went back to Furomei or Koga, or who ever he was, and asked the admiral's personal assurance that the killing and pillaging would stop. The Flag Officer agreed. Jim informed Ohnisi of the final deal:

To Lt. Col. Seiiti Ohnisi
In keeping with our agreement we are sending the Japanese Navy Officers and other sailors which crashed and now are in our hands.
They will leave here at daylight as it is too difficult for them to travel at night.
Sincerely yours, James M. Cushing[9]

The Japanese colonel answered as follows:

I have received your letter. The measure taken by you is a warrior like and admirable action.
I expect to see you again in the battlefield someday.
Your friend, Seiiti Ohnisi[10]

With the prisoner-exchange settled some of Jim's worries were over, at least if the Japanese kept their word. Somehow he had to inform Brisbane about the latest developments. He urged his radio operators to try to get a connection. Late that night Jim managed to send out a new message to SWPA:[11]

TO: GENERAL MACARTHUR
FROM: CUSHING
NR 12: 09 APRIL
JAP PRISONERS TOO HOT FOR US TO HOLD. DUE TO NUMBER OF CIVILIANS BEING KILLED I MADE TERMS THAT NO CIVILIANS ARE TO BE MOLESTED IN
FUTURE, IN EXCHANGE FOR THE PRISONERS. ALTHOUGH THE ENEMY DID NOT KNOW IT, WE HAD ONLY

25 SOLDIERS BETWEEN THE ATTACKING FORCE OF AP-
PROXIMATELY FIVE HUNDRED AND OUR POSITION. EN-
EMY NOW WITHDRAWING TOWARDS CITY IN SOUTHERN
CEBU—JAPS WERE REPORTED TWO THOUSAND STRONG,
LOOKING FOR PRISONERS.

At eleven o'clock the next morning, 10 April 1944, the only Prisoner of
War exchange on Cebu took place. On the guerrilla side a fighter with a
white flag acted as point of exchange. Lieutenant Pedro Villareal led the small
party down a dry riverbed. He was chosen because he
was not only an excellent soldier but he also spoke reasonable Japanese,
having served in the Japanese-supervised Bureau of Constabulary. Furomei
or Koga was carried in a chair upon the shoulders of the guerrillas. The nine
others walked. When the group reached a mango tree, standing prominent
and alone on an otherwise bare slope, they stopped. A group of about fifty
Japanese soldiers cautiously approached, armed only with swords and bayonets. Jim watched the ceremony through his binoculars, as the soldiers bowed
low in the presence of Furomei, shook hands with Villareal, then turned to
climb the ridges and return to Cebu City.

When he returned to base Villareal gave Jim two messages. One was
from Colonel Ohnisi, offering thanks for treating the prisoners "kindly." The
second was from the "general": "He extended his best regards to you and
men."[12]

When Jim returned to his headquarters there was still no message from
Australia. The next day was different as he received a message coded SWPA
NR 5:[13]

CONFIDENTIAL
REFERENCE TO YOUR MESSAGE NUMBER 8 DESIRE IF
POSSIBLE EVACUATION TO THIS HEADQUARTERS OF THE
SENIOR PRISONERS WITH AS MANY POSSIBLE CMA SE-
LECTED IN ACCORD WITH RELATIVE IMPORTANCE PD
NORTHEAST COAST CEBU IS NAVIGATIONALLY IMPOSSI-
BLE PD CAN YOU SEND THEM UNDER SAFE CONDUCT TO
A RENDEZVOUS SITE SOUTHERN BOHOL OR SOUTHERN
NEGROS CMA PREFERENCE OF RENDEZVOUS AREA IN OR-
DER NAMED PD HOW SOON COULD PARTY BE AT SITE PD

PARTY DELIVERED OF UTMOST IMPORTANCE BE ALERT
TO USE OF ASSUMED NAMES AND RANKS UNDER WHICH
SENIOR PRISONER MAY POSE AS JUNIOR PD DO ALL POSSI-
BLE TO KEEP THEM SAFE FOR EVACUATION AND PREVENT
RECAPTURE PD TO GIVE MATTER UTMOST SECRECY.

This was the answer to his message NR 8 sent on 9 April, two days earlier. A lot had happened in between. Why did Headquarters answer so late?
There was nothing much Jim could do anymore. The prisoners were gone.

SWPA in Disarray
General Richard K. Sutherland, MacArthur's Chief of Staff in Australia, was
furious when he read Jim Cushing's message NR 11 on the morning of 13
April. He could not understand how this could have happened. To let go a
Japanese flag officer, whoever he might have been, for whatever reason, was
unforgivable. He directed Courtney Whitney to send this message to the
poor colonel in Cebu:

> Your action in releasing important prisoners after negotiation with
> the enemy is most reprehensible and leads me to doubt your judg-
> ment and efficiency. You are hereby discharged from your functions
> as Commander of the 7th (?) Military District.[14]

To make it even worse, Sutherland ordered a second message sent, as a
warning to other guerrilla commanders in the Philippines:

> The Commander of the 7th Military District (?) captured a number
> of important prisoners and was directed to make every effort to re-
> move them to a place of safety. Captain (?) Cushing, however, after
> negotiations with the enemy, released the prisoners. He has there-
> fore been discharged from his functions as commander of the 7th
> Military District (?)[15]

Both messages carried the signature of General MacArthur. The messages contained several mistakes. In the first place Cebu was the 8th Military
District, not the 7th. Cushing was a colonel, not a captain as the message
said. Whether or not these mistakes were deliberate, meaning that the mes-

sages actually were some kind of warning or not, can no longer be established. There are no records about this issue.

After reading the messages, Cebu's fierce guerrilla commander broke out in tears. He cried unashamedly on the shoulder of Major Manuel Segura.[16] He took a bottle of Tanduay, prime Philippine rum, and disappeared with his dog Senta into the jungle for more than half a day.

But Jim had an important defender: Colonel Courtney Whitney, his former boss in the mining business in the Philippines, and a lawyer. Whitney spent the whole night working on a paper to defend Jim Cushing's actions.[17] He summarized all the radio messages at hand, including another that had come in overnight. He could prove to Sutherland that the release was effected on 9 April or two days before their message of instructions regarding the prisoners' disposition. This action was, according to Whitney, as a consequence not in disregard of specific instructions.[18] Whitney pointed out that Fertig's WAT station had delayed retransmission of the crucial messages from Cebu to Brisbane. He told Sutherland he was having the reasons for the holdup investigated.[19] The colonel concluded:

CUSHING's action was taken in the interest of the people. If he is discharged as Area Commander he would revert to the position previously held (guerrilla chieftain) and it would be impossible for this Headquarters to exercise any measure of control over him or coordinate his actions. It would be impossible furthermore to establish any other leadership over the people, who would look upon CUSHING's discharge as a penalty for serving their immediate interests.[20]

Whitney closed his argument: "I strongly recommend that no action be taken." Attorney Whitney won the case and Sutherland relented. The matter was dropped. As far as the GHQ was concerned, the "Koga Affair" was closed.

Jim was not aware of all that transpired in Brisbane. He had no idea that, thanks to his friend Courtney Whitney, the charges had been dropped. There was never any message about this to inform him. He was disappointed about the treatment he had received from Brisbane, but there was nothing much he could do about it. He thought he was fired, but did not act like it. He continued to do what he had done the last two years, and that was fight the Japanese.

There was one thing that kept bothering him: the question of who General or Admiral Furomei really was. Jim had never heard of an admiral or general Furomei, he knew only the name Koga, the Commander in Chief of the Imperial Japanese Navy. Jim had visited Japan several times and was fairly well familiar with Japanese customs. The fact that the Japanese prisoners on the beach kept on using the name "Koga" for their dead comrade made him lean toward the idea that it was really Admiral Koga who arrived dead on the beach in San Fernando. In Jim's mind the ferocity with which Col. Ohnisi conducted his operations was an indication that the admiral or general he had captured must have been highly important.

CHAPTER 5

THE HUNT FOR PLAN Z

G ENERAL FUROMEI, OR whoever he was, was back in Japanese hands. He was transferred immediately to Tokyo and kept immunicado. But headquarters kept on pushing to recover the documents that had also gone down on the plane.

Col. Ohnisi kept his word and left Jim's guerrillas, at least for a while, alone. For the colonel that was not a problem since he had enough targets left. Recovering the documents was his prime concern. He initially tried his luck by picking up random people in the hope they would break under torture. For this purpose he used so called *undercovers*, Filipinos who were willing to work for the Japanese. It did not help; the prisoners had no idea what the colonel was talking about. From picking up people at random he changed to picking up those with possible connections to politicians who had fled. He set his eyes on Governor Hilario Abellana.

Governor Abellana[1] initially decided, when the war broke out, to stay in office. He thought he could be of more help to the resistance movement by staying than by fleeing. For the resistance movement he was an asset as long as he stayed close to the Japanese. Gradually, however, his resspsonsibilities became more and more limited. In the end he believed he was only a figurehead who was misused by the enemy for propaganda purposes. He decided to escape. That was not easy because he was kept under close surveillance day and night. He made his move on Sunday, 17 January 1943. It was the day of the great procession in honor of *Santo Niño*, the patron saint of Cebu. The procession was the closing ceremony of *Sinulog*, the yearly fiesta of Cebu. The procession was always watched by tens of thousands of Cebuanos. During the procession Cebu City was closed for traffic. It was the ideal moment.

When the governor did not show up in his office the following Monday, the Japanese understood that he had escaped.[2] A great manhunt was organized, and all undercovers[3] were mobilized to get back the governor. It was all in vain as he could not be found. The governor was already on the neighboring Island of Bohol.

For more than a year the Japanese searched everywhere for the governor. Many friends, relatives and political associates were arrested, tortured and often executed in an attempt to find out where Hilario Abellana was. On 13 July 1944 Jovito Abellana, a cousin of the governor, was arrested. He was the only one of the Abellana family still around. He was brought to the Cebu Normal School,[4] headquarters of the dreaded Kempetai, the military police arm of the Imperial Japanese Army. There he was interrogated by Prince Yoshida Tadasi, chief investigator of the Kempetai, an officer said to be close to Emperor Hirohito.

For weeks Jovito was tortured to the extreme, but in the end, when the Japanese realized that he really did not know anything about the whereabouts of Governor Abellana, he was left alone in his cell to rot. He witnessed the day-to-day routine in torturing, saw the beaten-to-pulp-faces of his fellow inmates, and the mutilated bodies of those who did not survive the treatments. He was lucky to survive the ordeal. He was constantly afraid to be included in the weekly *Guindulman Express*.

Twice a week, on Wednesday and Saturday, a certain Japanese soldier showed up named Watanabe. He was always accompanied by two sadistic and wrestler-like Japanese men and more Japanese soldiers. Watanabe carried a long samurai sword and was dressed in a bloodied suit and wore blood-stained leather boots. He brought along a six-by-six San Miguel truck. They collected usually around 35 to 40 Filipino prisoners, bound them by ropes and either let them get in the truck, or, if they could not walk anymore, just threw them in the back of it. Once the truck left, the prisoners on board were never seen again. Fellow prisoners who stayed behind called it "taken to Guindulman" (in English: "becoming obscure"). In a remote place, somewhere near Cebu City, the prisoners on board the truck were beheaded by Watanabe and his associates. Nobody ever found out where the execution place was or what happened to the bodies of the poor victims;[5] probably they were just thrown in the sea.

On 3 September 1944 Governor Abellana was recaptured and brought to the Kempetai Headquarters in the Cebu Normal School. The governor was executed by the Japanese on 15 January 1945. His grave was never found.

Jovito Abellana, his cousin, was released by the Japanese on 3 September 1944, the day the governor was arrested. He was one of the very few who survived the ordeal of the Kempetai Headquarters in Cebu and was able to tell how cruel the Japanese and their Filipino helpers, the undercovers, were.

Often these undercovers captured a victim in a village, kept him for a while in the Cebu Normal School and then put a rice bag over his head, with holes in front where their eyes were. In this way they brought him back to his village, lined up all the male villagers and let him pick out those who were helping the guerrillas. Because of the rice bag he could not be recognized. If he did his best and picked out many guerrilla-helpers he was promised his freedom. This never happened as he was put on the next *Guindulman Express* for beheading and he was never seen again.[6,7]

The Japanese terrorized Cebu Island, and no place was safe. The guerrillas were very well aware of the fate that awaited them if they were captured. But why were there so many undercovers and Cebuanos who helped the Japanese?

The Greater East Asia Co-prosperity Sphere

Japan's sales slogan for the war in the Pacific was the establishment of a so-called *Greater East Asia Co-prosperity Sphere*. In simple words: "Asia for the Asians." The Western colonies in the Pacific area, such as the Netherlands East Indies, Burma, Singapore and of course the Philippines should throw off the yoke of colonization and join Japan in a close cooperation pact. In all these colonies it attracted attention, and followers. This included in the Philippines.[8,9,10,11,12]

It is not correct to think that the Philippines were 100 or, what some suggest, 120 percent pro-American. If we look at Philippine society before World War II, and as mentioned earlier, there was no segregation as was customary in large parts of the USA. But every job of importance was held by Americans. They were the mine-managers, even the mechanics, the officers in the Philippines army, the lawyers, the businessmen, very often even the professors at the universities. There were bars and restaurants where Filipinos did not go and the other way around. Philippines society was American-controlled. This created animosity; there is no doubt. Many Americans in the Philippines married Filipinas, and at the end of their contract, or just to retire or for any other reason, they brought their wives back to the US. In many cases these marriages were frowned upon or in practice made impossible. Jim Crow laws in many states enforced segregation. What happens if you can take the entrance "for whites only" and your wife has to take the "colored people entrance?" Inside the restaurant you would not even be allowed to sit and have dinner together. Anti-miscegenation or miscegenation laws criminalized inter-racial marriages. This created divorces and resentment. Parents and relatives who came over to visit their daughters and grandchildren were subjected to the same treatment.[13,14,15,16]

The arrival of the Americans in 1898 did not go without a struggle. Until 1913 guerrilla attacks plagued the American administration in the Philippines. It was a cruel guerrilla war with atrocities on both sides. In 1941, when the war with Japan broke out, there were still many who remembered the first years of American colonization.[17,18,19,20]

In other words, especially at the beginning of the war, not all Filipinos were adamantly against the Japanese. Another issue was food. Cebu was not self-sufficient in food production. Rice, for instance, had to be imported from other islands. Empty stomachs easily change rules or affection. The Japanese had plenty of rice and were willing to use this as barter for information and cooperation.

All things taken together it should not be a surprise that the Japanese so easily recruited undercovers, cooperators, helpers and informers. Jovito Abellana counted sometimes, at any given time, more than fifty undercovers in the Kempetai offices.

For the resistance movement it was difficult. They had little to offer and were hungry themselves. The end result was that the guerrillas had to be very careful; there could be a spy or collaborator behind every tree in the jungle. You just could not trust anybody. That the Japanese during the occupation of Cebu were cruel, there is no question. There are very few articles, reports or books concerning Japanese behavior in Cebu during World War II; however one of the few is Jovito Abellana's *My Moments of War to Remember.*

Notwithstanding all his efforts in scouring the Cebu countryside, Colonel Ohnisi was not able to recover the lost documents. Did they disappear with the wreck of the aircraft of "General Furomei"? And why were these documents so important?

CHAPTER **6**
JAPAN AND WORLD WAR II

J APAN (IN NATIVE language, Nihon or Nippon), is an archipelago located in the western Pacific Ocean. The characters which
make up Japan's name mean "sun-origin," which is why Japan is
sometimes identified as the "Land of the Rising Sun."

The main religion in Japan is *Buddhism*, apart from which there is Shinto,
the former state religion of Japan. Approximately 85 percent of the Japanese
population practices both religions. Shinto is characterized by polytheism
and animism, and involves the worship of *kami* or spirits. Most kami are local
and can be regarded as the spiritual beings of a particular place, but some
hold more universal roles.

For the West, the fifteenth century was the age of the Great Discoveries.
The Portuguese, in a succession of voyages, took possession of the Far East
and Japan. Then all of a sudden, on 20 April 1600, a strange ship appeared
on the northeast coast of the southern island of Kyushu. The Portuguese
Jesuits were perplexed: it was a Dutch ship, their protestant arch-enemies.
The ship was the *De Liefde*.[1] The newcomers soon became acquainted with
the Japanese ruler Ieyasu. He was impressed by the Dutch and noticed that
they were not interested in preaching their religion but only in trade. Gradually the Dutch took over the position of the Portuguese. In 1639 the shogun
officially closed off Japan from the rest of the world, limiting trade to the
Dutch merchants ensconced on the island of Deshima in Nagasaki. The iso-
lationist *sakoku* ("closed country") policy would eventually span two and a
half centuries.

On 31 March 1854, the American Commodore Matthew Perry and the
"Black Ships" of the United States Navy forced the opening of Japan to the

outside world with the Convention (or Treaty) of Kanagawa.[2] Adopting Western political, judicial and military institutions, the Empire of Japan (*Dai Nippon Teikoku*), changed into an industrialized world power that embarked on a number of military conflicts to expand the nation's sphere of influence.

The Greater East Asia Co-Prosperity Sphere[3]

Japan's transition from a feudal state into a modern Western-style industrial state was felt by many Japanese as a loss of face for Japan. But a smashing victory over Russia during the Russo-Japanese War of 1904–05 helped to rouse public enthusiasm. During these times the concept of *The Greater East Asia Co-Prosperity Sphere* was born. It represented the desire to create a self-sufficient "bloc of Asian nations led by the Japanese and free of Western powers." This concept would become in the middle and late thirties of the next century the banner under which the Japanese war-machine tried to conquer vast territories in the Far East. *"Asians for the Asians"* became the motto.

Japan's role in World War I was limited largely to attacking German colonial outposts in East Asia, and it took advantage of the opportunity to expand its territorial holdings in the Pacific. Japan went to the peace conference at Versailles in 1919 as one of the great military and industrial powers of the world and received official recognition as one of the "Big Five" of the new international order. It joined the League of Nations and received a mandate over Pacific islands north of the Equator formerly held by Germany.

Militarism

The Japanese parliamentary government was not rooted deeply enough to withstand the economic and political pressures of the late 1920s and 1930s, and during the Depression Japan became increasingly militarized. Party politics came under increasing fire because it was believed they were divisive to the nation and promoted self-interest where unity was needed. As a result, the major parties voted to dissolve themselves and were absorbed into a single party, the Imperial Rule Assistance Association (IRAA). Its creation was precipitated by a series of domestic crises, and the actions of extremists.[4] Twice in 1931 civilian ultranationalist elements attempted to overthrow the government. As a result of the ratification of the London Naval Treaty limiting the size of the Imperial Japanese Navy, a movement grew within the junior navy officer corps to overthrow the government and to replace it with military rule.[5] On 15 May 1932, the naval officers, aided by army cadets and right-wing civilian elements, staged their own attempt. Prime Minister Inukai Tsuyoshi was assassinated by eleven young naval officers.

The Run-up to War

In 1910 Japan annexed the Korean peninsula, and for the Koreans hard times followed. There were many uprisings and millions of Koreans were either killed or deported for forced labor in Japan. Korea also became a major source for sex slaves, euphemistically called *comfort women*, for the Japanese army brothels overseas.[6,7] The next target was Chinese-controlled Manchuria. This territory adjacent to Korea was an essential source of raw materials. Without occupying this country, the Japanese probably could not have carried out their conquest of South-East Asia or taken the risk of attacking Pearl Harbor.[8]

In the following years there were many skirmishes between Japanese and Chinese troops that were usually called "incidents." Eventually a full-scale war could not be avoided. It was the so-called Marco Polo Bridge Incident, on the night of 7 July 1937, that triggered a full-scale war between China and Japan.

It was a huge, hard war with extreme brutalities from the Japanese side, culminating in the Nanjing Massacre,[9] an incident in which up to 300.000 Chinese were mass murdered (by beheading or being buried alive). Initially the Japanese were successful, but later on things became difficult and battles were lost. Japan tried to solve its occupation problems by implementing a strategy of creating friendly puppet governments. However, the atrocities committed by the Japanese army, as well as Japan's refusal to yield any real power, made them unpopular and ineffective. By 1941, Japan had occupied much of north and coastal China, but the central Chinese government and military had successfully retreated to the western interior to continue their stubborn resistance.

From December 1937 events such as the Japanese attack on the USS *Panay* (a ship sunk by the Japanese without provocation) and the Nanking Massacre swung public opinion in the West sharply against Japan and increased fear of Japanese expansion, which prompted the United States, the United Kingdom and France to provide loan assistance for war supply contracts to the Chinese. Furthermore, Australia prevented a Japanese government-owned company from taking over an iron mine in Australia, and banned iron ore exports in 1938.[10] Japan retaliated by invading and occupying French Indochina (present-day Vietnam) in 1940, and successfully blockaded

China from the import of arms, fuel and 10,000 tons/month of materials supplied by the Western Allies through the Haiphong-Yunnan-Fou railway line. Furthermore, in order to pressure the Japanese to end hostilities in China, the United States, Britain and the Netherlands East Indies declared oil and/or steel embargos against Japan. The loss of oil imports made it impossible for Japan to continue operations in China.[11,12]

After the blockage of oil in mid-1941, policy debates in Tokyo narrowed sharply because the issue at stake had been reduced to its fundamental: *within a year the military would lack the fossil fuel necessary to continue fighting effectively.*[13,14]

Policy debates moved from grand strategic alternatives to narrow tactical analyses: how best to seize the Dutch East Indies and its oil wells. Analysts quickly concluded that the project must involve war not only with the British and the Dutch but also with the Americans. So planning focused on the question of how best to cripple Anglo-American war-making capacity in the Asia-Pacific region. The idea of a surprise attack on Pearl Harbor was first conceived in early January 1941 by Admiral Isoroku Yamamoto, Commander in Chief of the Japanese Combined Fleet.[15,16,17]

Yamamoto[18] was born as Isoroku Takano in 1884 in Nagaoka, Niigata, and graduated from the Imperial Japanese Naval Academy in 1904. Yamamoto was fundamentally opposed to war with the United States. He studied not only at Harvard University, but also served two times as naval attaché in Washington. He also served as Deputy Navy Minister. In 1939 he was reassigned from the Navy Ministry to sea as the Commander-in-Chief of the Combined Fleet.

On 1 December 1941 Hirohito finally approved a "war against United States, Great Britain and Holland" during another Imperial Conference, to commence with a surprise attack on the US Pacific Fleet at its main forward base at Pearl Harbor in Hawaii. The date was set for 8 December; because of the international dateline it would be 7 December in Pearl Harbor.[19]

The strike force which was going to attack Pearl Harbor set sail on the morning of 25 November 1941.

The attack on Pearl Harbor: war with America!
The attack fleet was the most powerful aircraft carrier force in the history of naval warfare at that time. The initial attack was scheduled for 0330 hours, X Day.[20,21]

Two hundred and thirty nautical miles north of Pearl Harbor, the carriers turned into a twenty-knot wind that swept straight down the flight decks. At six o'clock in the morning, green signals flashed and the 183 planes of the first wave took off.

Thirty-nine-year-old Commander Mitsuo Fuchida, a veteran of combat in China with more than three thousand hours of flying time to his credit, was picked to lead the attack on Pearl Harbor. Guided by his unsuspecting enemy's radio beacons, the music-filled frequencies of stations KGO and KGMB in Honolulu, in ninety minutes he would reach Pearl Harbor.[22]

The signal from Fuchida ordering to attack—*To! To! To!*—was heard clearly all the way back in Japan. Then a similar sounding code word—Japanese for "tiger"—as Fuchida let the carriers know the attack was actually underway: *Tora! Tora! Tora!*[23] The Japanese planes hit the first American ships and military installations on Sunday, 7 December 1941 at 0751. War with America was a fact.[24]

Overall, 9 ships of the U.S. fleet were sunk that day and 21 ships were severely damaged. Three of the 21 would be irreparable. The overall death toll reached 2,402, with 1,282 wounded, including 68 civilians. Of the military personnel lost at Pearl Harbor, 1,177 were from the USS *Arizona*. Japan would lose 29 out of the 350 aircraft used in the attack.[25,26,27]

CHAPTER 7

UNDER ATTACK!

I T WAS AROUND lunchtime on Sunday 8 December 1941, that Jim Cushing, together with his wife Fritzi, entered Café Imperial. The café was located on the second floor of the residence of Ramon "Moning" on the corner of Sikatuna and D. Jakosalem Streets in downtown Cebu City. Some of Jim's friends were already sitting at a table close by the window. Café Imperial was more or less the hang-out of Cebu's expats, mostly mining engineers employed somewhere in the southern Philippines. It was quiet; everybody was listening to radio station KZRC, Cebu's only AM radio station, broadcasting from the top floor of the Gotiaoco Building on M.C. Briones Street. The voice of Harry Fenton, the station's American anchor, sounded somber. Fenton repeated time and again that a few hours earlier the American Pacific Fleet in Pearl Harbor had been bombed by the Japanese. The damage and loss of life was tremendous, although exact details were lacking.

Harry Fenton was one of those expats that had fallen in love with the Philippines, having first arrived in 1938 with the US Army's medical corps. He worked for a while at Sternberg General Hospital in Manila before becoming a radio announcer in Cebu. There he found Betsy, his Filipina love. He married her and soon they had a baby boy named Steve. His *Amateur Hour* became the most famous radio broadcast in the Cebu area. He came originally from Schenectady, New York. His real name, Aaron Feinstein, betrayed his German-Jewish heritage. In the late 1930s the Jewish community in the Philippines numbered around 2,500 because of an influx of German Jews who were being prosecuted in Hitler's Germany. It is not known why he changed his name to Harry Fenton.[1]

Everybody looked somber. Rumors of war had been hanging in the air for long that it happening so soon and so suddenly was beyond anyone's expectation.

"What next, friends?" Jim broke the silence, "If there is really war I might enlist. I spoke already with General Chynoweth some time ago. He'd like to have me as a demolition officer." Others were not so keen on an assignment in the military. Escape to Australia was another option. They had lunch and a cold San Miguel beer.

An hour later Fenton broadcasted another news bulletin. The first Japanese attack in the Philippines had taken place at 1145 as pilots of the 11th Air Fleet attacked Clark Field just north of Manila. They caught two squadrons of B-17s dispersed on the ground and a squadron of P-40 interceptors just preparing to taxi. The first wave of twenty-seven Japanese twin-engine bombers achieved complete tactical surprise, striking the P-40s as they taxied. A second bomber attack was supported by Zero fighters strafing the field that destroyed 12 of the 17 American heavy bombers and seriously damaged three others. Only three of the P-40s managed to take off. A simultaneous attack on the auxiliary field at Iba to the northwest was also successful: all but two of the 3rd Pursuit Squadron's P-40s, short on fuel, were destroyed in combat or from lack of gasoline when the attack caught them in their landing pattern.[2]

The news became more somber with every new news bulletin. Many battleships in Pearl Harbor were lost, thousands of sailors had perished, and the damage was enormous. The destruction of airfields in the northern Philippines went on. The only lucky thing was that the American aircraft carriers, far more important than battleships, were out to sea and vital naval infrastructure (fuel oil tanks and shipyard facilities) had remained undamaged.

At 1230 p.m. on 8 December, 1941 (December 9 in the Philippines) American President Franklin D. Roosevelt addressed the American Congress in a speech that would be known as the *Day of Infamy Speech*. KZRC relayed the speech.

The Cebu expat community knew perfectly well what this all meant. Contrary to the US military they were here in the Philippines on their own, nobody had forced them to come or to stay. Even now, at this late hour, they could choose to stay or go. Australia was probably the best opportunity, certainly if one took into account that Australia was also a mining country. Staying, however, meant to go into hiding. There was no way to continue life as it was. Then there were their dependents. Most were married or had live-in partners; many had small children. It was not clear if they could bring those along, certainly not to the United States with its anti-miscegenation movements and its Jim Crow laws. It was too late to get passports, if that was possible at all. It was not an easy choice.[3,4]

Jim had the advantage that he and Fritzi had no children, so that at least made the choice easier. On the other hand there was no Japanese soldier on Philippine soil yet, and assuming they came from the north it was still a long way to Cebu. There would be time enough if things went wrong, was his philosophy. In the back of his mind he played with the idea of returning to his mine in Surigao since he could easily hide in the mountains and jungle of the northeastern tip of Mindanao.

The Japanese considered the Philippines as the westernmost bastion of American military power in the Pacific, so the country was clearly marked as one of the first objectives of their armed forces.[5] In addition, in the Japanese concept of the *Greater East Asia Co-Prosperity Sphere* the Philippines was of great importance. How could a great Asian country be against the idea of Asians for Asians? The Philippines was supposed to become a showcase for the Japanese. There was certainly the idea that the Japanese soldiers would be received with flowers for their kicking out the American colonialists.

The military point of view of the Imperial General Headquarters, in regard to the Philippines, was:

> To deny to American ground, sea and air forces the use of the Philippines as an advance base of operations.
> To secure the line of communications between the occupied areas in the south and Japan Proper.
> To acquire intermediate staging areas and supply bases needed to facilitate operations in the southern area.[6]

And then there was of course the mineral richness of the Philippines, especially in regard to copper, gold and chromite. In accordance with the overall plans the Southern Command allotted the mission of executing the Philippines invasion to the Fourteenth Army, under command of Lt. Gen. Masaharu Homma, peacetime commander of the Formosa Army.[7]

General Homma was a remarkable man. He was an amateur painter and playwright, and also known as the Poet General. Homma had a deep respect for, and some reasonable understanding of, the West, having spent eight years as a military attaché in the United Kingdom, including combat service in France in 1918 with the British Expeditionary Force.[8]

At dawn on 8 December 1941 the Batan Island[9] landing Force made an unopposed landing and seized the airstrip. On 10 December a second landing force landed at dawn at Aparri and Vigan against no opposition. The airfields were quickly occupied. Elements of the Vigan landing force pushed north, along the coast, and took the airfield at Laoag on 12 December.[10]

The successful exploitation of advance bases soon gave the Japanese air force overwhelming superiority. On 15 December, it was estimated that the combat strength of the United States Air Forces had been reduced to about ten bombers, ten flying boats and twenty fighters.[11] In less than a week the Japanese had gained control of the skies over the Philippines. Japanese air losses were negligible.

Amphibious operations also took place in Legaspi. Early on the morning of 12 December, the Japanese landed 2,500 men of the 16th Division in this city on the southern tip of Luzon Island. In the early dawn of 20 December the Mindanao invasion force, under Major General Shizuo Sakaguchi, landed near Davao. Resistance by the garrison of some 3.500 Filipino-American troops was quickly overcome and, by 1500 the same day, Davao and the airfield were occupied. A few days later, on 25 December, Jolo and its airfield were taken.

The main attack began early on the morning of 22 December as 43,110 men of the 48th Division and one regiment of the 16th drove north toward Manila where they would link up with forces advancing south toward the capital for the final victory.[12]

What could MacArthur do against the massive Japanese invasion force totaling close to 80.000 men? As of 30 November 1941, the strength of the US Army Forces in the Far East (USAFFE US), including Philippine units, was 31,095, consisting of 2,504 officers and 28,591 enlisted (16,643 Americans and 11,957 Philippine Scouts).[13] USAFFE was a mixed force of non-combat experienced regular, national guard, constabulary, and newly created Commonwealth units; the Japanese, on the other hand, used their best first-line troops at the outset of the campaign. It would be an uneven fight.

A Japanese division supported by artillery and approximately 90 tanks landed at three points along the east coast of Lingayen Gulf. A few B-17s flying from Australia attacked the invasion fleet, and U.S. submarines harassed it from the adjacent waters, but with little effect. There was almost no resistance from poorly equipped Filipino-American forces. The remaining Japanese units landed farther south along the gulf. The 26th Cavalry (PS), advancing to meet them, put up a strong fight at Rosario, La Union, but after taking heavy casualties and with no hope of sufficient reinforcements, was forced to withdraw. By nightfall on 23 December, the Japanese had moved ten miles (16 km) into the interior of the Island of Luzon.

The next day 7,000 men of the Japanese 16th Division hit the beaches at three locations along the shore of Lamon Bay in southern Luzon, where they found General Parker's forces dispersed, and without artillery protecting the eastern coast, unable to offer serious resistance. They immediately consolidated their positions.

With the landings in progress General MacArthur understood General Homma's strategy. It was obvious he sought to swing shut the jaws of a great military pincer, one prong being the main force that had landed at Lingayen, the other the units that had landed at Antimonan. The Japanese strategy envisaged complete annihilation of the Luzon defense force within a short period. With the principal island of the Philippines under their control, they could look forward to an easy conquest of the remainder of the archipelago.

MacArthur considered all options and concluded that only "WOP-3" (War Plan Orange 3) could save the situation for now. Under it, the Philippine Department headquarters, after the experience of numerous maneuvers, had selected certain delaying positions along the central Luzon plain. These positions had been reconnoitered and were considered fairly strong defensive lines along the route of withdrawal to the Bataan Peninsula.[14]

General Wainwright would fight a delaying action on the north to the neck of Bataan in the south. General Jones with his troops from Manila would be withdrawn into Bataan. On the peninsula, the main line of resistance would run from Moron, on the coast of the China Sea, to Abucay, on the shore of Manila Bay. Nine days of feverish movement of supplies into Bataan, primarily by barge from Manila, began in an attempt to feed an anticipated force of 43,000 troops for six months.

The next morning, 24 December, the USAFFE staff was called to a conference. General Sutherland, MacArthur's Chief of Staff, announced the decision and stated that the headquarters was to be moved to Corregidor that evening. General MacArthur, his wife Jean and son Arthur, were transferred to the fortress island of Corregidor off the tip of the peninsula. Top Filipino politicians, such as President Manuel Quezon and his family, Vice President Sergio Osmeña and Chief Justice Abad Santos, also went to Corregidor. On 26 December MacArthur issued a proclamation declaring Manila an open city. He hoped in this way to spare the city and population from the ravages of war.[15] The withdrawal to Bataan was successful.[16] The whole of Visayas, the center part of the Philippines, and Mindanao were still completely free of the Japanese.

CHAPTER 8

THE AMERICAN SURRENDER

W HEN THE JAPANESE generals studied their plans for the Philippines operation, somewhere in October 1941, Lt. Gen. Masami Maeda, later appointed Chief of Staff of the Fourteenth Army, asked what consideration had been given to a possible withdrawal of the enemy forces into Bataan. The question was brushed aside without discussion, and it was evident that Imperial Headquarters had formulated no definite plans to cope with that eventuality.[1]

On 2 January 1942, the advance guard of the 16th and 48th Divisions entered Manila. The occupation of the city went forward efficiently, and public order was gradually restored. With the capture of Manila only twenty-five days after the start of hostilities, the Japanese forces in the Philippines had gained possession of the foremost center of American influence in the Far East, and achieved the major objective fixed by Imperial General Headquarters. General Homma was convinced that the enemy force that had retired into the mountain fastness of Bataan could easily and rapidly be crushed by the Fourteenth Army.

While the Japanese units were engaged in preliminary operations against Bataan, Southern Army Headquarters at Saigon (Vietnam) decided to redeploy the 48th Division and the 5th Air Group, the backbone of the Fourteenth Army. The hasty and radical reorganization would have far reaching consequences.[2]

In the meantime General MacArthur regrouped his forces on Bataan into two corps. The I Corps under General Jonathan Wainwright occupied the left perimeter, and the II Corps under the command of General George Parker held the right. The left and right perimeters together formed the so-called *Mauban-Abucay Line*. Wainright had 22.500 troops, Parker around 25.000.[3]

The Abucay-Mauban line had to be abandoned on 22 January. Within four days, the *Orion-Bagac line* was formed. Against all odds General MacArthur was more than ever determined to hold on as long as possible. The longer the Japanese were stuck on Bataan, the more troops were tied up and could not be used anywhere else.[4]

At the end of January General Homma had to face the bitter realization that he was still far from his objective. It was clear that the offensive had failed miserably. Homma realized that to continue with it might well lead to disaster. The time for a decision had come. The alternative was to discontinue the offensive operations on Bataan and wait for reinforcements with which to launch a final offensive. Meanwhile, he would rest his men, reorganize the Army, and tighten the blockade.[5]

Thus, less than one month after the start of the offensive, 14th Army had been halted and forced back to a defensive line to await reinforcements.

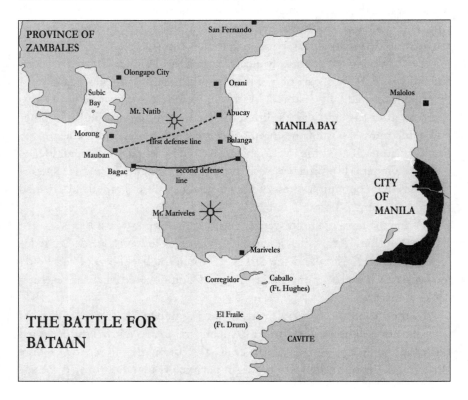

THE BATTLE FOR BATAAN

"The enemy has definitely recoiled," wrote General MacArthur. "He had refused his flank in front of my right six to ten kilometers and in other sectors by varying distances. His attitude is so passive as to discount any immediate threat of attack."[6]

KZRC remained the fastest and most reliable source of news for Cebu. Every day the expats followed the news in Café Imperial, one of the few places that had radio. Jim Cushing had kept his promise and signed up for the army. General Bradford Chynoweth welcomed the miner and gave him the rank of captain in the Corps of Engineers. As a mining engineer he was very familiar with explosives, and that was just what the general needed to carry out his extensive demolition plan in order to frustrate any attempts of the Japanese to occupy the island. There was little time for extended military training so after one week Jim was added to the demolition teams.

Instead of action Jim almost drowned under paperwork. Morale, especially among the Americans, was low. In April, when the Japanese finally started to close in on the Visayan Islands, Jim saw more action. Demolition was now in full swing and he enjoyed it. Bridges, storages, wharves, any facility that might have value for the enemy was destroyed. The most spectacular demolition was the destruction of the fuel depots on Mactan Island, the small coral island in front of Cebu City. Soon Jim became known as "Suicide Cushing."[7,8]

General MacArthur Leaves for Australia

Although Corregidor had seemed impregnable, survival on the beleaguered island fortress became increasingly difficult after Manila fell. The evacuation of the personnel of the civil government from Corregidor began on 19 February 1942. The Filipino politicians and their dependents all arrived safely in Antique, on the Philippine Island of Panay. President Quezon and Vice President Osmeña ended up first in Australia and later in the United States.[9]

Also General MacArthur's stay on Corregidor was soon to be ended. On February 21st General George Marshall in Washington notified him that President Roosevelt wanted him to go to Australia. In Australia he would start his new assignment as commander of the newly created Southwest Pacific Area.

MacArthur was not very keen on leaving Corregidor, and certainly not on leaving the Philippines. Finally he was more or less ordered by Presdident Roosevelt himself to leave immediately. MacArthur as a prisoner of war would have been a disaster of unmeasurable proportions.

On 11 March 1942 the general left, together with wife and son, on board PT-41, a 77-foot motor torpedo boat commanded by Lieutenant John D. Bulkeley.[10] He left General Wainwright in command and managed to leave Corregidor unnoticed.[11] MacArthur arrived safely on Friday, March 13 in Mindanao, and from the nearby Del Monte airstrip he left on the same day for Australia.[12] For his role in the defense of the Philippines MacArthur was awarded the Medal of Honor.[13]

The Fall of Bataan

General Homma's withdrawal in early February, and the escape of the Philippine government and General MacArthur from Corregidor, was a serious setback for the Imperial General Headquarters in Tokyo. This should never have happened. Fresh units from all directions, including special heavy siege artillery such as Type 45 240mm howitzers, arrived in Bataan. It underlined the philosophy of General MacArthur that resistance in Bataan was the best way to derail Japan's offensive in the south. It tied up battle hardened troops that could not be used elsewhere.

On 28 March General Homma gave the order setting 3 April, the death anniversary of Jimmu Tenno, the first Emperor of Japan, as the opening day of the offensive. The second and final phase of the Battle of the Philippines was about to begin.[14]

At 0900 on 3 April 300 artillery pieces and 100 aircraft opened with a devastating preparation that lasted 6 hours. Front line units jumped off on schedule at 1500. Mount Samat, a strategically located cone of Mount Mariveles, was stormed on 5 April and lost. By 8 April, the senior U.S. commander on Bataan, Maj. Gen. Edward P. King, saw the futility of further resistance, and put forth proposals for capitulation. The next morning, April 9, 1942, Gen. King met with Maj. Gen. Kameichiro Nagano and after several hours of negotiations, the remaining weary, starving and emaciated American and Filipino defenders on the battle-swept Bataan peninsula surrendered. It was the largest surrender in American and Filipino military history, and was the largest United States surrender since the Civil War Battle of Harpers' Ferry.[15]

With the fall of Bataan the Japanese captured some 60,000 Filipino and 15,000 American prisoners of war. The Japanese decided to bring all the prisoners to camp O'Donnel in Tarlac, some 130 kilometers from Mariveles. The prisoners had to walk most of this distance; this walk became known as the *Bataan Death March*.[16] Approximately 2,500–10,000 Filipino and 100–650

American prisoners of war died before they could reach Camp O'Donnell. The march was later judged by an Allied military commission to be a Japanese war crime.[17]

The Fall of Corregidor [18]

Bataan had fallen, but Corregidor held on. The small island, only 6 by 2 kilometers, was heavily fortified. Especially its huge 12-inch mortars were famous, but also obsolete as was most of its other artillery. After the fall of Bataan it lasted almost one month before General Wainwright realized that it was over. On 6 May 1942, at about 0130 p.m. he finally surrendered the Corregidor garrison.

The surrender was, after all, a complicated affair. Initially General Homma did not accept Wainwright's surrender offer. Wainwright offered to surrender all the troops on Corregidor and the small neighboring islands, while Homma demanded a surrender of all troops in the Philippines. Wainwright denied that he was the Commander in Chief of all USAFFE troops in the Philippines. In the end Wainwright had no other choice than to surrender unconditionally all USAFFE forces in the Philippines.

CHAPTER 9

THE JAPANESE OCCUPATION OF CEBU

THE CREATION OF the Visayan Force on 4 March 1942 had brought a change in commanders and a renewed vigor to the preparations for a prolonged defense of the islands in the Visayan group. Col. Irvine C. Scudder, commander of the troops on Cebu, where Visayan Force headquarters was located, had about 6,500 troops, including the 82nd and 83nd Infantry (PA, Philippine Army), the Cebu Military Police Regiment, a Philippine Army Air Corps detachment, and miscellaneous units. Their equipment, however, was very poor indeed. The Philippine Army received clothing that was of poor quality. Their rubber shoes would wear out within two weeks. There were shortages of nearly every kind of equipment such as blankets, mosquito nets, shelter halves, entrenching tools, gas masks and helmets. During August 1941, MacArthur had requested 84,500 Garand rifles, 330 .30-caliber machineguns, 326 .50-calibe machineguns, 450 37mm guns, 217 81mm mortars, 288 75 mm guns, and over 8,000 vehicles. On 18 September, he was informed that, because of lend-lease commitments,[1] he would not receive most of these items. As a result, the Philippine Army was forced to continue using Enfield and Springfield rifles, weapons originating from World War I.[2]

General Homma's preoccupation with Bataan gave General Chynoweth, the Visayan Force commander, an additional month in which to make his preparations. Much had already been accomplished when he assumed command, and under his direction the defenses were rapidly brought to completion. On Cebu the men had constructed tank obstacles, trenches and gun emplacements, strung wire, and prepared demolitions. Airfield construction was pushed rapidly on all the islands. Jim Cushing had been heavily involved in all of this.

Perhaps the most interesting feature of the preparations for the defense of the Visayas was the program known as Operation *Baus Au,* Visayan for "gets it back." Initiated by General Chynoweth[3] during his tenure as the commander of the Panay garrison and then adopted on Cebu, Operation Baus Au was the large-scale movement of goods, supplies, and weapons into the interior for use later in guerrilla warfare. Secret caches were established in remote and inaccessible places, and at mountain hideouts which could be reached only via steep, narrow trails barely passable for a man on foot. The program was completely in line with General MacArthur's original idea to go over to extensive guerrilla warfare if the Japanese landings could not be stopped.

Washington had told General MacArthur time and again that the war in Europe had the highest priority and, because of that, he could not expect the degree of supplies he had asked for. The heroic resistance on Bataan, however, softened up this hard position. The War Department dispatched Brigadier General Patrick J. Hurley, a former Secretary of War in the Hoover administration, to Australia with orders to take charge of a supply effort for MacArthur. Money was, according to the War Department, not an issue, it was purely a matter of logistics, of obtaining supplies and how to get them to Bataan. From the nine ships that were dispatched from Australia only two, the Philippine-registered SS *Doña Nati* and the Hong Kong-registered SS *Anhui,* were able to reach the port of Cebu City.[4] Each was loaded with food and ammunition, together almost 20,000 tons. By the time the ships had been unloaded at Cebu City and warehoused awaiting reloading onto coasters for the final run northward to Corregidor, Japanese naval patrols were in place within the approaches to Manila Bay. Evasion of those patrols by blockade runners had by then become virtually impossible.[5]

When it became impossible to reload the cargo on coastal vessels for transport to Bataan and Corregidor, USAFFE-Cebu used a fleet of trucks to haul the load of ammunition, hand grenades, mortar shells, small arms and canned goods to caches dispersed in the barangays Camp 7, Camp 8, Dita and other similar places in the interior of Cebu. This operation was not completely finished when the Japanese landed on 10 April. These movements then became dangerous; rather than risk enemy capture, trucks were driven or toppled into out-of-the-way ravines, creeks or gulleys. Supplies that could no longer be securely stowed away in the haste of movement were recovered by civilians who found their own hiding places with a thought of denying their use to the Japanese.[6]

The effect on the civilian population of Operation Baus Au and other measures for a prolonged defense in the interior was actually unfortunate. The Filipinos felt that they were being abandoned, and their faith in their American protector was badly shaken. What they expected was a pitched battle at the beaches ending in the route of the enemy. "They took great pride in their Army," noted Colonel Tarkington, "and having been indoctrinated for years with the idea of American invincibility, were all for falling on the enemy tooth and nail and hurling him back into the sea."[7]

Japanese knowledge of conditions in the Visayas was accurate and fairly complete. Though they did not know the exact disposition of the troops in the area, they knew which islands were defended and the approximate size of the defending force. Homma was confident that with reinforcements from Malaya and Borneo he could seize the key islands in the group. His plan was to take Cebu with the Kawaguchi Detachment and Panay with the Kawamura Detachment. These two forces, in cooperation with the Miura Detachment at Davao, would then move on to take Mindanao. That island conquered, the remaining garrisons in the Philippines could be reduced at leisure if they did not surrender of their own accord.

Given the fact that the fall of Bataan was imminent, no time was wasted in putting this plan into effect. On 5 April, four days after the Kawaguchi Detachment reached Lingayen Gulf, it was aboard ship once more, headed for Cebu. With 4,852 trained and battle-tested troops, General Kawaguchi had little reason to fear the outcome.

First word of the approach of the Japanese reached General Chynoweth on the afternoon of 9 April 1942, during a meeting with his staff and unit commanders. Three Japanese cruisers and eleven transports, it was reported, were steaming for Cebu from the south. All troops were alerted and a close watch was kept on the enemy flotilla. That night further news was received that the Japanese force had split in two, one sailing along the west coast, the other along the east. By daylight the enemy vessels were plainly visible, with the larger of the convoys already close to the island's capital, Cebu City, midway up the east coast. Shortly after dawn on 10 April, the Japanese in this convoy landed at the beaches of Talisay, some 20 kilometers south of Cebu City; at about the same time the men in the other convoy came ashore in the vicinity of Toledo, on the opposite side of the island.[8]

Defending the capital was the Cebu Military Police Regiment of about 1,100 men under the command of Lt. Col. Howard J. Edmands. Edmands'

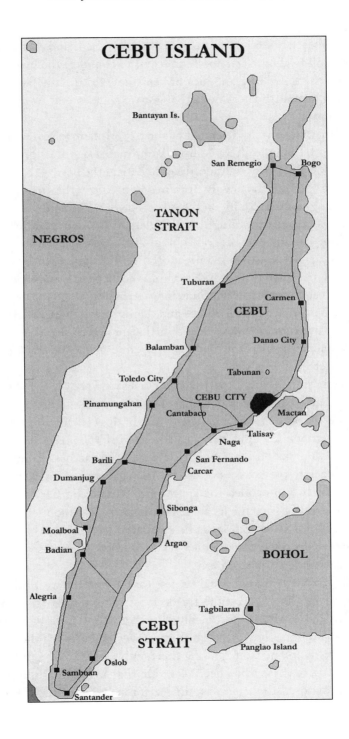

CEBU ISLAND

mission, like that of other unit commanders on the island, was to hold only long enough to allow the demolition teams to complete their work, then fall back into the hills. "I had no idea of being able to stop the Japs," explained General Chynoweth later, "but I thought we could spend two or three days in withdrawal."[9]

Southern Cebu was defended by the 82nd Infantry Regiment. Its commander, Col. Emigdio V. David from Pampanga, Luzon, assigned Company A, under 3rd lieutenant Salvador Ibay, to defend the beaches of Talisay. Ibay was also to prevent the enemy from marching down the Manipis road, the road leading to Toledo City on the other side of the island.

At seven in the morning the defenders of the Talisay beaches saw the first enemy landing barges approaching. There were ten of them, each with some 30 Japanese soldiers. With mortar and machinegun fire lieutenant Ibay's men managed to sink or damage all the barges. A second wave of nine barges was also covered in fire. Suddenly a squadron of ten Japanese bombers appeared and attacked with bombs and then strafed the defenders. Soon the Filipinos were running for cover and the Japanese occupied the beaches. The road to Toledo lay open, the road that went straight to General Chynoweth's headquarters in Cantabaco.

The fight for Cebu City lasted only one day. Faced by a foe superior in numbers and weapons, the defenders fell back slowly, fighting for the time needed to block the roads and destroy the bridges leading into the interior. By the afternoon the fight had reached the outskirts of the city and at 1700 the Japanese broke off the action. Under cover of darkness Edmands pulled his men back to previously selected positions about ten miles inland, along a ridge which commanded the approaches from Cebu City to the central mountain area. Though the Japanese were in undisputed control of the capital by the end of the day, Edmands had achieved his purpose. He had gained the time needed by the demolition teams, and his regiment was still intact and withdrawing in good order.

The Japanese enjoyed equal success that day on the west side of the island, in the neighborhood of the Toledo Western terminus of the cross-island highway. Toledo with its port facilities was an important military objective. On the assumption, however, that the narrow channel along the west would discourage an enemy from landing there, only a small force, the 3d Battalion, 82d Infantry (PA), had been placed in that area. The Philippine Army battalion opposed the enemy landing vigorously, but without success and finally fell back along the cross-island highway toward the town of Canta-baco, leaving the Japanese in possession of Toledo.

At Cantabaco, midway across the island, the highway split in two. One branch turned northeast to pass close to Camp X, where General Chynoweth had his headquarters, then southeast to Talisay. The southern branch led to Naga. At both places there was a defending force of Filipinos whose route of withdrawal depended upon the security of Cantabaco. Should the Japanese pursuing the 3d Battalion, 82d Infantry, gain control of that town, the defenders would be cut off.[10]

General Chynoweth understood fully the importance of Cantabaco to the defense of Cebu. Even before the Japanese landings, in anticipation of difficulty there, he had brought Colonel Grimes and his 3d Battalion, 83d Infantry, from Bohol to support the defenses of western Cebu. Now, on the afternoon of the 10th, he ordered Grimes to cover Cantabaco, and as an added precaution he sent a messenger with orders to his reserve battalion in the north to move down to the threatened area. Grimes, "eager to get into the fray started out with a gleam in his eye," and Chynoweth, confident that he had things reasonably well in hand, settled down for a good night's sleep.[11]

He got little rest that night. Time and again he was awakened by anxious staff officers who reported that the enemy was approaching from the direc-tion of Cantabaco. Despite these reports Chynoweth remained confident. He had received no message from Grimes, and he felt sure that if the enemy had broken through at Cantabaco, Grimes would have sent word. Moreover there had been no explosions to indicate that the demolition teams along the road were doing their work. He had inspected these demolitions himself and felt sure that if the enemy had passed Cantabaco, the charges would have been set off. But at 0330, when the sounds of battle became louder, Chyno-weth's confidence began to wane. The enemy was undoubtedly nearing Camp X. A half hour later all doubts vanished when large groups of Filipinos passed the outposts and appeared in Camp X. They seemed hypnotized, fired in the air, and refused to obey commands in their haste to flee. After a brief confer-ence with his staff, Chynoweth decided to pull back to an alternate command post on a ridge in Cantipla Forest, a half mile to the north, and await devel-opments there.

The collapse of the Cantabaco position had been the result of an unfor-tunate and unforeseen combination of events. The demolition teams in which Chynoweth had placed so much faith had waited too long, and when the enemy appeared, led by tanks and armored cars, they had fled. Like his commander, Colonel Grimes believed that the enemy would be halted by blown bridges and obstacles along the road. Not hearing the sound of explosions, he too, concluded that the Japanese were still at a safe distance. In his confidence he drove forward to familiarize himself with the terrain and was captured by an enemy patrol. Deprived of their commander, his men "stayed quite well hidden."[12] So well were they hidden that the Japanese were unaware of their presence.

The reserve battalion had never even started moving south. The messengers sent to that battalion failed to return, and if the battalion commander did receive Chynoweth's order to move to Cantabaco, he never complied. Instead, the battalion moved farther north, well out of reach of the enemy.

Opposed only by the retreating 3rd Battalion, 82nd Infantry, which was quickly dispersed, the Japanese had advanced swiftly from Toledo through Cantabaco and then along the Talisay and Naga roads. It was the Japanese force along the Talisay road that had scattered the Camp X outposts and forced upon Chynoweth the realization that his plans for the defenses of Cantabaco had miscarried.

With the enemy in possession of the cross-island highway, the fight for Cebu was over. Nothing more could be accomplished in central Cebu, and on the night of the 12th Chynoweth, with about 200 men, started north to his retreat in the mountains. From there he hoped to organize the few units still remaining on the island into an efficient guerrilla force.

The Japanese did not claim the complete subjugation of the island until 19 April, but Wainwright had already conceded the loss of Cebu three days earlier when he ordered General Sharp to re-establish the Visayan-Mindanao Force and take command of the remaining garrisons in the Visayas.[13]

In the meantime General Chynoweth tried to set up his guerrilla war. Apart from his unit in Cantipla Forest, there were all over the island several groups of soldiers, cut off in the early hours of the Japanese landings, who could form the main body of an organized resistance movement. To achieve this, however, was not easy. The interior of Cebu Island was rough, remote and inaccessible. There were no roads, no telephones, and no radio systems. All communication and transport had to be done by courier and by foot. In short everything was extremely time-consuming. But Chynoweth was in an upbeat mood and had high hopes for organizing a successful guerrilla outfit.

Although there was radio contact with USAFFE Headquarters on Corregidor, information about the war in the Central Philippines was scarce. Chynoweth had great respect for Harry Fenton as a newsman for KZRC and had urged him to continue as long as possible. But when the Japanese overran Cebu City it was the end for Harry. He fled, together with his wife Betsy and his baby boy to the mountains, just north of Cebu City.

Chynoweth would never have the chance to finish his work. While he was busy arranging his guerrilla activities the battle for Corregidor went on. It was a losing battle, and in early May came the climax.

At 1030 on the morning of 6 May 1942 General Beebe stepped up to the microphone of the "Voice of Freedom" and in tired but clear tones read a message addressed to General Homma "or the present commander in chief of the Imperial Japanese Forces on Luzon." The message was from General Wainwright and it contained his offer to surrender.[14] At 1100 and again at 1145 the message was rebroadcast, in English and Japanese, but still there was no reply. When the Japanese failed to reply to the noon broadcast or honor the flag of truce, Wainwright was faced with the terrible threat of the total destruction of his now defenseless force. He made one last effort at 1230 to reach the Japanese commander by radio, but the result was the same as before. There was only one method left: that was to send an officer forward under a white flag to the enemy lines to make arrangements with the local enemy commander.

For this assignment Wainwright selected, during a lull in the battle, a Marine officer, Capt. Golland L. Clark, Jr. Captain Clark was taken to a colonel he believed to be the Japanese troop commander on Corregidor. To him he explained that General Wainwright was seeking a truce and wished to discuss the terms of surrender with General Homma. The Japanese officer, after consulting his superiors on Bataan, told Captain Clark that if Wainwright would come to his headquarters he would make arrangements to send him to Bataan.[15]

Within an hour after his departure Clark was back in Malinta Tunnel with the Japanese message. Immediately General Wainwright, accompanied by General Moore and his aides, with Clark acting as guide, went forward toward the enemy lines. The man they met was Japanese colonel Nakayama, General Homma's senior operations officer. Homma had sent him to Corregidor the night before with orders to bring General Wainwright to him only if the American was ready to surrender all his troops.[16] It is not surprising therefore that when Wainwright explained that he wished to surrender only the four islands in Manila Bay, Nakayama replied with "an angry torrent of Japanese," the gist of which was that any surrender would have to include all forces in the Philippines. "In that case," replied Wainwright, "I will deal only with General Homma and with no one of less rank."[17] Nakayama thereupon agreed to take him to Bataan.

Together with his staff Wainwright was brought to the meeting place, a house about three quarters of a mile to the north. For almost half an hour the Americans waited on the open porch of the house, facing Manila Bay, a short distance away. At 1700 General Homma drove up in a Cadillac, saluted with a vague flourish of the hand, and strode up to the porch. Behind him were his principal staff officers, correspondents, and more photographers. The Americans followed silently. The meeting opened as soon as everyone was seated, without any exchange of courtesies. Wainwright made the first move by reaching into his pocket for his formal signed surrender note, which he tendered to the Japanese commander.[18]

After it was read, Homma stated through the interpreter that the surrender would not be accepted unless it included all American and Philippine troops in the Islands. To this Wainwright replied that he commanded only the harbor defense troops. Homma refused to believe Wainwright's explanation. Wainwright was in no position to bargain. Uppermost in his mind was the thought that the troops on Corregidor were disarmed and helpless. If Homma refused now to accept his surrender, these men faced certain death.

"I advise you to return to Corregidor and think the matter over. If you see fit to surrender, then surrender to the commanding officer of the division on Corregidor."[19] With these words Homma left the meeting.

There was little Wainwright could do on his return to Corregidor late on the night of the 6th but surrender under the terms dictated by the Japanese. There was no discussion of terms. The surrender was unconditional and the document drawn up contained all the provisions Homma had insisted upon. Wainwright agreed to surrender all forces in the Philippines, including those in the Visayas and on Mindanao, within four days. All local commanders were to assemble their troops in designated areas and then report to the nearest Japanese commander.

Promptly on the morning of 7 May 1942 Homma's intelligence officer, Lt. Col. Hikaru Haba, called on General Wainwright to discuss measures required to fulfill the terms of the surrender agreement. Wainwright decided to send Col. Jesse T. Traywick, his operations officer, to Mindanao with a letter explaining what had happened. In it he directed General Sharp to surrender the troops under his command.

The Japanese had still one more humiliation in store for General Wainwright. When the letter was completed, Colonel Haba announced that the general would go to Manila that afternoon to broadcast the surrender instructions. General Wainwright objected strenuously, but finally gave in.

Surrender in the South

Colonel Traywick and Colonel Haba reached Mindanao by plane on the 9th and arranged a meeting with General Sharp for the following day. During the afternoon of the 10th Colonel Traywick, with Haba met General Sharp at his headquarters at Malaybalay.[20] Traywick delivered Wainwright's letter and told Sharp the circumstances which had led to its preparation. He made clear that if the Visayan-Mindanao Force was not surrendered, the Japanese would probably reject the terms already agreed upon and would open fire on the prisoners on Corregidor. It was this threat that forced General Sharp to capitulate.[21,22]

General Sharp's surrender orders proved far more difficult to enforce than had been anticipated. His troops were scattered among many islands; most of them were untrained Filipinos; and those who were safe in their mountain hideouts showed no disposition to give up their freedom. Communication between the islands was poor and it would be some time before the last troops laid down their arms. Until then the fate of the Corregidor garrison hung in the balance.

The detailed instructions to each commander were sent by courier on the 11th. General Chynoweth, for example, was to bring his men to the northern outskirts of Cebu City. All commanders were warned against the destruction of military or civilian property and urged to accord the Japanese "courteous and prompt obedience."[23]

The surrender of Chynoweth's troops on Cebu was not accomplished easily. Chynoweth had heard Wainwright's surrender broadcast on 6 May and received General Sharp's clear text message to surrender four days later.[24] He next received a letter from the commander of the Japanese forces on Cebu urging immediate surrender to save lives. Chynoweth acknowledged receipt of the letter but made no move to surrender his force.[25] Copies of the correspondence were sent to the various units on Cebu, and the men were told that they could surrender individually if they wished to do so.

Only two Filipinos and two Americans took advantage of this opportunity. General Chynoweth then made plans to move to Panay to join forces with Colonel Christie.

Chynoweth could no longer put off the difficult decision. He did not wish nor did his situation require him to surrender. But both Generals Wainwright and Sharp had directed him to do so. On 15 May General Sharp's courier arrived in Cebu. He gave Chynoweth the written terms of surrender, Sharp's order directing surrender, and a letter from Wainwright stating that "on no account were any commanders to make any attempts to evade the terms of surrender." The courier also told Chynoweth that the Japanese had concentrated the Americans on Corregidor under their guns and would kill them "if the surrender was not faithfully executed." Chynoweth thereupon decided to surrender and immediately notified the Japanese commander of his decision. The next day he assembled the organized elements of his force and marched down out of the hills.[26]

During the next week the troops on outlying islands submitted to the Japanese, and by 9 June 1942 all forces in the Philippines, with the exception of certain small detachments in isolated areas, had surrendered. On that day General Wainwright was notified that all organized resistance had ended. "Your high command," the Japanese told him then, "ceases and you are now a prisoner of war." The six-month-long struggle for control of the Philippine archipelago was over.

The victory which Homma had hoped to win by the middle of February was finally his on 9 June, four months later. Each day's delay had meant a loss of face for the Japanese, and General Homma paid the price. The campaign was hardly over when Imperial General Headquarters relieved him of command and brought him back to Tokyo, where he spent the rest of the war on the sidelines, as a reserve officer.

With the conquest of the Philippines,[27] the Japanese gained the best harbor in the Orient, excellent bases from which to stage and supply their garrisons to the south and east, as well as a large population to contribute to the Greater East Asia Co-Prosperity Sphere.

Cebu City fenced

Soon after the Japanese occupation became a fact the first guerrilla activities showed the resilience of Cebu. Under the leadership of Jose Macabuhay the struggle started as early as July 1942 with the stealing of Japanese weapons.

It was a group of ten people, all from the Cebu City barangays Mambaling and Duljo. Their first succss was the stealing of four Nambu (Luger-like) pistols with sixty bullets, two samurai swords, three Japanese rifles with ammunition and two bayonets. The Japanese reacted furiously and constructed a bamboo fence all around the city in order to have better control over who went where. The fence started from the seashore of Duljo up to the suburbs of Guadalupe traversing the hills north of the Capitol down to Mabolo and on to the seashore again. The laborers involved in the building were paid eighty centavos a day. There were gates where sentries were placed. The gate near Mambaling, for instance, was placed at C. Padilla Street, a distance of about seventy meters away from the Kinalumsan Bridge.[28,29]

PART TWO

GUERRILLA WARFARE IN CEBU, PHILIPPINES

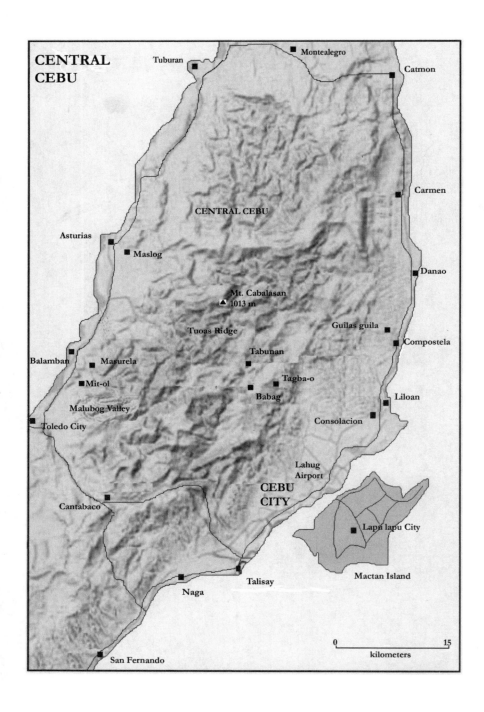

CENTRAL
CEBU

Tuburan

Montealegro

Catmon

CENTRAL CEBU

Carmen

Asturias

Maslog

Danao

Mt. Cabalasan
1013 m

Tuoas Ridge

Guilas guila

Compostela

Tabunan

Balamban

Masurela

Tagba-o

Mit-ol

Babag

Liloan

Malubog Valley

Consolacion

Toledo City

Lahug
Airport

CEBU
CITY

Cantabaco

Lapu lapu City

Naga

Talisay

Mactan Island

San Fernando

0   15
kilometers

CHAPTER **10**

THE BIRTH OF A GUERRILLA ARMY

T
HE FIRST THING the Japanese on Cebu Island stumbled over
was the extent of the damage done by demolitions. Every bridge,
railway or other asset that could be of any use to the Japanese
war machine had been destroyed. It caused delays and hindered an expedient
occupation of the island. The Japanese were angry and put the blame on the
guerrillas. Guerrillas that, by all means, were not even organized or operating,
but someone or something had to bear the brunt of their anger. Twenty-four
hours after the first Japanese landings in Talisay the tone of what was to be
expected from the Japanese occupation was set.

The American submarine USS *Swordfish* unloaded the Filipino politicians she had picked up on Corregidor at San Jose de Buenavista, in Antique,
at 0240 on 22 February. The SS *Don Esteban,* the Filipino ship with the other
half of the party, reached the same port an hour later. From there President
Quezon traveled to Australia. Before he left he authorized Chief Justice Abad
Santos to act as acting President of the Philippines. The Chief Justice went
on to Iloilo, Negros, and finally Cebu, where he arrived on 7 April.

On 8 April Abad Santos and his companions were captured by Japanese
advancing on the road in barrio Tubod, Barili. Major General Kiyotake
Kawaguchi, commander of the Japanese forces that took Cebu, and Colonel
Kawakami, chief of the military administration in that province, took turns
interrogating Santos. Having ascertained who he was, they blamed him for
all the acts of sabotage and demolition on the island. When asked to cooperate with the Japanese, he refused to do so.

The Japanese military administration in Manila under Major-General
Yoshihide Hayashi was informed of Abad Santos's refusal to cooperate. It

was most unfortunate that Santos's capture coincided with the visit of Field Marshal Sugiyama at the headquarters of the Japanese Army in Orani, Bataan. He was extremely angry at General Homma for the delays concerning the Japanese conquest of the Philippines. Informed about Abad Santos's intransigence, Sugiyama is said to have ordered Hayashi "to liquidate all leaders who were opposed to the Japanese military administration."

On or about 26 April 1942, Abad Santos was brought by ship to Mindanao. After days of travelling he ended up on May 1 in Malabang, Lanao. The next day was 2 May, and after lunch, behind a coconut grove at a turn of the road, near a river bank, Abad Santos was summarily shot. The murder in cold blood, without any form of due process, of an acting President of the Philippines, set the tone for what Cebu could expect of the Japanese occupation.[1]

After the final surrender of General Wainwright, Jim Cushing went, together with wife Fritzie and his huge dog Senta, a Great Dane, into hiding in Cebu's hinterland. They moved around in the south and in the center of the island, but stayed usually in barangay Babag. General Chynoweth had warned him that the Japanese would kill any non-surrendered straggler on sight, certainly if it was an American. He could not expect any form of clemency. Jim was convinced that it would not take long before the Americans would be back to kick out the Japanese. There were very few Americans who did not surrender, and because of their Caucasian looks they had to be extremely cautious. For Jim it was slightly easier. As half Mexican and half American he could, sun-tanned as he was, easily pass for a Filipino. Only his height might be a problem.

It did not take long before everywhere small bands of men, often ex-members of the Filipino units of USAFFE, presented themselves, under various names, as guerrillas. The first was probably Jose Macabuhay from Mambaling, a group that was closely related to Governor Hilario Abellana.

Another early group was an armed unit organized around USAFFE Captain Leoncio Minoza. Probably they were the first ones who assassinated a Filipino collaborator. They killed the man, who was responsible for betraying USAFFE Captain Carmichael.[2]

In the northern part of Cebu, in Barrio Awayan above the Lusaran Valley where two rivers meet, Sergeant Marcial Banate gathered 280 men, most of whom had firearms. In the southwestern town of Dumanjug, Mayor Jose S. Amadora, a reserve officer, organized the town's resistance group that numbered 200 men. In the town of Tuburan, on Cebu's northwestern coast, news about guerrilla groups filtered amoung the officers and men who had returned from their broken units and evacuated with their families to the interior. Prominent among these groups were Lieutenants Ricardo Mascariñas, Manuel Allego, Columbus Parilla and Sergeant Simon Maxilom. Far to the north on Bantayan Island there were soldier returnees like Colonel Franciska Roska, Colonel Francisco Villacasten, Colonel Buenaventura de Leon, Lieutenants Venancio "Bening" Sevilla, Eliodoro C. Calgado and Bernardino "Danding" Rivera. In the Tabogon-Borbon areas, Captain Domingo Y. Recio, a doctor, organized 90 officers and men. In the town of Carcar in southeastern Cebu, Lieutenant Ramon D. Castillo and Lieutenant Ireneo Racoma gathered 100 officers and men.[3] Mayor Pascual Derama organized 50 men in Borbon. While in Alcoy, Lieutenant Leonilo O. Hamoy took the lead. On the west coast at Balamban, Lieutenant Nicasio San Juan in June organized a unit with 27 rifles. He moved to Pinamungajan where his unit grew to 118 riflemen. In the Ronda-Alcantara area in southwestern Cebu, Lieutenant Eutiquio Acebes who was an officer of the 82nd Infantry Regt. organized 76 men. Lieutenant Domingo B. Cuizon grouped 46 ex-USAFFE men with 36 rifles, 2 machineguns, 5 shotguns and 18 assorted sidearms. Lieutenant Antonio Cuizon formed a group in Dalaguete in southeastern Cebu. Captain Jose O. Ponce in San Fernando had 200 men with 63 rifles and 15 sidearms. Lieutenant Castor Zamora assembled 56 men in Alegria.[4]

In other words, from all corners of Cebu Island men wanted to participate in the armed struggle against the Japanese invaders. Not all of these groups were real guerrillas; some were just plain criminals, thugs and bandits who used the situation to enrich themselves. Others saw a chance to settle old scores. In order to get food and money they did not shun methods such as blackmail, intimidation and extortion. The big problem was how to unite the good groups and get rid of the bad eggs. First and foremost it was necessary to have leaders who could organize a real guerrilla movement.

During the first months of the occupation, June and July, local leaders such as politicians, mayors and barangay captains in the southern part of Cebu tried to find someone who was without stains to take the initiative for the resistance movement. It proved to be very difficult.

In the end Jim Cushing seemed to be a useful candidate. For the local leaders he had a few advantages. He was an American of mixed blood, he looked very much Filipino, he was not from Cebu and he was married to a woman from Leyte, another island. He was also a captain in the Corps of Engineers of USAFFE. Many knew of his daring activities as "Suicide Cushing." They approached him and he turned them down. To be a leader of a bunch of unorganized Filipino guerrillas was the last thing that attracted him. He had been in the country long enough to know how difficult that would be.

Jim preferred to work on his own or with a very small team. But actually he had in mind to return soon to his mine in Surigao and from there try to reach Australia. He thought that with his intimate knowledge of the Philippines that he could be of more use to General MacArthur in his campaign to retake the islands than by staying in Cebu.

In the meantime Jim also heard the stories of the cargos of the Allied supply ships *Doña Nate* and the *Anhui*. The Japanese tried feverishly to get their hands on these supplies. Some traitors knew of the disposition of the cargo of both ships and the enemy organized search patrols, which penetrated the interior mountain barrios in efforts to locate and collect the arms and ammunition. The Japanese did not shy away from intimidation, torture and other horrible acts to force inhabitants of the mountain barangays to give up their weapon and food caches.

At Barrio Tagba-o, just north of barangay Tabunan, there was a school teacher who had gone over to the Japanese. He led a company of the enemy to Tagba-o to help them locate the arms and ammunition that were left by the USAFFE in the area. At Tagba-o they caught Felomino Cugay, a resident who was suspected of knowing where the firearms were. He was tortured but refused to talk. Finally he was tied to a stake; they poured gasoline over him and struck a match. Poor Felomino died a horrible death. That was how the Japanese dealt with these Filipinos.

In mid-August 1942 the Japanese came back. This time they collected enough firearms and ammunition to load a full *balsa*, a local sledge, pulled by a caraboa. As the group left, taking the trail to Cebu City, they were ambushed by local residents. The Japanese and their Filipino traitors were killed and the firearms recovered.

The mayors and barangay captains kept on pressing their points to Jim Cushing. After a while Jim, understanding the problem, thought he could not refuse anymore. He had to help the resistance movement. He started to work in southern Cebu, in towns such as Ronda, Alcantara, Dumanjug and Barili. He managed to get people such as Captain Eutiqio S. Acebes, and his close associates Lieutenant Francisco R. Kintanar and Lieutenant Ricardo Gabuya, as well as Cayetano Villamor, who acted as legal officer for this group, into a common effort. Later Dumanjug's Mayor Attorney Jose Amadora and 3rd Lieutenant Nene Ciano participated also. In no time they assembled some 200 to 300 men, most of them armed. By the end of August Jim managed to organize a number of these groups into the *Cebu Patriots*.[5,6,7]

In the northern part of Cebu it was radioman Harry Fenton who was very active. General Chynoweth, a great fan of Fenton, had warned him to stay as far away as possible from the Japanese. He knew that Fenton was on the top of the list of persons to be arrested once Cebu was under control. During the months before the surrender of Cebu, Fenton had proven to be extremely anti-Japanese and had voiced his opinion time and again over the radio. Just before the fall of Cebu Fenton took his wife Betsy and baby Steve and hid in sitio Ga-as of barangay Tabunan, almost in the center of the island. Here he started to work on organized resistance against the Japanese occupation. He associated himself with groups in Tuburan, on Cebu's west coast, where a band of guerrillas was formed around lieutenants Ricardo Mascariñas, Maruel Allego, Columbus Parillo and Sergeant Simon Maxilom. They formed an initial group of about 20 men, armed with rifles and revolvers of various calibers. But there were also groups in Bogo, Tabuelan, Lugo, Catmon and Danao.

Sometime in early September 1942[8] Jim was informed about the activities of Harry Fenton in Tabunan. From Babag, where he was at that time, to Tabunan was not very far as the crow flies, but over the narrow trails through the mountains and tall cogon[9] grass areas, it was a march of several hours. On 8 September he decided to pay Harry a visit. Although they knew each other casually they had never had a serious talk. There were other people around, such as 3rd Lieutenant Nene Ciano, Franklin Ciano, 1st Sergeant Paulino Ciano (father of the two other Ciano's), Sergeant Sebastian Augusto, doctor Alejandro Blathazar, attorney[10] Quirico del Mar and attorney Alfredo Vargas. Fenton's residence was a hidden hut in Sitio Ga-as of Tabunan, where he stayed with his Filipina wife Betsy and his baby son.[11]

Three days of conferences followed, with the main topic being the immediate consolidation of the various armed groups of resistance against Japan in the province of Cebu. At the end the participants agreed to consolidate existing guerrilla groups under a joint command. Fenton and Cushing, considered to be of equal standing, were both designated commanding officers. Cushing would handle military affairs, Fenton would administrate the command. The organization would operate under the name *Cebu Area Command* and have its headquarters in barangay Tabunan. Simultaneously, the various officers from the local guerrilla units were constituted into a General Staff. Subordinate leaders were, on the other hand, given minor commands and allotted areas under their control, with their troops formed into battalions. It was believed that the coalition of Fenton and Cushing was a move that bolstered immensely the position of the guerrilla movement in Cebu. With centralized direction and control, the movement, which otherwise could have assumed a desultory nature, broken as it was into small local groups, achieved greater efficiency. Most guerrilla leaders realized this and were in fact highly receptive to the union of the two sectors.[12] The establishment of a single Cebu Command also brought into full play the administrative and propaganda skills of Fenton and the combat ability of Jim Cushing.[13]

The organizational structure formulated as a result of the establishment of the Cebu Area Command was as follows:[14, 15]

Lt. Col. James M. Cushing	CO, Combat Operations
Lt. Col. Harry Fenton	CO, Administrative
Lt. Col. Ricardo T. Estrella	Chief of Staff
Major Marcial Banat	Adjutant and G-1
Capt. Ramon Durano	G-2
Lt. Col. James M. Cushing	G-3
Capt. de Leon	G-4
North Sector:	CO—Lt. Col. Fabian Sanchez
Northwest Cebu Sector:	CO—Capt. Bernard Hale
Northeast Cebu Sector:	CO—Lt. Col. Ricardo T. Estrella
Central Cebu Sector:	CO—Lt. Col. Olegario H. Baura
South Cebu Sector:	CO—Major Marciano Calderon

G-1: Deputy Chief of Staff
G-2: Deputy Chief of Staff for Intelligence
G-3: Deputy Chief of Staff Operations
G-4: Deputy Chief of Staff Logistics

To further strengthen the coalition, officers were sent to various parts of the island to inform other smaller units what had transpired at Tabunan and to convince their leaders to submit to the new leadership. Among those sent out to undertake this mission were, among others, lieutenants Maximo M.

Albinda and Pantaleon P. Ciano, who were sent to the towns in the south; and Lt. Garcia, who proceeded to the northern areas. These missions were for the most part successful. Many of the local leaders came to meet with Fenton and Cushing and pledged their cooperation and support to the larger undertaking envisioned by the two commanding officers.

The David Rivera Group

Although most guerrilla groups were easily convinced to merge with the Cebu Area Command, there were also some that were initially hostile to Jim Cushing's and Harry Fenton's organization. One of these was the David Rivera Group.

When General Chynoweth decided to surrender, Staff Sergeant Manuel Bacud was one of those who thought surrender was not a good idea. He went into the mountains above Lutopan, not very far from Toledo City. He stayed there quietly with his girlfriend Manuela Rivera and passed the time in collecting rifles and other weapons left behind everywhere. He deposited these in a huge cave not far from where he was hiding.

Time passed. Some Filipinos collaborated with the enemy for whatever reason they could think of. For most probably it was just a matter of survival. David Rivera, the brother of Manuela, was one of those. David, a miner, tried to do buy-and-sell business with the Japanese garrison in Tina-an, Naga. At a certain moment the Japanese found out that they were being cheated by David. They arrested him and he was tortured in a way only the Japanese could have invented. When they were finished they crucified him against an electric post at Tuyan, Naga, and left him there as an example to others.

Upon hearing all of this Bacud decided to save David. He brought the miner to his hideout in the forest near Lutopan, and Manuela, his sister, nursed him back to life. Fearing that the Japanese would find out what he had done, Bacud assembled some armed men around him so at least he could put up a fight if necessary. This group became soon known as the David Rivera Group. They started to harass the Japanese and became quite successful. The group became bigger and bigger.

It was at this stage that Lieutenant Habacon contacted Bacud, after discussing the whereabouts of the group with Jim Cushing in Tabunan. Jim thought that in the interest of the resistance movement it would be better to integrate the group into the Cebu Area Command. He picked some men to go with him to Lutopan to bring the David Rivera Group down to Ming-

lanilla for a joint operation. The plan was to ambush the trucks which peri-
odically brought Japanese soldiers who relieved the garrison at the town of
Naga and the Apo Cement Factory.[16] Lt. Fernillamor, Lt. Manuel Segura,
Lt. Bernard Hale, Lt Pantaleon Ciano and Lt. Eusebio Habacon accompanied Jim Cushing.

It was the first week of October 1942 when they left Tabunan. They
passed through the forest of Cantipla, Sudlon, Mara-ag, Gabi, Pangamijan
and finally reached the outposts of the David Rivera Group. A guide brought
the group to the main camp in a cave some 70 feet up the mountain, the entrance of which was guarded with two water-cooled Browning machineguns.
The greetings were polite but not necessarily cordial, though there was no
visible animosity. After a long discussion Jim convinced David to join the
Cebu Area Command, and to celebrate the cooperation they decided to
attack the Japanese in Minglanilla together as a joint operation.

The next day, 6 October 1942, they moved out, and the following morning everybody took his ambush position at Lawa-an. The site was a portion
of the road leading away from the south end of Mananga River Bridge. Lt.
Villamor commanded the men on the east side; Lt. Segura commanded the
group that would close the road on the south. The ambush became a big success as the Japanese suffered severe losses, and the guerrillas only had a few
superficially wounded men. The success of the operation sealed the deal for
the Rivera Group to accept the authority of Tabunan.[17]

Civilian Support

No guerrilla war can last long unless there is support from the local population. In the case of the Cebu guerrillas there was from the very beginning
ample support from the local population. In the first place there was little
sympathy for Japan to begin with, as the Japanese ideas about a Greater East
Asia Co-Prosperity Sphere did not appeal to the Cebuano's. They were more
American-focused. The first stories about inhumane treatment, the summary
killing of Abad Santos, and the Japanese order that they could not harvest
their rice and corn without a permit were the last drops in the bucket. The
Cebuano's offered *en masse* their allegiance to the resistance movement. Many
signed up to became a guerillero. Aside from its manpower contribution to
the resistance movement, the civilian sector likewise provided much needed
supplies, and assisted in intelligence work.

Another substantial factor was the effort of Hilario Abellana, pre-war governor of Cebu, to maintain a free civil government in Cebu. Abellana for a time served as a puppet governor under the Japanese, but later escaped and joined the guerrillas in the field. Abellana was a colorful figure in the province and was beloved throughout the island. He was especially important for the raising of funds for the guerrilla movement.[18]

CHAPTER 11
TABUNAN

C EBU'S MOUNTAIN BARANGAYS, such as Lusaran, Babag, Sudlon, Tagba-o and Tabunan have always felt somewhat mysterious. They are only, as the crow flies, a handful of kilometers away from the city proper, but in reality it is hours walking over difficult and remote trails. It used to be the territory of the *Kaingeros,* indigenous people who cultivated the area until such time that the soil was no longer good for planting. Then they transfered to another area and burned forest again. It is often called a slash-and-burn system of agriculture.

Tabunan is in the middle of the island, near Cebu City's boundary with the town of Balamban to the west. Today it is an agricultural village with a land area of about 1,110 hectares and a population of about 600 people. The barangay consists of the sitios: *Fenton,* with only a few households, the larger *Batalyon,* located near the Bangbang River, *Awayan, Odlom, Cantipla I, Cantipla II, Litio* and *Tabunan Proper.* The name sitio Fenton, pronounced *Pengton* in the area, refers to radio man Harry Fenton who used to live there during World War II. Not far away, in sitio Batalyon, used to be the camp of Batallion II, led by 3rd Lieutenant Pantaleon "Nene" Ciano.

I visited the area for the first time in the mid-1980s with a copy of Manuel F. Segura's *Tabunan: The Untold Exploits of the Famed Cebu Guerrillas in World War II* in my pocket. From Cebu City proper I walked one slippery trail after another via Busay, Babag, Malubog, Sibugay, Sirao, Taptap to Tabunan. I passed through the Cabadiangan Valley at Sak-on, via Barrio Pannagban and Mulao and the plains of Barrio Tag-ube. I saw Mount Asiotes in the distance and had to cross the Bangbang River. Instead of *Nipa*[1] many houses used cogon grass as building material. The people I met often smoked home-made cigars or cigarettes made of the *lomboy* (Duhat)[2] tree. I was told that, if I was lucky, I could see a Black Shama (Copsychus cebuensis), one of the rarest birds on earth which only lives in the Tabunan forest. It was a distance of some 20 kilometers and it took me several hours. I must admit that, at that time, I did not know that the area was infested with deadly snakes, such as the Philippine cobra, the world's third deadliest snake.[3] I recently came across an American study about the danger of snake bites to (rice) farmers of three rural sites in the Philippines. The result of this study for those three places was 107 deaths per 100.000 farmers per year![4] That means over one death per 1,000 farmers per year. And then there are pythons many meters long.

I had a look at the place where Fenton's house supposedly had been. Close by was a spring inside a cemented structure, which was where Fenton's men got their drinking water. Not far away from the site where Fenton lived was the place where those who were executed "in the name of justice" were buried. According to local people there are some 135 people buried here.

After my first visit I accompanied my colleague, the late Professor Harold Olofsson, San Carlos University, a few times on his anthropological research in the area. Not long after my first visit some roads were constructed nearby, mainly to give the military a better chance against units of the New People's Army who were said to camp in the area. It took, however, until the early 1990s before the area was really opened up by the Cebu Transcentral Highway, the famous road that was constructed on the orders of former Governor Lito Osmeña. Today Tabunan is easy reachable.

It is a mystery why Tabunan became the Headquarters of the Cebu Area Command. It could have been any other place in the area. There were a few advantages, such as the proximity to Cebu City and the difficult access. It was at that time impossible to reach Tabunon by car or tank; even by motorcycle. On the other hand the forest and brush around the village made it easy for attackers to close in without being spotted. Another big advantage was the Bangbang River; it meant that there was always sufficient water. The headquarters was located under big trees. It could not be seen from across, much less from above, for the green canopy of the forest hid it from view. The houses were constructed with the trunks and branches of small trees found in the area. Each framework was bound together with rattan or other vine, or in some areas, buri. Cogon grass made up the walls and the roof. Some houses were built on big rocks, others on tree stumps. Trails that cut through the underbrush of the forest connected the houses.

Life in Tabunan during the war was very simple. Most of the people, including Col. Cushing and Col. Fenton, walked around in their bare feet. Going into the mountains they often put spikes in their shoes, because of the slippery trails. Jim Cushing usually wore shorts, but he always had his .45 cal. hanging on his hip. His Great Dane Senta accompanied him whenever possible.

Weapons

Most of the guerrillas' weapons were of the military type which had been left behind by USAFFE members. Most common was the Lee Enfield Rifle, a heavy weapon with bolt-action. It loaded five rounds of .3006 caliber.[5] There were also a number of US Army Springfield rifles, also bolt-action with five-round magazines. Grenade launchers were very rare. Here and there you saw a few hunting rifles, some .22-cal. rifles, and a great variety of shotguns, often homemade (*paltik*).[6] In the beginning of the struggle there was plenty of ammunition, mainly thanks to the large supplies brought in by the ships *Doña Nita* and the *Anhui*. However, many encounters with the enemy took a heavy toll on the ammunition supply. Soon some handy guerrillas managed to reload empty shells with yellow powder from recovered Japanese naval mines. There was a large variety of handguns. Some were Army-issue pistols and revolvers, usually of .45 cal. But there were also many police handguns around, usually .38s. Those who had no firearm equipped themselves with bolos.[7]

At first there were no heavy weapons. After a while, however, Simeon Cortes managed to construct mortar tubes from ordinary water pipes which he reinforced with steel plates so they could withstand high pressure on firing. On several occasions, such as combats in Babag, Toledo, Malubog and Danao they were successfully used. There were no locally made shells; all the shells used came from the supplies of the *Doña Nati*.

Medical Care

There was a small but quite reasonably equipped hospital in Tabunan with doctors and nurses, all under the charge of Doctor Ramon Torralba. Acquiring medicine was a problem. This was the more important because apart from wounds as a result of attacks and skirmishes, diseases such as malaria, dengue fever and hepatitis were endemic. Jim Cushing suffered often from malaria, but also from arthritis. It was not uncommon to see him from time to time hobbling around on crutches. In many cases the doctors had to fall back on old local remedies based on herbs and medical plants. The most common medical problems were, apart from malaria and dysentery, boils and carbuncles. Due to lack of disinfecting materials wounds often had to be burned out. It is a painful but necessary procedure. It was usually done by dried tobacco leaves which were dipped in oil and then alighted. In remote places the men often had to rely on the local *mananabang*.[8] Snake bites occurred and there was no antivenom; the Philippine cobra (*Naja philippinensis*), a very aggressive snake, was especially feared by the men.

Food

Food was always a problem, as it was both scarce and simple. Although Filipinos are rice-eaters, in Cebu corn is the staple food. The main reason for this is the fact that there is very little land in Cebu that is suitable for rice farming. In other words, rice has to be brought in from other islands. Corn was normally cooked and eaten whole grain. Sometimes there was rice, but not very often. If there was no rice and no corn, which happened regularly, root crops such as sweet potatoes became the main food. Sometimes there was cassava (*camoteng kahoy*) or cooked bananas.[9]

Meat was extremely scarce, with only chicken and sometimes pork available in minimum quantities. Sardines in tin were the most common form of protein. Coffee and tea were extremely scarce, so a common drink was *salabat* or boiled ginger. There was enough water from small creeks or streams and an occasional waterfall or small lake.[10]

Many guerrilla officers had come directly from civilian life with no previous military training. Others had military training years before the war so it was thus necessary to conduct basic training for the former and refresher training for the latter. Thus CACOTS was born. The school site was a secluded level area below the cliffs of Met-ol, not far from the headquarters of Colonel Almendras at Caba-asan. Head of the school was Captain Santiago Garcia, who was assisted by Captain Julio Martinez.[11]

The CACOTS turned out four classes during its existence. The students included ranking non-commissioned officers. Apart from standard military knowledge, such as discipline and tactics, the students were trained in weaponry and the use of cover, concealment and other forms of fieldcraft.[12]

Communications

A huge problem was to allow the different units to communicate with each other. There were no telephones available in the mountain barangays so in the beginning everything had to be done by messenger or courier. That took time. For units that were not too far off, Philippine ingenuity brought a solution. Clever members of the Cebu Area Command installed barbed wire as telephone cables, isolated from the surroundings by bottles that connected some units with the headquarters in Tabunan. They managed in this way, for instance, to connect the headquarters of Major Albinda in Hagnum with the headquarters in Tabunan. Later they even managed to connect units over distances up to 30 or 40 kilomers away.

CHAPTER 12

JAPANESE COUNTERATTACKS

The Japanese Organization in Cebu

I N THE MEANTIME the Japanese had put their operations in Cebu on a sound footing. In Cebu City, the *Subetai* (Fighting Unit) was housed in the University of San Carlos building on P. del Rosario Street. The notorious *Kempetai* (Military Police) was located in the Normal School Building on Jones Avenue. Its Chief was Captain Kanimoto Tsureyama, who was later replaced by Captain Yamamoto. An interesting figure was also Prince Yoshida, Chief Investigator of the Cebu Kempetai, who was closely related to Emperor Hirohito. The *Konobutai*, another fighting unit, had its headquarters in the University of the Philippines Cebu College Building on Gorordo Avenue; its Chief of Intelligence was Captain Otsuka. The Japanese marines were housed in the Gotiaco Building on M.C. Briones Street. The Japanese Navy had its headquarters in the Cebu Trade School buildings near the piers, and the Navy also controlled the Talisay Sugar Central. The Japanese motor pool was housed in the Cebu Provincial High School (now Abellana High School), while the Cebu Normal School grounds was used as a stockyard for gasoline drums.[1]

Soon after the occupation force had settled in, a Japanese proprietor opened a comfort station for the soldiers in Cebu City. In the station worked approximately 12–16 women to take care of the sexual needs of the Japanese soldiers.[2]

The Battle of Babag

Through their agents, who operated out of Cebu City and out of their garrisons at the towns of Toledo, Danao, Carcar and the Asano cement plant at Tina-an, Naga,[3] the Japanese authorities in Cebu had got wind of the developments in the mountains. There had been already a number of small skirmishes between guerrilla units and the Japanese. Although the resistance movement was not yet really a threat, it had become at least a nuisance.

On 24 October 1942 the first real encounter between the Cebu Area Command and the Japanese took place. Lieutenant Rogaciano C. Espiritu and Sergeant Ramon Climaco led two platoons, some 50 men, down to Lahug at the outskirts of Cebu City. They halted for a while at Laguerta in order to finalize their plans. When all was sorted out Espiritu ordered one of the platoons to attack the Japanese who were housed in the U.P.[4] Cebu College. A second platoon was ordered to head for the hill northeast of U.P. and attack the Japanese at the Lahug Elementary School. The rest of the men were ordered to deploy, as a blocking force, at the junction leading to Lahug airfield. There was a large contingent of Japanese soldiers at the U.P. because of the American civilians that were interned there. The Japanese at the Lahug Elementary School guarded the British nationals locked up in that place.

The two platoons moved carefully. They kept checking and rechecking their weapons as they trod the trail leading down to Lahug. Near the junction the two platoons separated from the group and proceeded to their objectives, leaving men posted at the junction.

The two platoons had not gone very far when the men at the junction saw a column of Japanese moving toward them from the direction of the airfield. They took cover and prepared an ambush. The Japanese had no notion of the upcoming danger, and when they walked straight into the trap the first salvo from Lieutenant Espiritu's men downed 30 Japanese soldiers. Upon hearing the firing from Espiritu's men the two platoons, as was prearranged, withdrew immediately from their positions near the schools towards the hills. The guerrillas had no casualties.

The Japanese were furious at what had happened, and decided to root out this resistance once and for all. They assembled a force of some 400 men and went up to Babag. It was 26 October 1942. The terrain of low jungle, forest, brush, narrow muddy paths (it was rainy season), small rivers, ravines, mosquitoes and snakes, was more favorable for defenders than for the attackers. Upon approaching the hills at Tigid and Paypay, they were met by Lieutenant Espiritu and his men. Taking advantage of their knowledge of the terrain, the first sergeants, Climaco and Severino Mabini, managed to cut off some enemy units and wipe them out. In the meantime Japanese planes dropped supplies for their troops by air. Due to tricky wind conditions not all these supplies reached the Japanese, and in many cases the guerrillas managed to catch them. The good air-dropped food and the success against the enemy brought Jim's troops into high spirits. The battle raged for a number of days, but the Japanese could not get the upper hand. Gradually activities wound down and the Japanese withdrew. The guerrillas did not lose any member while losses for the Japanese were heavy. They lost a battle, but the war was still going on.

Attack on Japanese Garrison in Toledo City[5]

In November, just after the Battle of Babag, Jim planned a raid on one of the Japanese garrisons. He chose the garrison in Toledo City on Cebu's west coast. He was convinced the Japanese could be surprised. From Pandongbato, the site of the Central Headquarters, they took the trail skirting Malubog, and thence to the plain of Magdugo. Major Olegario L. Baura, the area commander, together with Captain Crispin Ramos, was in the lead. By the evening they arrived in the foothills above Toledo where they were joined by Jim and Captain Nene Ciano, Lieutenant Eusebio Habacon and a few others. Company C, under Lieutenant Saturnino P. Acuña, was chosen to make the main thrust. Most of the guerrillas were from the same area and knew every inch of the territory. After a final conference on the evening of November 24 the men tried to get some sleep as the attack was planned for first morning light.

The objective was the Japanese garrison housed in the Central School of Toledo. The enemy strength was supposed to be one company. They were armed with rifles, automatic weapons, trench mortars and knee mortars. The "Knee mortar" or Heavy Grenade Discharger was one of the most feared weapons in the Japanese arsenal. This weapon received the dangerously unfortunate English nickname of "knee mortar"; the curved base plate was meant to be braced against a solid foundation (the ground, a log, etc.), NOT one's knee, as the recoil would result in broken bones or worse.[6]

Jim's aim was to harass the Japanese; he had no intention of taking over the garrison. Just before everybody was in place a number of dogs, apparently smelling the intruders, started to bark and the element of surprise was gone. The Japanese hastily formed reconnaissance patrols. When one patrol came close to a platoon of Company C, fire was opened up. Many Japanese dropped dead or wounded. The Japanese dragged their fallen comrades in the school.

After a while, the battle died down to sporadic rifle fire and an occasional mortar round.

Jim, Ramos and a few others occupied a foxhole beside the trunk of a huge mango tree. Cushing was looking through his binoculars to observe the progress of the attack when suddenly he decided to move his position somewhat more to the right and the rest followed him. The movement must have gone unnoticed to the Japanese because a new and bigger group of enemy soldiers tried to break out just at that spot. They were met with heavy fire and that took quite a toll on their number. They quickly retreated to their garrison. By late afternoon, Baura gave the order to withdraw. The guerrillas lost two men, the Japanese many more.

While Jim was leading the attack on the Toledo garrison, Major Harry Fenton was with another group of guerrillas from the Northeastern Cebu Sector in a two-day attack on the enemy garrison in Danao. That action was costly for both sides.

Other ambuscades and raids followed. The enemy started to realize that they had an opponent in the mountains that meant business.

The Battle of Babag continues . . .

But the Japanese did not give up in Babag. They licked their wounds and prepared for another attempt. On 29 November 1942, early in the morning, the guerrillas came under fire from a cannon[7] mounted in the vicinity of Club Filipino.[8] The shelling was followed by heavy bombing and strafing by eight Japanese planes of the Val type,[9] which were stationed at the nearby Lahug airfield.

After a softening up period of a few hours the Japanese launched a massive attack. Hundreds of soldiers followed the narrow paths into the foothills. Enemy planes continued to drop bombs and strafe the area. The fight continued well into the night. On the second day it was a repetition from the day before. The guerrillas maintained their positions but the pressure was heavy. Jim Cushing visited the frontlines and, after sizing up the situation, sent out messengers with orders directing the nearby sectors to send reinforcements. Lt. Pedro Zuñega came with men from the Cebu Central Sector. Major Baura, the CCS commander, also came. Lt. Dominador Acantilado came in from the group of Major Albinda. Lt. Bordalba brought in some 50 men and Sergeant Climaco guided them to occupy the *ga-ang* (rocky area) near his unit. Captain del Pilar came in from GHS with his long- and short-range mortars. Jim appointed Major Baura as overall commander.

The Japanese did not give up that easy. They too reinforced their troops, brought in a mountain gun,[10] and tried to surround the guerrillas from all sides. The battle went on for ten days up to 8 December 1942. When the enemy finally withdrew the guerrillas had suffered two dead and a few wounded, but they had killed dozens of enemy soldiers, including a full colonel.

The withdrawing enemy buried their death along the slope towards the Busay Elementary School after first beheading the corpses. The heads were loaded on trucks and brought to the compound of Colegio de San Carlos, on P. del Rosario Street. There the heads were cremated and the ashes put into small white boxes. After the battle, in which hundreds of guerrillas were involved, Jim Cushing delivered a speech in which he thanked his men for their brave and glorious battle. He ordered the slaughter of some pigs for a traditional *lechon* party.

Toledo Again

A month later, on 20 December 1942, Jim launched another attack on the Toledo garrison. It was planned for dawn, and this time there were no dogs to give away the positions of the guerrillas. Lieutenant Abel Trazo led the attack. He let the men wait until the Japanese left the school for a bath in a nearby spring. Most of the Japanese wore only G-strings. Although some armed guards covered the scene, most did not bear any arms at all. Just when they wanted to step in the water the signal for the attack was given. In one salvo all the Japanese dropped dead. The attack was a complete surprise for the enemy. Within seconds the rest of the garrison took its positions and started firing from the bushes around the school. The mortars of the guerrillas began to lob grenades into the compound. The Japanese answered with their notorious knee-mortars. The guerrillas suffered casualties, but Jim had no idea at that point how many. For hours the battle went on. Sometimes the Japanese broke through the lines, but with reinforcements from elsewhere the holes in the line could be repaired. As the sun began to set, Major Baura decided to break off the action. Within a short time the guerrillas faded away in the surrounding hills.[11]

The Battle of Inayawan Crossing

Hardly a week later there was another clash. It was on 28 December 1942, just after Christmas. This time the guerrillas had focused their efforts on the railway between Danao and Argao. This narrow gauge railway was constructed somewhere between 1890 and 1910. The Japanese were regular users of the train, but the guerrillas attacked it time and again.

On 28 December a train, fully loaded with Japanese soldiers, was expected to run from Carcar to Cebu City. There would be a stop at Naga, in the area under the control of guerrillas led by Lt. Nestor Legaspi. In Barrio Inayawan, where the railroad tracks crossed the provincial road from the south to Cebu City, Legaspi's company had set up an ambush. Legaspi's troops were hiding on the land side, assisted by two platoons led by Lt. Eufronio Abella and Sgt Java. Legaspi expected a fully loaded train and had asked headquarters for reinforcements. Jim had sent Lt. Jesus Navarro and Lt. Jose Macabuhay as assistance. Navarro let one of his platoons under Sgt Beltran take positions on the seaside behind a cluster of young coconut palms. When the train approached, Lt. Legaspi saw that there were not only soldiers riding on it, but next to the slow-moving train, on the seaside, marched a column Japanese soldiers. To prevent guerrillas from attacking the train the Japanese lobbed indiscriminate mortar rounds on the left, or land, side of the railroad tracks. Apparently the Japanese soldiers thought that guerrillas would come only from that side, from the foothills. The Japanese had no idea that Sgt Beltran and his men were on the sea side of the rail tracks. Actually the Japanese were using the train as a moving barricade against attacks from the hills. The train itself was also heavily barricaded with sandbags on the flat cars. Legaspi could see that there were also mortars and machineguns behind the sandbags. When the train reached the crossing, its rear being directly in front of the reinforcement companies of Macabuhay and Navarro, the guerrillas opened fire. The train screeched to a stop and the Japanese soldiers tried to find cover. With the guerrillas firing at almost point blank range, the Japanese stood no chance and most dropped dead after the first salvo. It was a short, but heavy, fight that left 180 Japanese soldiers dead on the spot. Legaspi's men suffered no casualties at all.[12] [13]

The Battle of Tabok-Canal
Days after the battle of Inawayan, Cebuanos were still drinking toasts to Jim's guerrillas for their impressive performance against the Japanese. But the guerrillas were on guard, since they knew that somehow and somewhere the Japanese would try to avenge the humiliating affair of Inawayan.

After all the harassment by the guerrillas the Japanese had learned their lesson and built a huge fence around the city to keep infiltrators out. One of the gates in the fence was in Lahug, on the northern side of the city; another was in Mambaling, on the southwestern side. Early in the morning of 30 December 1942, the people near the Mambaling gate woke up to the sound of hundreds of Japanese soldiers leaving their camp in Mambaling. Some 200 soldiers left in the direction of Pardo and Basak. Volunteer guards immediately warned Lt. Nestor Legaspi at his bivouac on Campar Hill, some 300 meters behind and above the church of Pardo. His company was known as "X" company.

In front of the Pardo church the Japanese soldiers, who knew where the guerrillas were camping but could not reach them, started to yell at them and to challenge the guerrillas to fight it out. At the intersection of Tabora Street and the road to Inayawan they turned right again heading towards Inayawan. They passed Barrio Tugas and took the road to Barrio Tabok-Canal. There, at a lone house with a stable for horses for tartanillas,[14] they stopped and took a rest.

Legaspi quickly discussed with his platoon leaders the plan of action. This was a chance to teach the Japanese a lesson that could not be missed. They managed quietly to surround the house with the stables. Around 0830 that morning Abella opened fire, quickly followed by Beltran and his men. The Japanese had hardly any cover and were dropping in great numbers. Corporal Nicolas Valerio had an especially good time with his automatic rifle. Lt. Macabuhay with his men acted as a blocking force between Mambaling and Cebu City to prevent any Japanese reinforcements from reaching the scene. Around three in the afternoon the fight was still going on when Col. Cushing arrived with reinforcements for the guerrillas. The fight lasted well into the night. According to some witnesses only 11 Japanese soldiers managed to return alive to their camp in Mambaling. Jim and his men collected more than 100 rifles, plus some mortars and automatic rifles from the site. Jim considered this battle a bigger victory then than the Battle of Inawayan where 180 enemy soldiers were killed.[15,16]

The Battle of Kinasang-an
A few weeks later, in more or less the same area, another battle broke loose. This time the fight took place near the road fork where the provincial road from Cebu City to Talisay separates from the road to Inawayan and Tabok

canal. A large Japanese force, armed with mortars, mountain guns and machineguns, took part. Lt. Arcilla, Lt. Abella and Sergeant Beltran with their forces managed to pin the enemy down. The Japanese made several *banzai* [17] charges, but could not prevent losing heavily. Some reports counted 114 dead soldiers on the battlefield. After a few hours the guerrillas withdrew back to Tabok-canal and reassembled in Inawayan.[18] The Japanese did not pursue them.

CHAPTER **13**
GUERRILLA WARFARE IN THE PHILIPPINES

F ROM THE DAY of his confident parting message to the Filipinos, "I shall return," no deviation from MacArthur's single-
minded plan is discernible. Every battle action in New Guinea,
every air raid on Rabaul or PT-boat attack on Japanese barges in the Bis-
marck Sea, was a mere preliminary to the retaking of the Philippines. In the
field of intelligence, the development of the Philippines guerrilla movement
over the years was a calculated prerequisite for MacArthur's return. The Philippines "underground" was in position to assist MacArthur's landing forces
on Mindanao, Leyte or Luzon. Information direct from the Philippines
ranged from inside government dope (furnished by Manuel Roxas, who had
cover as a collaborator) to the guest lists of the Manila Hotel—an infallible
clue to high-level Japanese military or naval conferences.[1]

After General MacArthur's staff arrived in Australia in March 1942,
radio contact was maintained with Corregidor for a short while. With the
surrender of Corregidor, all communication with the Philippines was cut off.
A virtual wall of silence appeared to enshroud the country, with no information reaching the outside world.

Then suddenly on 10 July 1942, a weak signal addressed to MacArthur
was picked up on the enemy-occupied island of Java (part of the Netherlands
East Indies, now the nation of Indonesia) and passed on. The message read:

Detachments of Fil-American forces, we have not surrendered, are
actively raiding northeast barrios and towns of Pangasinan including Dagupan. Radio censorship by Japs very rigid resulting in complete ignorance of Filipinos of the true and correct status of the

war... Our people, nevertheless, are undaunted and continue to seek correct information. Your victorious return is the nightly subject of prayer in every Filipino home.

Lieutenant Colonel Nakar.[2]

According to Col. Courtney Whitney, MacArthur's confidant, "Probably no message ever gave MacArthur more of an uplift." Obsessed with his "second homeland," the SWPA chief closely followed developments and personally interviewed American refugees who began to arrive in the autumn of 1942.

The last message received from Lt. Col. Nakar was dated 22 August 1942. On 29 September he was captured and eventually imprisoned in Fort Santiago. Even as a prisoner, Nakar remained defiant. He bluntly refused his freedom in exchange for signing surrender papers and swearing allegiance to the Japanese. On 2 October 1943, a year after his capture, Nakar was executed by beheading.[3]

The first direct personal information from the Philippines was brought by Capt. William L. Osborne and Capt. Damon J. Cause. When Bataan surrendered on 9 April 1942, Osborne decided not to surrender. He linked up with an Air Corps pilot, Capt. Damon J. Gause, who had soldiered until the fall of Corregidor as an infantryman. They located an old 22-foot sailboat with a one-cylinder engine. After a hazardous 3,000-mile journey through Japanese-patrolled open seas, buffeted by storms and a typhoon, and strafed by enemy planes and patrol boats, they reached Australia on 11 October 1942. They were both awarded the Distinguished Service Cross by General MacArthur personally for their exploits.[4]

An almost parallel feat was accomplished by Captain Frank H. Young, a messenger for Col. Claude Thorpe, a guerrilla leader of remnant groups in central Luzon. Young left in July 1942 and travelled via Bicol, Samar, Leyte, Cebu, and Negros to Panay, there he joined Albert Klestad, a German civilian, and came to Australia via Zamboanga. They arrived in Darwin on 12 December 1942. As did Osborne and Gause, they brought important and lucid information of the enemy and guerrilla activity in the areas through which they had passed.[5]

From November 1942, radio calls gradually started to emerge. The first was a call from Major Ralph B. Praeger, a guerrilla commander in Northern Luzon. In December 1942 there were already twenty-two calls. From then on the number increased steadily, reaching a peak of 3,700 at the time of the landings in Luzon in January 1945.[6]

The First Guerrilla Activity: Walter Cushing Ambushes the Japanese in Candon

But without any knowledge of General MacArthur and his staff in Australia, there was already extensive guerrilla activity in the Philippines even before the Americans surrendered. The first serious engagement between the Japanese army and the Philippine guerrillas was initiated by Jim Cushing's brother, Walter.

It happened in Candon, Ilocos Sur, on 19 January 1942. Candon was a small town in the province of Ilocos Sur, located some 25 miles south of Vigan and 60 miles north of the major Japanese landing sites at Lingayen Gulf. On 9 and 10 December 1941, only days after the Japanese landings in Lingayen Gulf, Philippine Army Lieutenant Feliciano Madamba (13th Infantry Regiment, 11th Division) and Candonino Gaerlan, a graduate of the Mapua Institute of Technology in Manila, came on the idea to ambush some of the many Japanese military convoys using the coastal highway. They assembled a sizeable group of volunteers and managed to get hold of a large cache of Lee Enfield rifles from US Army stores in nearby San Fernando.[7] In the hills beyond Candon, were a few hundred American civilians. Among them was Walter Cushing, Jim's older brother.[8]

Gaerlan and Cushing met in the Candon area and discussed their options. They scheduled an ambush for a Monday, 19 January 1942. At 8:00 a column of open trucks approached, at moderate speed, with Japanese soldiers riding in the back. The guerrillas opened fire on the vehicles, the trucks crashed, and most of the soldiers were immediately killed, including their commander, a full colonel. The body count was sixty-seven dead Japanese and the destruction of nine vehicles (several of them captured U.S. Army trucks). The guerrilla injuries were practically non-existent.[9]

Colonel Russell Volckmann, who later headed all guerrilla forces in North Luzon, praised Cushing, calling him the "granddaddy" of the Luzon resistance. In the military literature, the statement by Colonel Baclagon in his *Philippine Campaigns* (1952) is typical, referring to Cushing as having the "Distinction of being the first guerrilla leader to lead an ambush against the Japanese."[10]

The subsequent careers of Cushing and Gaerlan were exciting, brilliant, deadly and brief. Cushing's career came to a bloody end on 19 September 1942, at Jones, Isabela, where he was finally surrounded by Japanese forces. After shooting a few of the enemy, Cushing killed himself, which apparently so impressed the Japanese commander that he permitted the villagers to give Cushing a formal funeral and memorial service in line with his own religion.[11]

Candonino Gaerlan, in late 1942, was betrayed by a local chief of police. The Japanese surrounded his house, and Gaerlan was killed in the ensuing gunfight. The Japanese cut off his head, stuffed it in a jar of alcohol, and exhibited it in town plazas en route to Candon.[12]

MacArthur's Intelligence Set-Up

One of the first decisions of MacArthur, when he arrived in Melbourne, was to create the Central Bureau, a joint American-Australian SIGINT (Signals Intelligence Gathering) organization. Part of the Bureau was a group known as No. 5 Wireless Section; this group was to be involved in the interception of Japanese naval and military traffic.

In order to collect intelligence and conduct guerrilla warfare against Japanese forces in the South West Pacific, the Allied Intelligence Bureau *(AIB)* was established in June 1942.[13] This small but highly efficient organization was designed to train, equip and dispatch agents to operate behind enemy lines from the Solomons to Singapore.

First Mission to the Philippines: Jesús Antonio Villamor Lands in Negros

As a result of the GHQ desire to retain a direct and personal relationship with Philippine planning and operations, a special Philippine Sub-section of AIB was formally set up on 21 October 1942. Plans for Philippine intelligence penetration were immediately developed. General MacArthur decided that the first landing in the occupied Philippines would be carried out by Captain Jesús A. Villamor, a highly decorated Filipino pilot.

Jesús Antonio Villamor (1914–1971) was a Philippine Air Force officer assigned to lead the 6th Pursuit Squadron. Villamor and his squadron were credited with four kills: one Mitsubishi G3M bomber and three Mitsubishi A6M Zeros. Two of them were personally shot down by Villamor himself. After his squadron was destroyed, Villamor continued his war against the Japanese as an intelligence officer. Promoted to Major, Villamor served as a commander in the Allied Intelligence Bureau.[14] On 27 December 1942 Major

Villamor, with five other Filipino officers, was inserted by the submarine USS *Gudgeon* (SS-211)[15] into the southern Philippines. Villamor's assignment (code name: *Planet Party*) was to develop an intelligence net based on the "cell" system, independent of guerrilla organizations and possible guerrilla nets, for security and to provide a neutral source of information.[16]

After departing Fremantle, USS *Gudgeon* set out towards her destination on the southern part of the island of Negros. The first night, high winds and seas prohibited approaching the original landing site, so the submerged *Gudgeon* moved quietly along the coast into the next day, scanning for a new location. Finally on the third night, 14 January 1943, a deserted beach was identified near Cansilan Point at the end of Tolong Bay, and Villamor successfully loaded his men and supplies into rafts and landed ashore. He found a number of guerrilla units who often fought against each other and areas that had no commander at all. Villamor was immediately recognized by the local population as a war hero, which in a way jeopardized his mission. Nevertheless, in order to straighten things out he assumed command of the Negros guerrillas and began to build a network as he had been instructed to do. He appointed as his deputy commanders Major Salvador Abcede and First Lieutenant Ernesto S. Mata.

Radio Contacts with Guerrillas

After the call from Major Praeger's station WYY on 4 November 1942, it took until 11 January 1943 before the connection between WYY and SWPA's (Southwest Pacific Area) station KAZ was properly working. KAZ was at that time the Royal Australian Air Force (RAAF) station in Darwin, Northern Australia.[17]

Shortly after receiving Praeger's call, calls from other Philippine areas came in. The activity of the Cebu radio station was one of the more unfortunate incidents in the history of radio contacts in the Philippines. The first information concerning the existence of this radio station came in the War Department's message 1138, 14 February 1943. The radio was then reporting, in the clear, information of value to the enemy and would not cease despite War Department orders. Attempts were then made to contact the Cebu station WJE from SWPA contacts on Negros and Panay, but without success. The station was operated by Harry J. Fenton, the former radio announcer in Cebu City, who was very outspoken in his hatred of the Japanese and their associates. After a month's transmission the radio went off the air.[18]

On 28 February 1943, the War Department in message 1527 to SWPA reported that they were developing codes with a guerrilla transmitter in southern Negros. The radio was made from a Silliman University set that had been carried to the hills by the physics professor H.R. Bell (Diliman University) before the Japanese occupation of Dumaguete.[19] Direct contact with KAZ and this radio, KZCB, was established in mid-March 1943. The radio became part of the Negros net in April.[20] In addition to this, radio contact with Major Villamor on Negros was established on 26 January 1943.[21] By mid-1943 radio contact with the most important guerrilla units was fairly well established.

Second Mission to the Philippines

Just after Villamor had left, on 4 January 1943, three Americans in a small boat arrived in Darwin, northwestern Australia: Capt. Jordan A. Hamner, Capt. Charles M. Smith and Albert Y. Smith. They had been sent from Lt. Col. Fertig's headquarters in Mindanao to contact SWPA forces and to bring information concerning the Mindanao guerrillas. This development was an important link in future plans for intelligence gathering. Hamner and Smith told SWPA authorities that Fertig had a radio and was attempting to contact Australia. He did not succeed until about 20 February 1943.

They told the authorities also that Lt. Col. Fertig, actually a mining engineer, and his guerrillas controlled a large part of Mindanao. The Japanese were simply not capable of occupying the huge Filipino island.[22]

After the arrival of the Americans from Mindanao, the receipt of messages covering wide areas from Col. Macario Peralta (Panay) and development of radio contacts with northern Luzon and Negros opened a new vista of the possibilities for penetration of the Philippines through guerrilla units. The first guerrilla organization to receive active consideration was in Mindanao. Plans were made to supply this organization and develop in it a major base for future assistance to the Philippines. Commander Parsons, USNR, took an active part in these plans. He would lead a fact-finding mission to the island.

Commander Charles ("Chick") Thomas Parsons, Jr.

Chick Parsons was born on 22 April 1900 in Shelbyville, Tennessee. At the age of five he went with an uncle to Manila. In 1908 he returned to the USA. At the age of 21 he went back to the Philippines, this time to stay. He worked in a number of jobs in a variety of places in the country and served for a number of years as a US naval officer. In 1929, Chick took a job managing the Luzon Stevedoring Company; he also became Honorary Consul for Panama in Manila.

MacArthur and Parsons had a history. Their friendship began in 1936, when the General came to Manila as Chief of Staff, Philippine Armed Forces. In 1932, Parsons joined the U. S. Navy Reserves. In December 1941 he was called to active duty in Manila as a lieutenant in Naval Intelligence. After a period of internment at Santo Tomas University, they permitted him to leave because of his Panamanian diplomatic status, and after a journey of many months Parsons reached New York City. Chick reported to the Navy Department Headquarters in Washington, D.C. and was sent to Brisbane, Australia, where he was assigned to the Allied Intelligence Bureau (AIB). He would become MacArthur's "Man in Manila." Comdr. Parsons left Australia on 8 February 1943 Fremantle on the submarine USS *Tambor (SS-198)* and landed at Tukuran, Zamboanga. Here he made contact with Col. Fertig.[23] Parson's code name was "Fifty Party," his activities would become known as project "SPYRON." He would make numerous trips by submarine to many parts of the country.[24] He was never caught by the Japanese.

Military Districts: Jurisdictional Limitations
Before Comdr. Parsons left for Mindanao, the general problem of area jurisdiction of guerrilla organizations had come up. Increasing reports of conflicting spheres of activity between guerrilla leaders continued to arrive, particularly from Major Villamor, and it became obvious that some decision would have to be made by GHQ to define commands.

The problem of finding commanders suitable for the overall situation was a difficult one and would take time and trouble. Recognition of individual local commanders appeared to be the most satisfactory solution, and G-2 (Willoughby) unhesitatingly recommended the establishment of island commands on the basis of pre-war Military Districts. This was an important step as it revived authoritative territorial entities well known and respected by former PA (Philippine Army) members. Formal letters dated 13 February 1943 to Col. M. Peralta and Col. W. Fertig were carried by Comdr. Parsons when he left Australia, appointing them CO of the 6th and 10th Military Districts, respectively. On 21 February, radio messages were sent to Peralta and Fertig announcing their appointments as Commanders of Panay (6th MD) and Mindanao (10th MD).[25]

Frictions Between the Various Commanders

Only fragmentary information on the general guerrilla picture in early 1943 was available when the Military Districts were being recognized. In truth, there were unknown problems and rivalries.

In the first place there was the friction between Panay and Mindanao, or between Peralta and Fertig. Jealousy was originally thought to be the cause. In 1943 Col. Peralta organized the "IV Philippine Corps," but senior officers were threatening the command and suggesting that Col. Fertig, as senior known American officer in the islands, take command of the Corps.[26] Col. Fertig accepted Col. Peralta's offer, but GHQ in Australia knew nothing about this. Neither Fertig nor Peralta was really prepared for a Military District arrangement; both appeared dismayed and thought that GHQ had no faith in their abilities. It was an understandable reaction in able men, although their military phraseology appeared ambitious.[27]

Before Fertig was aware of Peralta's intentions to establish an independent "IV Corps," he had units established on Negros under Major Placido Ausejo. Ausejo's forces were later released from Fertig's command and Fertig instructed Col. E.E. McClish, his commander in northeastern Mindanao, to establish contacts on Leyte and Samar. In the meantime Peralta's men had already established contacts there. In some cases these conflicted interests fanned local animosity and even led to inter-guerrilla strife. The position of Samar's overall guerrilla leader, Ruperto Kangleon, was also not clear. On Bohol, Major Ismael Ingeniero was believed to have held undisputed command. There were, however, indications that this was not entirely the case.

The Peralta-Fertig dispute over spheres of influence extended to Negros and obscured more legitimate parallel confusion over the command on that island. Lt. Col. S. Abcede was backed by Peralta and Maj. Villamor; Ausejo was backed by Fertig. But there was also Col. G.R. Gador, who saw in Cebu the Fenton-Cushing combine hold undisputed control of the island from the earliest stages of guerrilla activity there. Although there was a certain amount of killing and destruction, it appears possible that this feature was exaggerated by Kangleon, Fertig, Parsons, and Ingeniero, who had ambitions regarding Cebu. Recognition of the Cebu Area Command at an earlier date apparently could have had a beneficial effect on Visayan guerrilla activity. Actually during this stage, Cebu seems to have been left out of the discussions. But Jim Cushing must have known about the attempts to create kingdoms left and right. Because of the central location of Cebu, couriers from all sides must have passed by regularly on their way to the other islands. These couriers for sure must have used the facilities of the Cebu Area Command; therefore Cushing must have known what was going on. Cebu was by far the most important island in the Visayas, and Peralta, Abcede, Fertig, Kangalon and Ingeniero would have considered it as the prize to catch.[28]

Guerrilla Developments Elsewhere

Apart from the few messages from Nakar in July and August 1942, GHQ in Australia did not, as of early 1943, have any contact with the central and northern part of the country. This did not mean that nothing was going on there.

Apart from the actions of Walter Cushing in northern Luzon there was the organization of Col. Claude Thorp who, in January 1942, worked his way from Bataan through the Japanese lines to establish a headquarters in the Zambales Mountains. From this retreat, Colonel Thorp attempted to centralize operations in the various regions of the island including northern Luzon and the Bicol Peninsula. Though he made substantial progress in this direction, his efforts were brought to an untimely end. In October 1942 Colonel Thorp and several of his staff were trapped in a Japanese raid and subsequently executed. After Colonel Thorp's death, a multiplicity of independent guerrilla commands began to develop throughout the provinces of Luzon.[29]

In the southern half of Luzon, three units were particularly outstanding in their growth and operations. These were the forces of Maj. Bernard L. Anderson in the eastern region, of Maj. Robert Lapham in the central region, and the "Marking Guerrillas" in the sector east of Manila.[30] Especially Lapham was so successful that the Japanese army put a $1 million bounty on his head. Marking's guerrillas formed in the Sierra Madre mountains east of Manila under Col. Straughn's umbrella, and became an independent organization when Straughn was captured in August 1943. Straughn was beheaded by the Japanese. Marking's organization developed a reputation for ruthlessness, and was often in open conflict with the Hunters ROTC Guerrillas, nearby.

Then there were the Hukbalahaps in Pampanga, the East-Central Luzon Guerrilla Area (ECLGA) units of Colonel Edwin P. Ramsey in east-central Luzon, the Hunters in Cavite, the Fil-American Irregular Troops in Rizal, and President Quezon's Own Guerrillas in Batangas. These units were of varying quality and effectiveness.

The guerrilla situation in the northern half of Luzon remained generally obscure until well into 1944. Distance, difficulty of communications, and the extensive countermeasures of the Japanese hampered any effective SWPA penetration of the upper provinces either for liaison or supply.

After Colonel Nakar's execution by the Japanese and the subsequent loss of contact between his headquarters and Australia, a series of successors attempted to carry on his work in the northern mountains and in the Cagayan Valley. The Japanese in these areas were particularly watchful, however, and, as each new leader arose, he was tracked down and eliminated. In a heroic and desperate effort to continue the movement, Colonel Nakar's intrepid lieutenants, Lt. Col. Arthur Noble, Lt. Col. Martin Moses, Maj. Ralph B. Praeger and Lt. Col. Manuel P. Enriquez, were killed or captured by the enemy before the close of 1943.[31]

In early 1944 the command of the main guerrilla forces in northern Luzon fell to Maj. Russell W. Volckmann, an unsurrendered American officer. Major Volckmann designated his organization the United States Army Forces in the Philippines, North Luzon (USAFIP, NL).

Major Volckmann's forces grew rapidly and by the end of 1944 numbered some 10,000 men.[32] The greatest drawback to the full realization of his efforts, however, was the lack of radio contact with General Headquarters, SWPA. Finally, in September 1944, he succeeded in putting a makeshift radio into operation and, through this lone channel of communication, messages began to be sent and received.

CHAPTER 14

THE BATTLE FOR TABUNAN

B Y THE END of 1942 it was very clear to the Japanese that the Cebu Area Command was the enemy to beat and Jim Cushing the great architect of the Cebu Resistance Movement. A price was put on his head and the Japanese went to great lengths to capture him. They were convinced that once the headquarters in Tabunan was destroyed the resistance movement would soon die out. In early 1943 they made several large-scale attempts to dislodge the Cebu Area Command.

The Battle of Malubog
The first attempt came early in January 1943 when a sizable Japanese fighting force left Cebu City and proceeded south along the provincial road to Naga. There were some skirmishes with rebel forces, but no large-scale fighting. The following day, reinforced with seasoned troops from the Naga garrison, the enemy force moved quickly over the central mountain range to Toledo City on the west coast of the island.

At the Central Cebu Sector Headquarters in Pandong Bato, information filtered in about the increased strength of the enemy garrison at Toledo. Major Baura, sector commander, dispatched a message to Lt. Quiumpo at Minglanilla to move his entire company towards Toledo. Baura, thinking something might be in the air, also ordered other companies to head there.

On the 29th of January Baura received word that a very large Japanese force was on its way from Toledo to Sangi, a road crossing just outside of the town. At the Sangi crossing the Japanese took the road to Magdugo in the Malubog Valley. It was clear to Baura that this was another attempt on the GHQ at Tabunan, but this time from the west. Messages went up and down to the GHQ in Tabunan and Jim dispatched mortars, including a specially made 81mm mortar, to the threatened area. By the time the enemy arrived in the Malubog Valley the guerrillas had already taken positions on the ridges around the valley. The mortars were ready. The first enemy assault was beaten back and the Japanese suffered heavy casualties. With the advantage of the height the guerrillas could inflict heavy damage on the enemy. By midafternoon four Japanese planes made bombing runs, but they could not prevent their own troops from being decimated. The night was rather quiet, but the next morning the battle resumed. That day the fighting was sporadic. Again Japanese bombers made a number of runs, but the guerrillas were well dug in and the planes did not do much damage. The second night was quiet until at dawn on the third day the enemy was nowhere to be seen. The Malubog Valley was littered with temporary shallow graves, dug by the Japanese. Here and there hands or feet were sticking out of the graves, which was a horrible sight, but the battle was won. According to Segura the Japanese suffered 750 casualties in this battle.[1] The guerrillas tried to catch up with the fleeing Japanese in order to inflict more damage, but they quickly withdrew to Naga and Minganilla.[2,3,4]

The Battle of Guila-guila

Guila-guila is a sitio of Barrio Bagalnga, municipality of Compostela, 25 kilometers north of Cebu City, on the east coast of Cebu Island. Beyond the town proper to the north is a bridge over the Canamocan River, and a hundred meters after the bridge is the junction at Sitio Guimbal, where a feeder road branches to the west from the provincial road. About four kilometers from the junction the open terrain ends and the road enters between the hills at Sitio Guila-guila. Not far from here was the command post of Major Fabian M. Sanchez. In the early morning of 5 March 1943 Sanchez received a message that a Japanese column was sighted near Liloan, some 10 kilometers to the south and marching northward. Sanchez ordered Lieutenant Pedro Pusta to set up an ambush in Liloan with his platoon.

There was a skirmish between Pusta's platoon and the Japanese at Barrio Lo-oc in Liloan. Seeing that he was outnumbered, Pusta ordered his men to withdraw, and the Japanese followed. Other guerrilla units joined the battle, but they could not prevent the enemy from slowly gaining terrain. The Japanese spread out and used the sugar cane fields along the road as cover for their advance.

At his command post in Basak, Sanchez surmised from incoming reports that the enemy was approaching in massive numbers. He was not sure whether the Japanese were on their way to reinforce their garrison in Danao or if it might be an attempt to penetrate his area and attack GHQ at Tabunan. For sure the Japanese wanted revenge for their miserable operation in Malubog where they suffered the loss of hundreds of men.

Major Sanchez had prepared positions at Sitio Guila-guila for just such a move by the enemy. His men occupied the high positions with a clear view of the feeder road, which the Japanese would surely take. Sanchez was lucky to have three machineguns and more than a hundred men. There was a fall-back position at Barrio Panagban with another 100 men.

In the meantime Lieutenant Pusta had withdrawn from Liloan to Estaca, just south of Compostela proper. After a while he broke off the skirmish at Estaca and fell back towards Compostela. He left some men behind to delay the Japanese before withdrawing along the Guimbal-Dapdap road. The Japanese followed the guerrillas and turned inland along the feeder road with open level fields on both sides. After passing the first bridge they saw the low hills ahead and then came to the second bridge. Beyond the bridge Lieutenant Admana's men were waiting, the trap was set. Once the Japanese started to cross the bridge a murderous fire broke loose. The freedom fighters used every weapon they had, the three machineguns firing continuously. The Japanese were completely surprised and dozens were killed by the first guerrilla salvos.

But the enemy kept on coming. Late in the afternoon Japanese reinforcements arrived in trucks and the guerrillas began running low on ammunition. The sun was setting. A few hours later, while the battle was still sporadically going on the Japanese air force started bombing the guerrilla positions. After the planes left the Japanese attacked again but the guerrillas were gone, having nearly run out of ammunition. Major Sanchez reported to GHQ that he had counted 232 dead Japanese soldiers. Civilians in the town of Compostela said they counted nine Japanese trucks with dead enemy soldiers. The battle of Guila-guila was another victory for Jim Cushing and his men.[5]

The Fall of Tabunan

Notwithstanding the lost battles the Japanese did not give up in their attempt to capture the guerrilla General Headquarters at Tabunan. A few days after the battle of Guila-guila they were ready again. This time they came in mas, with five Japanese columns marching in the direction of Tabunan. They broke through the first defense lines. All guerrilla units became mobile; many of these were directed to act as a blocking force against the approaching enemy. In order to get a better grip on the situation Major Baura pooled all his runners at his headquarters. The enemy used aircraft for strafing runs and bombings; their heavy gun at Magkagang Hill above Camp 4 also directed its fire to the area. Initially the enemy directed its attacks especially to the area of Cantipla, the gateway to Tupas and Tabunan. The battle raged for many days, but slowly the guerrillas lost their grip on central Cebu. The enemy came closer and closer to GHQ in Tabunan. Around March 20, in the Maraag area, Baura and Cushing discussed their options. They were concerned about the Women's Camp near Tabunan where Mrs. Fritzi Cushing, Mrs. Betty Fenton and little Steve, Fenton's son, were staying. At all costs it had to be prevented from falling into the enemy's hands.

Once they arrived Cushing sent the women off to a new hiding place. Just after they left Jim was informed that the Japanese had reached the Tabunan area from the east. Another enemy column had broken through Colonel Albinda's units in the north and was expected to link up with the force already in Tabunan. Jim sent some men to different areas in an attempt to take out the various telephone lines the guerrilla used for their communications. He was afraid the Japanese would follow the telephone lines to get to the GHQ. The men were only partly successful; in some places the Japanese had discovered the lines already.

Jim and his staff withdrew to a place deep in the forest on Sunog Ridge, west of Tabunan. Suddenly Jim became mad; his men had never see him so angry when he found out that the officer in charge of the .50-cal. machinegun guarding the north entrance to GHQ at Tabunan had left his post when the Japanese column was coming in.

That night there was little sleep for the men in hiding. The next morning they ate only sardines while not daring to make a fire since it might be spotted by the Japanese. Some men familiar with life in the jungle gathered "pacol," banana-like fruit that is usually eaten by monkeys. Cushing and Baura discussed the situation, after which Jim decided to follow a lie-low policy for the time being. A runner was sent north to try to find Harry Fenton, from or about whom they had heard nothing for quite a while.

A few days later, on 26 March 1943, Tabunan was taken by the Japanese.[6] Nothing much was left for them because all major officers of the guerrilla forces escaped. Jim went to Masurela, on Cebu Island's west coast, somewhere between Asturias and Toledo. From there he went down to Mitol (near Balamban), also on the west coast, where he stayed for some time. Fenton transferred to Maslog, a mountain Barrio of Asturias on Cebu's west coast. Meantime, upon hearing that the patriots were regrouping in the Asturias area to continue their resistance, the Japanese became determined to penetrate the place.[7]

CHAPTER **15**

THE STRUGGLE FOR RECOGNITION

Radio Contact With Australia!

A LREADY AT AN early stage of the resistance movement it was clear to Jim Cushing that contact with the outside world was a necessity to survive. In the beginning they had sufficient weapons and ammunition, thanks to the supplies taken from the SS *Doña Nati* and the SS *Anhui*. After a while, however, stocks dwindled and they had to revert to Philippine ingenuity. Shells were manufactured from Japanese sea mines, mortars from steel pipes, and simple shotguns from scrap iron. This was not a long-term solution. Cebu Island is very centrally located in the Visayas, so whoever wants to go from Panay, Negros or Bohol to Leyte, Samar or other islands has to pass through Cebu. These colleagues-in-arms often used the facilities of the Cebu Area Command to stay out of the hands of the Japanese. They told Jim about contacts they had with other groups and about small arms shipments, ammunition and other supplies from Australia.

The first requirement for contact was a radio. Harry Fenton kept on broadcasting until 9 April 1942, the day before the Japanese landed in Cebu. He was very proud of the telegram he received from General MacArthur, on the eve of his last broadcast, congratulating him for relaying the Voice of Freedom to the southern areas.[1] Fenton's very caustic anti-Japanese broadcast made him a marked man, however. He could count on being arrested or shot on sight if the Japanese ever found him. Fenton was a broadcaster, not a technician, though, and without someone to manage his equipment nothing could be done. When the Cebu resistance movement began to take shape he tried to locate "Joe" Esplanada, who had been a member of the technical staff at KZRC. He found Joe at his hideout in Cabadiangan, Compostela. Together with Sebastian Augusto they set up a small receiver for

Fenton at his hidden camp at Kabakhan in Tabunan, and soon other technicians followed. They found their first transmitter, an American-made RCA one, hidden in a cave in the Central Cebu Sector. But there were lots of parts missing. They managed to get the missing parts and the transmitter was set up in Mabini. Together with a receiver from the Bureau of Mines they were now able to hear news broadcasts from outside the country, especially from KGEI in San Francisco.[2]

In order to make contact with other stations they needed, however, a much stronger transmitter. After a while they found in Basak, Cebu City, a strong transmitter from KZRC which was supposed to be destroyed by the Japanese. They had done their job very sloppily though, and with some ingenuity the resistance managed to repair it. The transmitter was set on the 49m band, a very broad band covering 3,000 to 4,000 kilocycles. For safe transmission they needed a code, but did not have one. By transmitting for very short periods, to avoid discovery by the Japanese, they decided to transmit in the open. Working in shifts they tried to contact KFS, Palo Alto, in California. It did not work. Getting fed up, Lieutenant Perez tried another frequency, 3,800 to 3,600 kilocycles. Suddenly he got an answer. It was 13 February 1943. They were quickly ordered not to broadcast in the clear and to maintain radio silence until further instructions.

The next day, however, Fenton could not resist the temptation to try again. He identified himself and asked that his family in Schenectady, New York be informed that he was still alive and well. Three days later an angry answer told him, "By order of the War Department, keep silent for security reasons."[3] Three weeks later the Tabunan headquarters was overrun by the Japanese. This ended for a while all communications with the world outside Cebu.

Upon hearing that the patriots were regrouping in the central mountain barrios to continue their resistance, the Japanese determined to penetrate the place. Fenton was distrustful of the fairly open area near his camp and therefore slept in a house at Bae. Nearby was Lieutenant Sebastian Augusto, who had set up a radio station.

A rift growing between Fenton and Cushing?
At the very beginning of the armed struggle the relations between Jim Cushing and Harry Fenton were very cordial. They shared things and disagreements were rare. After the fall of Tabunan the situation gradually changed.

Maybe the fact that they used separate headquarters played a role in this. Fenton's spy-hunting and the executions that followed also became worrisome for Jim.

In late March an incident occurred that made things worse. Marcario Peralta, commander of the Panay guerrillas, had sent a liaison officer to Cebu with orders for the promotion of Jim and Harry to the rank of Lieutenant Colonel. This officer, Captain Alfredo de los Reyes, handed the order to Jim Cushing who quickly dispatched a messenger to locate Fenton, who was then in southern Cebu, to show him a copy of the orders. The messenger missed Fenton, who was already on his way back to his headquarters. When the two met again, a few days later, Jim was wearing the colonel's insignia. Surrounded by his bodyguards Fenton strode up to him and stuck a revolver in Cushing's neck.

Jim looked calmly over his shoulder and said, "Why Harry, you are a colonel now!"

Disregarding that, Fenton answered, "So, in my absence you accepted orders without consulting me!"

"Well, Harry, I sent a messenger to you in the south, but he apparently missed you."

The incident underlined Fenton's suspicious nature quite clearly. After this incident it was never the same as before.[4,5]

Worries over Cebu

A few weeks later, in April 1943, out of the blue sky an American arrived in Central Cebu. He was Roy Bell, a professor from Silliman University in Dumaguete, Negros. Bell came as a representative of Major Jesus Villamor, Chief of the Allied Intelligence Bureau's advance party in the Philippines.[6]

Major Villamor landed on Negros on 14 January 1943. As mentioned earlier, it took him some time to clear up the mess the resistance movement on Negros was in. Villamor's assignment was developing an intelligence net based on the "cell" system, independent of guerrilla organizations and possible guerrilla nets, for security and to provide a neutral source of information.

Before turning to his main job he felt obliged to sort out the situation on Cebu. Alarming rumors had reached Australia, before he left, about random killings and harsh treatment of civilians by the resistance movement in Cebu. During his first weeks in Negros the stories only got worse. He was impressed by the work Bell had done for the Negros guerrillas.[7,8]

Who Was Roy Bell?

When the Americans occupied the Philippines in the early years of the 20th century one of the first things they did was reorganize education. Thousands of teachers and professors were shipped to the Philippines to take part in this effort. There were also new schools founded. Apart from this the Philippines, as a strong Catholic country, offered an excellent challenge for Protestant missionaries. Silliman Institute was founded in 1901 in the city of Dumaguete, on the southern tip of the Island of Negros, by the Presbyterian Board of Foreign Missions. It became a university in 1938.

Roy Bell was born in 1896 in Kansas, USA. In 1921 he ended up, together with his young wife Edna, in Dumaguete as a teacher and missionary at the Silliman Instute. He liked his work and when the war broke out he did not go back to the US but stayed behind in the hope of being able to continue his work. After the fall of Cebu it took more than six weeks before any Japanese showed up in southern Negros. Eventually on 26 May 1942 a smiling Captain H. J. Tsuda of the Japanese army stepped onto the Dumaguete dock. It was not a massive invasion, as the captain was accompanied by only 40 soldiers. The first few months of the occupation happened in a rather friendly way. Roy and his family took the precaution to move to a log cabin in the mountains; this was safer because Americans were being picked up and sent to Manila for imprisonment. Meantime Roy had a large hand in setting up the resistance movement in southern Negros.[9] He helped Villamor to straighten out the problems with the resistance on the island and to bring it under a single command.

Villamor was very happy with the work of Bell and consulted him about what to do with Cebu. As a Filipino, Villamor was well aware that Filipinos from a certain island have difficulty interfering with Filipinos from other islands. That was why he was reluctant to go personally to Cebu on a fact-finding mission; you never knew, maybe he would be shot on suspicion that he was a spy. Bell told him what he knew about the situation and mentioned also that he was reasonably acquainted with Harry Fenton. Villamor and Fenton also knew each other rather well. Just before he left for Australia the two had met in Cebu and exchanged passwords for later use in retaking the Philippines. A few days later, in mid-April 1943, Bell left, together with Lieutenant Juan Dominado, Lieutenant Vail, and Arne, a stranded Norwegian sailor. They crossed Tañon Strait, the stretch of water between Negros and Cebu and landed in a small village on the other side.[10]

Meeting Cushing and Fenton

Once they landed they were immediately surrounded by a group of local guerrillas. Their leader, Jose, did not trust them at all. Roy Bell explained the purpose of their arrival and asked to be brought to Harry Fenton. Jose took their weapons and agreed to inform Fenton of their arrival.

They were brought to a local Catholic priest where they stayed two days before they received a message from Fenton to bring them to his headquarters. Fenton even directed Jose to furnish the visitors with an old car for much of the journey. But when they reached the vicinity of Toledo, Roy's party had to turn inland by foot to avoid Japanese patrols. The rest of the journey was through difficult and rough terrain. They crossed rivers and walked through jungle until after a long and arduous march they arrived at a clearing. Roy noticed a number of huts and small, rough buildings, and, in the middle of the clearing a set of gallows. When he asked the guard about the structure he answered: "Oh yes, we finished off all of the mayors on Cebu who stayed in office for any time after the surrender of American forces on 7 May 1942."[11]

He was brought into a primitive office with a nipa roof. Fenton recognized him immediately. "Mr. Bell, why did you come here?"

Roy explained his mission and gave the password Major Villamor had given him. Fenton was surprised that he had the password. He confirmed that they had executed a number of civilians and explained that many were in fact helping the Japanese in their counter-insurgency measures. There was no other choice, he said. The Japanese considered Cebu an important location and kept occupation forces of up to 10,000 men, apart from navy and air force units. They did do all they could to wipe out resistance fighters by the roots. They had even fenced in Cebu City in order to be able to control who went in and out. It was a matter of an eye for an eye. It was difficult to trust anybody. Freedom fighters that were caught were tortured and executed, sometimes with their whole family, in the most horrendous ways.[12]

They exchanged a lot of information about the armed struggle on both islands. The visit led to radio contact with the WSK station in Negros, and eventually with KAZ, through which communications with SWPA in Australia could be established.

Roy informed Fenton that SWPA in Australia would like to have a single command on all the islands. So far Cebu was an exception with its double command. This situation made it difficult for Australia to recognize the Cebu Area Command, and that made it a problem to send supplies and money.

The next morning Roy found at the breakfast table an unexpected guest, Governor Hilario Abellana. Roy knew him by name, but had never met the governor before. Abellana told him that initially he had stayed in office after the Japanese occupied Cebu. "But I was a complete figurehead with no chance to help the people in Cebu City. The Japs have thousands of troops there—it is the second largest city in the Philippines, after Manila. I could not stop the brutal treatment of the people so I fled into guerrilla territory."[13]

Later in the morning Roy met Jim Cushing and repeated his story about Villamor, the worries about the Cebu guerrillas, and recognition. Jim acknowledged the problem and said that he would look into it. He added: "I hope your report about us to Villamor won't be all bad. We have been rough on our dealings with many people but Villamor must try to understand that there are many collaborators in and around Cebu City. It has been difficult to identify them here in the largest city outside Manila. But I agree it cannot go on like this much longer."[14]

Neither Fenton, nor Cushing was interested in accompanying join Roy Bell to Negros to tell their own story to Major Villamor. They said they could not leave their men so soon after losing their headquarters in Tabunan. Their organization had to be put back in shape and adjust to the new situation. Roy proposed bringing Governor Abellana to Negros. This proposal was also rejected. The governor had only joined the guerrillas only a short while ago and Fenton as well as Cushing were not sure he was the right person to represent them.

A few days later Roy and his men returned to Negros. On the one hand he was disappointed; on the other he had come to realize that the situation in Cebu was completely different from the situation in Negros. Negros was not only almost three times the size of Cebu, but its population density was only half. The importance of Negros was only sugar, while Cebu was an important trading and communications hub. Then there was the psychological issue. Cebu was the second largest city, a historic site of importance, and vice president Osmeña hailed from there. The Japanese kept a garrison of 10,000 to 12,000 in Cebu and less than 1,000 in much larger Negros. Compared to other islands, such as Bohol, Panay, Leyte and Samar, it was the same. These islands had only small Japanese garrisons; large parts of the islands never saw Japanese at all. Mindanao, 20 times the size of Cebu, was actually only partly occupied. Col. Wendell Fertig, the guerrilla commander of that island, occupied more territory than the Japanese. Compared to other islands Cebu was in a serious war while they were, to a certain extent, only playing hide and seek.

Fenton's fears were confirmed when Japanese troops almost caught him early on 17 June 1943. He just managed to jump out of a window from the house where he was staying. His wife Betty was not so lucky; she was caught and taken prisoner, together with their second child David, then only a baby. Betty Fenton was brutally handled and terribly humiliated by the enemy.[15] Mother and child was both imprisoned in Cebu City. Two Bataan veterans who had recently returned to Cebu were also captured and hanged without any due process. The capture of his wife and son made Harry Fenton bitter and vindictive.[16]

The guerrilla district commander in Pangasinan (Northern Luzon) was Major Charles Joseph Cushing, Jim's brother. He joined the US Army at the age of 14 in New Mexico (1933) and served with General Pershing there. In 1941 Charles was in the Philippines, and when the USAFFE surrendered, he joined the movement of Lieutenant-Colonel Thorpe and eventually became commander of the Pangasinan guerrilla. In March 1943 the Japanese proudly announced that Cushing had learned the error of his ways and surrendered to Imperial troops. This was partly true. The Japanese had captured his wife Mercedes, but he disappointed his captors by walking in alone.[17] They brought him to Cebu and up to Babag. A letter purportedly written by Charles was delivered to Jim Cushing in the mountains, and was also published in *Visayan Shimbun*, the Japanese-controlled newspaper (edited by Napoleon Dejoras) published and circulated in Cebu. The headlines read:

CUSHING, MRS FENTON URGE
ALL GUERRILLAS TO GIVE UP
Advise Men Up in Arms to Offer Services to Building of New PI,
Guerrillas Should Aid in Construction of New Philippines."

A photo on the front page showed Charles seated between Lieutenant Kaneko and Sergeant H. Yoshita, both of the Cebu Military Police (Kempetai).

The letter drew laughter from Jim Cushing. "This was written under duress," he said. "My brother does not mean what he writes here. Why, he has always called me Jimmy. Here he writes 'Dear James.' And he was always Charley to us. Here he signs 'Charles'!"

The same issue of the Japanese paper carried a letter addressed to "All who have taken up arms," purportedly written by Betty Fenton, wife of the co-commander of the Cebu Guerrilla Force. A photo on the inside showed Mrs. Fenton with Japanese officers Captain Akao and Lieutenant Kaneko, the paper's editor Napoleon Dejoras, and baby David Fenton. Addressed to: "To Whom it May Concern."[18]

Fenton and his loyal followers fled to the northern part of Cebu, establishing his hideout in a pleasant valley among the gentle hills of Barrio Montealegre, a mountain Barrio of Asturias. It was a very remote place, in the middle of Cebu Island and actually closer to Sogod than to Asturias. The Barrio was within the limits of the Northern Cebu Sector with Major Agaton Medina as its security.

The units around the general headquarters were left at Yutan-on, a mountain Barrio between Balamban, Cebu, and Cebu City. The headquarters battalion was under Captain Alipio Macarolia. The 1st Battalion of the Eastern Cebu Sector was under Col. Gracias C. Espiritu; and the 2nd and 3rd Battalions were under Col. Maximo M. Albinda. The Northwestern Cebu Sector was under Major Bernard Hale, also a former mining engineer. These four battalions were called the X-Battalion, remnants of the units left by Col. Fenton. This battalion was under direct command of Col. Jim Cushing.[19]

When the two supreme guerrilla leaders were separated, and immediately after the organization of Battalion X, Col. Cushing and his fellow officers discussed at length the possibility of contacting Major Villamor after all. Apart from weapons, ammunition, medicines and radio spare parts, there were lots of other issues that had to be solved that would otherwise hinder operations. An important issue was money. They knew that other guerrilla groups, for instance those on Mindanao, printed their own money. Jim was in favor, Fenton was against. After days of long discussions the final vote was unanimous in favor of contacting Villamor. Jim decided to go to Negros, the neighboring island, where Villamor had his base.

Before he left Jim appointed Lt. Col. Ricardo Estrella as his caretaker. He gave him a long white sealed envelope in which was a letter with instructions in case he did not return from his mission to Major Villamor. Jim limited the party to four officers. He selected Major Abel Trazo, a Bataan veteran who knew Villamor personally, Lieutenant Lucio Carniga, who knew the way, and Lieutenant Ricardo Valenzuela. He also took Major Baura because he knew that Baura and Estrella often quarreled. They did not bring any major weapons; just sidearms.

Jim disguised himself as a priest and wore a soutane. During the trip this sometimes caused hilarious complications because people in the villages they passed through asked Jim if he could baptize newly born babies, or marry a couple.

They proceeded up to Moalboal without any incident. They crossed the Tañon Strait at night in Alegria, and landed in Manjuyod, just north of Bais City in Negros Oriental. This was the area controlled by Col. Gabriel Gador. The colonel gave them a guide to Kabangkalan, on the west coast of Negros, where they expected to see Major Villamor.

On the way from Manjuyod to Bais, an old wound in Jim's leg started to give him trouble. During one of the battles at Babag, a piece of shrapnel had lodged there and the wound was now getting infected. In the area above the sugarcane fields of Bais, he could no longer walk. The leg appeared to be gangrenous. A pharmacist in the area opened up the leg and removed the small piece; it turned out to be the size of a corn grain. The group rested long enough to allow the leg to get in better shape before resuming the walk.

Major Villamor was unfortunately not in Kabangkalan, and they were told he moved to Mariculum. He was not there either; he was now in the area of Tolong, they were told. Because Major Trazo knew Villamor personally he was sent ahead. They did not want to take the risk of being shot as spies or meeting some imposter acting as Villamor. The stakes were high and a small mistake could be disastrous.

The precautions proved to be unnecessary. Major Trazo found Villamor in Tolong and they recognized each other right away. Trazo doubled back and brought Jim to Villamor. They arrived in mid-September 1943 in Villamor's headquarters.[20] Jim's arrival must have been a shock for the camp occupants. Here was the famous rebel from Cebu, dressed as a priest in a soutane,[21] his body racked by pain, ridden with malaria and faltering about on a pair of bamboo crutches because of his injured leg. But he had made it.

After Jim had briefed Villamor on all the ins and outs concerning Cebu, a number of telegrams went back and forth between Negros and SWPA. Villamor, who now understood the situation on Cebu, did his best to push Jim's case to GHQ, but he was never able to get a commitment from Brisbane.

Villamor arrived in Negros on 15 January 1943 and left on 20 October 1943. He wrote in his mission report over Cebu the following:

In Cebu, trouble between FENTON and CUSHING, who had actually been operating satisfactorily during the early days of the guerrillas, began to manifest itself until it got so that an open break finally resulted, beginning with CUSHING's travel to my place against FENTON's wish and ending in FENTON's arrest. From all reports I have had about Cebu, it was apparent that the FENTON-CUSHING team was very much liked by all people on that Island. It was not until FENTON began to get scandalously involved with women that his popularity began to decrease. This started about February this year. CUSHING, on the other hand, whose popularity was somewhat dimmed by FENTON's due to the latter's more intimate knowledge of bombast and ballyhoo, now began to be regarded by the people as a better leader than previously thought. His popularity was greatly increased by the common knowledge of the fact that he personally used to lead the troops in most of their encounters with the enemy.[22]

ACTIVITIES

Activities in [Cebu] are now mainly limited to the perfection of organizations, training, ambushes, armed demonstrations, intelligence and, in the case of some units in Luzon, attempts at the elimination of Quislings and suspected pro-Japanese elements. In some localities (Cebu is a noteworthy example) killing of suspects and supposed collaborators has reached a point as to make even the loyal people sick. Also in Cebu, and to a limited extent Panay and Negros, ambushes often developed into pitched battles lasting for two or three days with the enemy finally employing field pieces and airplanes. Leaders in these localities refuse to admit that their forces were involved in anything but defensive measures. CUSHING for instance, stoutly maintains that the fighting in which he and his troops were involved were not battles but merely series of ambushes.[23]

OVER JIM CUSHING HE WROTE:

a. CUSHING, James (Cebu). Personally known to me. Miner. Possesses a dual personality—one cold, hard and unforgiving; the other, soft, sentimental, almost childish. Part Mexican. Easily blows up but just as quickly repents. Curses hard but is fond of quoting the "Good Book." Speaks English with a slight accent. Pronounces the suffix "ed" distinctly, as "attack-ed." Hates the Japs as much as he loves his "Cebu Patriots" of whom he refers with tear filled eyes. Courageous. Leads men in combat. Lacks administrative ability. Regards civil government as not feasible. All Cebu is behind him. All the Japs in Cebu are after him.

b. ABCEDE thinks he is a great fellow.

c. FERTIG, Wendell W. (Mindanao): Cushing regards him suspiciously. Believes he is "maneuvering" for the eventual control of all guerrillas. Dislikes him.

RECOMMENDATIONS

1. I cannot emphasize too strongly how much the recognition by GHQ means to the guerrillas. Failure of several leaders to get this recognition has led to a general breakdown of morale and caused them to lose men by the hundreds. In Cebu, for instance, despite the fact that FENTON and CUSHING had a closely knit organization, the prospect of getting into a recognized unit caused many of their officers and men to leave for other areas, particularly when they believed there was no longer any hope that Cebu would be recognized in view of the scandalous activities of FENTON.

2. This eagerness to be in one of the recognized units is general in all areas. The longer recognition is delayed, the more the guerrillas feel that GHQ has no interest in them. Eventually, they assume that their true status is nothing short of bandits with no hope of recognition now or later when our forces return. This question of recognition is one of the biggest causes for any feeling of hopelessness that seems apparent in some units.

3. I, therefore, strongly recommend that recognition be extended as early as possible to independent guerrilla units in the Islands. Numerous difficulties will undoubtedly be encountered before this recognition can be extended to all units and there will be no way of surmounting most of these difficulties unless a more flexible and practical policy be adopted than that which presently exists as regards the recognition of guerrilla units.

4. I further recommend that great care be exercised so as not to discredit representatives in the field. In my own case, a little detail

like the handling of radio traffic made my position at one time rather difficult. In this instance, CUSHING had left a sick bed and crossed enemy territory to reach my headquarters. GHQ's order, however, directing him to proceed to FERTIG's headquarters came through ABCEDE who was then using my station for his traffic. Likewise, the request for ABELLANA to proceed to FERTIG's headquarters was not handled through me but FERTIG (who had sent a man by boat to deliver the message) although I had radio contact with ABELLANA in Bohol. This resulted in CUSHING and ABCEDE believing that I had been relieved and discredited.[24]

Conference in Mindanao

At the time Jim Cushing returned to Cebu instructions were sent that he should attend a conference in Mindanao, at the headquarters of Col. Fertig. Participants in this conference were supposed to be Col. Fertig and other "guerrilla leaders." The purpose of the conference was to attempt to reach some working solutions between commanders in the southern Philippines. The conference was actually a series of conferences around the first of December 1943. Those present were: Major Ingeniero and officers from Bohol; Colonel Kangleon and officers from Leyte; Pedro Lopez, Hilario Abellana, and possibly a Santiago Q. Garcia, from Cebu; and also Fertig and Commander Chick Parsons. All Cebu representatives went without Cushing's knowledge or permission but were treated and acted as official representatives. Lopez and Abellana were actually in disfavor on Cebu as possible collaborators at the time. Lopez's notes:

> . . . Right now, the recognition of Cebu is out of the question," replied Commander Parsons. "As a matter of fact, General MacArthur was disgusted with the atrocities, killings, USAFFE-ings and G-fouring in Cebu. Just now it is better not to activate Cebu." Then he went on to inform us how he had gotten long before firsthand reliable reports that made sweeping attacks against the Cebu force and its command in their treatment of the civilian population. From what Commander Parsons told us, I could gather that he and General MacArthur had already made up their minds that the Cebu force, although doing good fighting, had not behaved properly and failed

to live up to the good name of the Army, and that they would have nothing to do with it until its policies and actuations were revised to conform with law and justice. . . .[25]

Based on the above it is not surprising that Cebu's recognition by SWPA did not push through. It was huge disappointment for Jim.

Back to Cebu

Jim left Negros on 9 October 1943 to return to Cebu from where he was supposed to go to Mindanao to attend the above-mentioned conference. He brought three American soldiers, ex-prisoners of war, with him: Russell Snell, Jim Dyer and Irving Joseph. The three were getting bored at Villamor's head-quarters, as they were not allowed to participate in guerrilla activities, and were hoping that the legendary Jim Cushing would provide more action. The three men had been taken prisoner on Bataan but were put to work by the Japanese as car mechanics in Bacolod on the Island of Negros in the Visayas Region.[26,27]

From the very beginning the three discussed endlessly the possibilities of escape. In Bataan there was no chance at all, but in Bacolod chances looked a lot better. On the night of Sunday, 4 July 1943 they got their chance.[28] That night the they realized suddenly that there were, because of Sunday night, only three Japanese guards. A quick check found that one was doing his laundry; the two others were taking a bath. The three Americans threw some weapons in the best of the trucks available, put Japanese helmets on their heads and put on the gas. When they reached the foothills, they stopped, disabled the truck, pushed it into a rice field and went on by foot. They ended up in the area under command of Colonel Ernesto S. Mata. Instead of being allowed to join the guerrillas in their battle against the Japanese, Mata kept them away from the fighting. He did not want any interference with his guerrilla work by Americans.[29]

When one day in October 1943 Jim Cushing hobbled out of the jungle into their camp they saw their chance. They had heard a lot about the famous guerrilla leader and thought that under his command they had a better chance of participating in the struggle against the Japanese. Jim was delighted since there were very few Americans on Cebu and he welcomed the presence of a few compatriots. On 25 November he led his new recruits over the mountains of Negros to the Tañon Strait to Cebu.[30]

The results of his meetings with Major Villamor were meager, to say the least. Actually the only concrete result of the trip was radio codes inside a War Department envelope written in invisible ink. This was carried by Trazo. Jim was actually bitterly disappointed.[31] He did not know the picture in Cebu at this time, but knowing it could have changed radically in a very short time, Jim sent Baura ahead to check the situation. Baura landed near Barili, on Cebu's west coast. There he was almost killed by Japanese who were waiting for him. He narrowly escaped. How could this have happened? Who had betrayed them? News of the incident filtered back to Jim with information about possible treason. Jim was supposed to land at Tangil, Dumanjug, south of Toledo City, but instead sailed further north to a little known point between Asturias and Tuburan.

The Fenton-Cushing Conflict

Harry Fenton and Jim Cushing were two very different persons. Fenton first arrived in the Philippines in 1938 with the U.S. Army's medical corps and worked for a while at the Sternberg General Hospital in Manila. Like so many Americans he was captivated by the Philippines. He purchased his discharge and went to Cebu to become a radio announcer for KZRC. His *Amateur Hour* became one of the most popular shows on the air in the time before Pearl Harbor. When war broke out he was pulled back into the service, commissioned as a first lieutenant and put to work as a censor. It did not last long; he was so suspicious of everything that came across his desk that after a short while he was out again and back in Cebu.[32] He simply did not fit in the military.

He was extremely anti-Japanese and let no occasion pass to ventilate his opinion. It was clear that if ever the Japanese arrived in Cebu he would be a marked man. He was also fiercely loyal to his country, the United States of America.

As a guerrilla leader he was difficult to approach and usually dealt with his subordinates via his adjutant, Captain Marcial Banate. He had a small circle of trustees around him, but most other officers feared him. From the very beginning of the guerrilla struggle he was afraid of treason, spies, collaborators and anybody involved with or suspected of helping the Japanese. He ordered his men continuously to round up those who could not be trusted, and after a short trial, often less than a few hours, executed them. Hanging was his favored punishment, but he also used firing squads.[33] He sported a long yellowish beard and moustache which caused some guerrillas to name him *Jesus Christ*.

In many ways Jim Cushing was just the opposite. He was very much approachable, and shared whatever he had with his fellow guerrillas, regardless of rank. He spoke softly and mildly, sported a well-trimmed black beard and fought fearlessly side by side with his fellow guerrillas. The only thing he had in common with Harry Fenton was his hatred of the Japanese and his loyalty to his country, America.

To a certain extent it was natural that they grew slowly apart. After all, they had different jobs within the Resistance Movement. Jim was always fighting; Harry stuck his nose in the papers.

The first real conflict was over money. Fenton was strictly against printing their own money to pay the troops and for purchasing food and other necessary things. He insisted that real money should be used and that they had to try to get that wherever possible. It was Governor Abellana who was most often tasked to do just that. In the beginning they had the supplies from the *Doña Nati*, so the problem was not that urgent. But the supplies did not last forever; and as they started to dwindle the money problem became serious. Jim had a different philosophy. He knew that on other islands the guerrillas printed their own money and it worked quite well, so why not give it a try?

In October 1943 the food situation became critical. Attempts to get rice from Panay Island failed. Actually Macario Peralta, the commander on Panay, was only willing to provide rice if the Cebu Area Command was willing to integrate into the Fourth Philippine Corps, which he commanded. This proposal was, for Cebu, non-negotiable. A little later a liaison officer for Col. Fertig showed up in Cebu. He told the Cebuanos that Col. Fertig wanted to place Cebu under his command. Also the Leyte units made overtures to put Cebu under their wing. Cushing and Fenton together declared a hands-off policy for Cebu.[34]

With Fenton's headquarters in the Bago-Maslog-Bae area, and Cushing's in the forests of Masurela-Sunog-Tabunan, although the distance was only 7 kilometers, the rift gradually grew deeper and deeper. Without the calming effect of Jim's presence, Fenton's witch-hunt executions increased dramatically.

Spies, Collaborators and Undercovers

Was Harry Fenton really mad? Had he lost control, or was he only over-reacting? There are different views on this subject. Reading *Tabunan*, the book written by Manuel F. Segura, one gets the impression that Fenton really went too far in his attempt to root out all the evil of cooperation with the enemy. Cayetano M. Villamor (no relative of Major Jesus Villamor), a lawyer and judge, has a completely different view. In his *My Guerrilla Years*, he also covers the Fenton issue extensively. On the first page of the first chapter of his book he writes:

> Contrary to the enemy's high-powered showmanship and propaganda, the Japanese soldiers were brutally killing old folks and innocent children in their efforts to subjugate summarily our people. This was war and the members of my family knew it—a war forced on us by an arrogant neighbor.

The Philippine Oligarch System

The Philippines is an oligarchy, a society where a handful of people or families rule the rest. From the state, the province, the city or the village, you frequently see the same names as political leaders. A politician who cannot be reelected because of term limits simply takes care that the name of his wife, his son or daughter, or even uncle or cousin, replaces him or her on the list of candidates. This system is often referred to as the *dynasty-system*. President Cory Aquino, in an attempt to adjust the Philippine political system to meet the requirements of the 21st century proposed a law to abolish the dynasty system. A law like this has to pass the House of Representatives. In this House the important families and landowners make the rules, and Aquino's law is, after 30 years still stuck there.[35,36,37,38]

Because of this dynasty-system most mayors in the cities and rural areas of Cebu, during the war, were mayor in the first place to continue the dynasty in order to protect their properties and business interests. Fenton's philosophy was that those mayors were not interested in joining or helping the resistance movement; they might lose their wealth if they disappeared in the jungle. If staying, Fenton thought, means doing business with the Japanese, so be it.

In other words, in Fenton's view any mayor, or person of any importance who stayed in office, must be a traitor. You simply could not take any chances, it was him or you. There was no room for benefit of the doubt.

Fenton's Dilemma

Fenton made lists of people who could not be trusted and should either be arrested or shot on sight. Cayetano M. Villamor, a lawyer and a member of the Cebu court system before the war, and an active guerrilla during the war, had a totally different view of Fenton then those who criticized the American radioman. He wrote:

> I must commend Col. Harry Fenton when he issued a black list of the persons who were to be shot on sight. Before its issuance to the different guerrilla units, the victims' cases were carefully studied and investigated.
>
> The persons therein listed were misguided irresponsible. They were false Filipinos—men who could not be depended during critical hours. These nobodies disastrously cooperated with the yellow rats for pecuniary purposes at the expense of the noble cause and of their own people.
>
> I must, in equal fervor, blame the resistance authorities. At times, they caused unnecessary misery to their own people. Even for slight provocations they killed those whom they suspected to be working with the enemy. Their motives were not square and honest.
>
> Sometimes our resistance leaders acted thru the impulses of the moments. They took action hurriedly, possibly because they were also aware that their certain death by the enemy was just around the corner.
>
> It is true that the killings produced good results at that time for the cause. Our countrymen hesitated to disastrously render effective service to the enemy. Were it not for the executions, what would happen to the cause and to the resistance movement in our province during the Japanese occupation?
>
> Let me repeat, there were unnecessary executions. They were executions to advance personal interests, not for the cause. These executions were disastrous and deplorable.[39]

Manuel F. Segura in his book *World War II in Central Visayas*, tells us the following of the Military Justice Courts:[40]

> The move was taken to keep in line or control the Cebu guerrillas and the civilian population including those living in Japanese controlled areas. Authorities in GHQ at Tabunan arrested both military

and civilians who allegedly committed transgressions against the laws, most especially, loyalty to country.

Suspects were tried on regimental level by Special Court Martial composed of three officers for minor offenses or by General Court Martial composed of five or more officers with a law member, often a lawyer. The trials were held at the General Headquarters in Tabunan for serious offenses.

In his book Segura reproduces a list of the Court Martials over the periods 7 July 1942 to 23 March 1943 and 16 September 1943 to 26 July 1944. There are no records for the period 26 March 1943 (the day Tabunan Headquarters was captured by the Japanese) until 15 September 1943. The list contains 155 death sentences.[41] In the same period, based on the testimony of Jovito Abellana, among others, the Japanese Kempetai office in the Cebu Normal School executed around 7,000 Filipinos. This figure is based on around 70 a week.

Fenton was confronted with a situation in which the enemy exercised extreme pressure on Cebu's population, abused, raped, tortured and beheaded at will anybody they did not like, a population that not only, to a certain extent, had reservations over the Americans, but that also was confronted with food shortages. Furthermore there was the political dynasty-system that forced leaders to choose between wealth protection and loyalty to their country. In this atmosphere of mistrust, betrayal and uncertainty in combination with the fall of the headquarters in Tabunan and the capturing of Fenton's wife and baby-son, Harry Fenton had no place in his heart for leniency.

Fenton Arrested and Court-Martialed
Soon after Jim left for Negros, ranking officers of the resistance movement held a series of conferences near a big Dakit (Indian rubber) tree on the ridge above Adlawon. Two weeks later a force of some 600 guerrillas proceeded north. About 300 men were from the Eastern Cebu Sector under Lt. Col. Espiritu. The rest were Lt. Col. Albinda's men. They were going after Fenton,[42] who was believed to be hiding in Montealegre.[43]

Fenton was not in Montealegre, he was in Lugo, villagers told them. The men marched three days through rough terrain to Lugo. He wasn't there either, and some people said he might be in Cabalawan. The men marched another two days back southward to Cabalawan, which was actually within

Barrio Montealegre. There they found the camp of Captain Marcial Banate, Fenton's adjutant. Banate was not there, however they found Quirino Torres, one of Fenton's bodyguards. Torres was not willing to talk, he was very afraid of revenge from Fenton. Only after being threatened with summary execution if he kept on refusing to tell where Fenton was, Torres told the men where to find the colonel. Fenton's hiding place was a small hut on a hillside, about half a kilometer away. Col. Almendras and his men crept up the hill and surrounded the hut. "Harry! Come out and surrender!"

After a short while he did just that. They tied him with a rope and searched the hut.

To everyone's surprise they found a suitcase with some P250,000 in cash. They also found a 14-year-old girl, a mestiza. A number of Fenton's followers were also arrested and tied up.

A few days later the 600-man column arrived back at Adlawon, near the old headquarters in Tabunan. During the march back Fenton was not treated very well. He was blindfolded, spat upon, hit, kicked in the head, and someone even set his beard on fire. The guerrillas were split over the capture of Fenton. There were a number who had special grudges against him, one of whom was Col. Estrella. He believed or was convinced that at one time Fenton had taken advantage of his wife, and that shortly thereafter Mrs. Estrella had been taken by the Japanese in a manner that, according to Estrella, did not leave Fenton entirely blameless. Since then, Estrella had become fired with the obsession of putting an end to Fenton. This was his chance.

Estrella opened the sealed envelope Jim Cushing had given him in case something happened to him. The envelope contained a note from Cushing authorizing him to take over command of the Cebu guerrillas. Estrella was in a hurry; he was aware of an intelligence report stating that the Japanese had offered him, Estrella, a cash advance of P60,000 for selling out the entire Cebu guerrilla command to the enemy. If this leaked out he would be in trouble.

Estrella quickly organized a conference of battalion commanders, before whom he charged Fenton with violating several provisions of the Articles of War (AW). The majority shared his view. Fenton was condemned to death on a violation of AW 67, 93, 94, 95 and 96. Before he faced the firing squad he wrote to Jim Cushing:

Dear Jimmy

After the war, please take Steve [his son] to my folks in the States. I am sure this is all a misunderstanding.

Good luck to you. Harry

And so, on 16 September 1943, Harry Fenton was executed by firing squad in Caba-asan, Cebu.[44,45]

The Treason of Colonel Estrella

Before the war Café Imperial in Cebu City was the favorite hideout of Cebu's expat community. At the start of the war these expats, most of them Americans, disappeared. Their role as customers in the café was taken over by Japanese officers.

Early in September 1943, Captain Alvin Lasala went to the café to see two Japanese officers. These men were Prince Yoshida, the chief investigator of the dreaded Kempetai in Cebu, and Tsureyama, the head of that organization. Captain Lasala was a guerrilla officer working undercover as a buyer and seller of war materials. It had taken him time and a few bottles of real American White Horse Whiskey to become friends with Yoshida and Tsureyama. Japanese are big drinkers but, as most Asians, they do not have much stomach for hard liquor and they easily become drunk. The Japanese needed Lasala for the supply of badly needed war materials and, of course, as a source of information. Information was what Lasala was after. There were rumors of treason within the ranks of the guerrillas. Especially around the towns of Tuburan, Asturias and Balamban, on Cebu's west coast, many guerrillas had recently surrendered to the Japanese. Why was that happening? There must be a reason.

The more whiskey was poured into the glasses of the two Japanese officers the more they started boasting about the successes of the Japanese army and the Kempetai. On the subject of the "bandits," the Japanese tried to convince Lasala that the problem would be soon solved.

"May be one month . . . less than one month, no more guerrillas. American Cushing now in Negros," Prince Yoshida said. "Fenton already killed. Commander guerrillas now Estrella. We offer gift to Estrella P250,000. We have advanced P60,000 old money."

"Cushing arriving Cebu," he continued, "mountain soldiers of Estrella will capture Cushing. Cushing will be executed by guerrillas. After Cushing killed guerrilla forces surrounded by Japanese forces and guerrilla surrender."

Lasala almost froze when he heard this. He let the waiter fill the Japanese glasses again and waited for a good excuse to leave. The guerrilla headquarters had to be informed immediately. Although Lasala had his own couriers he had to be very sure and asked the older brother of Manuel F. Segura, one of the key officers of Jim Cushing's staff, to bring the message to Col. Espiritu, one of the Cebu Area Command staff officers he trusted. A special commando was sent to Negros to warn Jim Cushing.[46]

The commando sent to Jim on Negros arrived in time to warn him about the things that had happened in Cebu since he left. It confirmed the funny feeling he had. That was why he sent Major Baura ahead. He left Negros for Cebu on 25 November 1943. Instead of landing in Tangil, near Dumanjug, he landed at a secret obscure point between Asturias and Tuburan. A few days later he arrived, together with the three American ex-POWS's, at his headquarters. He was briefed on the situation by several of the unit commanders. He was shocked and outraged over the treatment of Harry Fenton.

Col. Estrella was arrested and charged with treason. He was found guilty and on 2 January 1944 and executed by a firing squad under the command of Jim Cushing himself. The firing squad was composed of only American officers.[47,48,49]

The events of that autumn added another strain to Jim's already shaken health. With his body wracked by arthritis, malaria and the wound in his leg, his health could not take any more. He fell seriously ill for the next two months and was confined to the quarters of guerrilla doctor Torralba.

In January 1944 he gradually improved, and started to work on the rebuilding of his forces. The Japanese attacked in full force in late January 1944 and nearly captured the headquarters again; in fact they came close to destroying the entire organization. Finally, on 12 February 1944, the long awaited recognition of the Cebu Area Command came from Brisbane, retroactive to 22 January 1944. The official recognition of the Cebu Area Command was an important measure to bolster the morale of the forces. They were no longer "bandits."[50]

Shortly after this recognition, supplies were sent via Mindanao and Bohol, and Cushing established direct radio contact with GHQ in March. By February 1944, the forces had been reorganized, an effective intelligence net was in operation, and an increasing volume of important intelligence was being sent with the establishment of direct radio contact. The new set up was as follows:

Commanding Officer	Lt. Col. James M. Cushing
Chief of Staff	Lt. Col. Olegario L. Baura
Adjutant General	Maj. Manuel F. Segura
AC of S, G-1	Maj. Daniel M. Iway
AC of S, G-2	Maj. Jesus R. Ybañez
AC of S, G-3	Maj. Fernando M. Villamor
AC of S, G-4	Maj. Agaton Medina
Chief of Civil Affairrs	Lt. co. Fabian M. Sanchez
Chief Surgeon	Maj. Alejandro Balthazar
Chief Judge Advocate	Maj. Quirico del Mar
Chief Signal Officer	Maj. Eulogio Bonsukan
Chief Ordinance Officer	Maj. Carlos del Pilar
CO, Hq Service Company	Capt. Alipio Macariola
CO, MP Battalion	Maj. Bernard hale
CO, 85th Inf. Regt	Lt. Col. Rogaciano C. Espiritu
CO, 86th Inf. Regt	Lt. Col. Maximo Albinda
CO, 87th Inf. Regt	Lt. Col. Abel Trazo
CO, 88th Inf. Regt	Lt. Col. Alejandro D. Almendras

Part of the revamp was reorganizing the existing eight battalions into four regiments, the 85th, 86th, 87th and 88th. The weapons they had at hand were some 2,700 assorted pieces including 14 machineguns, 6 mortars, and 33 auto-rifles. They also maintained a few ordnance shops for manufacturing small amounts of ammunition and making repairs. Jim maintained strict discipline, and most of his officers had the respect and admiration of their men. As instructions from GHQ emphasized intelligence rather than offensive effort, the general policy became to "lie low."[51]

Rough Riders

After being driven out of their Tabunan headquarters in March 1943 the movement set up a new headquarters near Asturias, on Cebu's west coast. Gradually, however, the movement moved back to Tabunan. Tabunan had a number of advantages that could not be found elsewhere. By the end of 1943 the old headquarters was again in full use.

In Tabunan, deep in the forest, was a large stockade overflowing with prisoners, at times some five or six hundred. These were Filipino spies, thieves, all sorts of criminals and shady characters. For many, proof was insufficient for a solid conviction, but because they were not fully trusted they could not be released. They were a problem for Jim.

Somewhere at the end of 1943 he came on an idea to do something about these unfortunate inmates. He gave them an option to serve in a special unit so they could prove they could be trusted. If they survived a dangerous action they could earn their freedom.

Many of the stockade inmates volunteered. The prospect of fighting was definitely better than the near hopelessness that was their lot in the stockade. Jim gave the company a name: the Rough Riders. Their commander became Lieutenant Lorenzo Buenaflor, a soft-spoken Ilongo (from Panay Island), originally an airplane gunner. He was an experienced soldier, brave and several times wounded in action. The Rough Riders would go on to play an important role in the liberation of Cebu at the end of World War II.[52]

PART THREE

THE Z-PLAN

CHAPTER 16
THE CODE BREAKERS

Breaking the Enemy's Codes

WAR IS A complicated affair. Numerous parties have to communicate with each other in order to achieve a common goal. Orders have to be drafted, based on information and intelligence, and next the orders have to be issued in such a way that the enemy is not warned. Over the ages mankind has developed a number of systems to communicate with each other over long distances. Of course, especially in the case of a war, you cannot send your messages in plain text. You have to use a secret code.

The Japanese Codes[1]

The Japanese did not place so much emphasis on codes and cipher systems as their language was totally different to most European languages and so thought to be unlearnable. Japanese is usually written as a mixture of Chinese characters *Kanji* and two alphabets, *hiragana* and *katakana*. It is written in Chinese polysyllabic characters written from the top right hand corner going down in columns progressing to the left.

Nevertheless, the Japanese during World War II used many different codes and ciphers. All of these cryptosystems were known differently to different organizations; there was little or no coordination between the systems. The main reason for this lack of cooperation was simple distrust. The military did not trust the civilian government and the navy did not trust the army, or the other way around. The two most important systems were the *Purple cipher*, used by the Japanese Foreign Office, and the *JN-25 system*, in use by the Imperial Japanese Navy (IJN).

The Purple cipher had no cryptographic connection with any version of

JN-25, or indeed with any of the encryption systems used by the Japanese military. Purple traffic was exclusively diplomatic, not military.

The Japanese believed throughout the war that Purple was unbreakable, and even for some time after the war, even though they had been informed otherwise by the Germans. In April 1941 Hans Thomson, a diplomat at the German embassy in Washington, D.C., informed his bosses in Berlin that the Americans had broken the Japanese diplomatic Purple cipher. The message was duly forwarded to the Japanese; but use of the code continued.[2,3,4,5]

When, on 7 December 1941, Admiral Kichisaburu Nomura, the Japanese Ambassador to the USA, submitted the so-called 14-Part-Message, in fact Japan's Declaration of War, to United States Secretary of State Cordell Hull, the Americans already knew exactly what was in the paper.[6]

The JN-25 System

JN-25 was introduced in 1939. It was used for high-level naval operations and was a superencrypted code, eventually a two-book system, and joint cryptanalytic progress was slow. It proved to be extremely difficult to break this code. British, Australian, Dutch and American analysts were cooperating in attacks on JN-25 well before Pearl Harbor, but because the Japanese Navy was not engaged in significant battle operations before then, there was little traffic available to act as raw material. Publicly available accounts differ, but the most credible agree that the JN-25 version in use before December 1941 was not more than perhaps 10% broken at the time of the attack. Just before the Japanese attack on Pearl Harbor a new edition of the system went into effect and sent all the cryptanalysts back to the beginning.

OP-20-G—Signals Intelligence Command

The American effort to crack JN-25 was directed from Washington, D.C. by the U.S. Navy's signals intelligence command, called OP-20-G (*Office of Chief of Naval Operations, 20th Division of the Office of Naval Communications, G Section/Communications Security*). Its mission was to intercept, decrypt, and analyze naval communications from the Japanese, German and Italian navies.

Much of its work in the Pacific area was directed against Japan, but there was the problem of finding personnel who could speak Japanese. The Navy had a number of officers who had served in a diplomatic capacity in Japan and could speak Japanese fluently, but there was a shortage of radiotelegraph operators who could read Japanese Morse code communications sent in *kana*.

Fortunately, a number of US Navy and Marine radiotelegraph operators operating in the Pacific had formed an informal group in 1923 to compare notes on Japanese kana transmissions. Four of these men became instructors in the art of reading kana when the Navy began conducting classes in the subject in 1928. By June 1940, OP-20-G included 147 officers, enlisted men and civilians, linked into a network of radio listening posts as far-flung as the Army's outposts.

A problem was that over the years OP-20-G and its army counterpart, the US Army Signals Intelligence Service (SIS), had become fierce rivals, competing with each other to provide their intelligence data to high officials. These data were distributed under the codename "MAGIC."

Although this situation improved somewhat during the year, it was never solved properly. For the Pacific area, OP-20-G used two stations: Station HYPO, located at Pearl Harbor in Hawaii, and Station CAST in Cavite, near Manila in the Philippines.[7]

After the attack on Pearl Harbor, HYPO and the Dutch at Batavia, in conjunction with CAST in the Philippines and OP-20-G made steady progress in breaking JN-25. The breakthrough came during Japanese preparations for the attack on Midway Island. This allowed Admiral Nimitz to gamble on an ambush which resulted in the Battle of Midway, the loss of four Japanese carriers and many naval aviators, and what is generally agreed to have been the turning point of the Pacific War.[8]

Allied Translator and Interpreter Service (ATIS)[9,10]

The fact that the enemy was Japanese created difficult translation problems for the different intelligence services. In order to cope with this ATIS was created. ATIS, The Allied Translator and Interpreter Service, was a combination of Australian and American intelligence personnel placed into an integrated structure. Most of the 2,000 Americans who served in ATIS were *Nisei*, second-generation Japanese-Americans. Because very few Japanese soldiers surrendered, the emphasis for ATIS was mainly in connection with the translation of Japanese documents written in the complex and polyalphabetic Japanese language. The War in Europe required three times as many interrogators as translators. But in the SWPA the ratio was the other way around. Almost all of the personnel in the US Navy section of ATIS graduated from the US Navy Japanese/Oriental Language School, University of Colorado at Boulder.

For Marshal Admiral Isoroku Yamamoto,[11] Commander in Chief of the Combined Fleet during World War II, the defeat in the Battle of Midway was a bitter pill to swallow and a huge loss of face in Japanese culture. That Yamamoto, the architect of the attack on Pearl Harbor, remained as Commander in Chief, was at least partly to avoid diminishing the morale of the Combined Fleet. However, the Naval General Staff was disinclined to indulge further gambles. This reduced Yamamoto's philosophy to pursuing the classic defensive "Decisive Battle" strategy he had previously attempted to overturn in favor of offensive operations.

MacArthur's Central Bureau

General Douglas MacArthur escaped from Corregidor in the Philippines in a PT boat to Mindanao and flew to Australia from Del Monte on a Boeing B-17 Flying Fortress. He made his way to Melbourne, arriving there on 22 March 1942.

One of his first decisions, when he arrived in Melbourne, was to expand the SIGINT (Signals Intelligence) operations already existing in Australia. MacArthur was not happy to depend on the Navy's discretion in handling his SIGINT requirements. He therefore created two new groups: A Research and Control Centre known as the Central Bureau, and an Intercept Organization known initially as No. 5 Wireless Section. Major General Charles A. Willoughby became MacArthur's Intelligence Officer (G-2).

A top secret mission (*Operation Vengeance*) was authorized to try to intercept Yamamoto while he was traveling in the air and to shoot down his plane. A squadron of Lockheed P-38 Lightning aircraft, stationed on the island of Guadalcanal, was assigned the task. Pilots from three units were informed that they were intercepting an "important high officer" with no specific name given.

On 14 April 1943, Section 51 Wireless Section operators intercepted Japanese signals that contained Admiral Isoroku Yamamoto's itinerary for an upcoming trip to Rabaul, on the Island of New Britain. The message was immediately passed on to the Central Bureau in Brisbane where it was decrypted. From there it went straight to Admiral Chester W. Nimitz.

The decrypted message[12] contained specific details regarding Yamamoto's upcoming tour, including arrival and departure times and locations, as well as the number and types of planes that would transport and accompany him on the journey. Yamamoto, the itinerary revealed, would be flying from

Rabaul to Ballalae Airfield, on an island near Bougainville in the Solomon Islands, on the morning of 18 April 1943.[13] Admiral Nimitz informed U.S. President Franklin D. Roosevelt, who ordered "Get Yamamoto."

On the morning of 18 April, despite urgings from local Japanese commanders to cancel the trip for fear of ambush, Yamamoto's two Mitsubishi G4M fast transport aircraft left Rabaul as scheduled for the 315-mile (507 km) trip.

Sixteen P-38s were launched by the Americans to intercept the Japanese admiral's transport and its Zero escorts. One flight of four was designated as the "killer" flight. These planes were flown by Captain Tom Lanphier and lieutenants Rex Barber, Jim McLanahan and Joe Moore.[14] They intercepted Yamamoto's plane over the southern tip of the Island of Bougainville, close to the town of Buin, and after a dogfight with his escorts shot it down. Yamamoto was killed in the attack.

For the Japanese Imperial Navy it was quite clear that code JN-25 had been broken and they immediately changed over to a new one. From now on they would be much more careful in using codes.

Mineichi Koga

Yamamoto's successor, the 57-year-old Admiral Mineichi Koga, took over the position as Commander in Chief of the Combined Fleet on 23 April 1943. He was a conservative officer and a firm believer in the Decisive Battle philosophy of American naval theorist Alfred Thayer Mahan. He knew the chances of success were small, but it was Japan's last hope. Just like his predecessor, he kept his headquarters aboard the battleship *Musashi*. Admiral Shiguru Fukudome, the 53-year-old Chief of Staff of the Japanese Imperial Navy under Admiral Yamamoto, remained in position.

On 8 March 1944, Koga issued his final operations plan for the Decisive Battle, *Plan Z*. Once the advancing American fleet broke into the Philippine Sea by way of the Marianas or the Palaus or New Guinea, the Combined Fleet would sally forth in full strength. In his efficient, methodical way, he set about concentrating the bulk of Japan's surface force in the positions he thought most appropriate. Part of his plan was the transfer, at the end of March 1944, of his headquarters from the battleship *Musashi*, anchored at Palau, to the Philippines.[15,16]

CHAPTER **17**

THE DOCUMENTS THAT CHANGED THE WAR IN THE PACIFIC

A DMIRAL KOGA, THE new Commander in Chief, arrived at Truk on 23 April 1943. He kept his headquarters aboard the *Musashi*, which at that time, along with its sister *Yamato*, was the largest battleship ever built. On 23 May he arrived with his flagship at Tokyo for discussions with headquarters.

Fukudome, who remained chief of staff, had known Koga for a number of years and considered him a conservative and cool officer who thought logically but was strong willed. These traits were evident in the plans he was shaping for battle with the American fleet. From the very beginning, Koga insisted that their one and only chance for success lay in a decisive naval engagement.

Koga's strategy was spelled out in detail in a document presented on 25 August 1943, called the "Z Plan." It outlined defensive plans against Allied attacks on Japan's South Pacific possessions and made provisions for engaging the American fleet in a decisive battle. In early February 1944, Koga won approval from the General Staff to modify the plan by redistributing Japanese forces around a revised "last line of defense." He also won approval to command the fleet at Truk rather than staying in Tokyo.[1]

While Koga was still in Tokyo, American aircraft attacked Truk on 16–17 February 1944 and sank several Japanese warships and merchant ships and destroyed more than 275 aircraft. Truk was now, apparently, too vulnerable. On 23 February, Koga boarded the *Musashi* and set sail to Palau in the

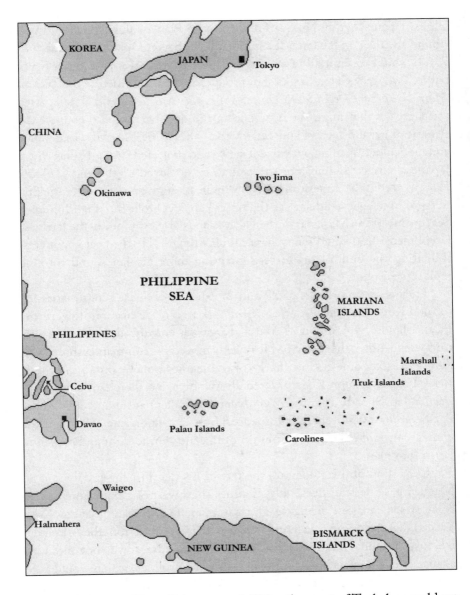

western Carolines. From Palau, some 1,500 miles west of Truk, he would set the Z Plan into motion. Admiral Koga waited at Palau with the main force of the fleet held in readiness; Admiral Ozawa's Air Fleet and the Second Fleet under Admiral Kurita were also ready for all that could happen. But the American Task Forces failed to make an appearance and nothing came of it.[2]

At Palau, Koga and his staff refined the Z Plan, issuing a final draft version to the fleet on 8 March (Combined Fleet Secret Operations Order No. 73). It would commit all remaining Japanese naval power to one last major battle. Two weeks later, Koga's staff produced a paper entitled *"A Study of the Main Features of Decisive Air Operations in the Central Pacific."* It suggested aerial tactics that might be used during the decisive battle to counter the American naval offensive and destroy the U.S. Pacific Fleet. It was detailed and meticulous, spelling out current status and projected strength, plus where Japanese surface and air strength was to be deployed by the end of April. Koga expected the Americans to show up in strength any time after the first of April.[3] He believed that once the American fleet broke into the Philippine Sea, by way of the Marianas or the Palau Islands or New Guinea, the Japanese Combined Fleet would meet them in full strength. He then set about consolidating the bulk of his forces, obtaining more airplanes, and training replacement pilots.[4]

During the mornings of 28 and 29 March, Japanese scout planes informed Koga that the American fleet appeared to be heading toward the Palau Islands. By noon on 29 March, Koga was convinced that the Americans would attack the next day. He quickly moved his command ashore, with Admiral Fukudome taking charge of the leather pouch containing the Z Plan. That afternoon Koga ordered all warships and merchant ships away from Palau. Shortly after the *Musashi* left the Palau harbor and entered the Pacific around 0540, she was torpedoed by a US submarine. Although the damage was not major, the ship was not in condition to fight and set sail to Japan for repairs.[5]

Koga did not dwell long on the fate of his flagship, for at dawn on 30 March the American fleet, only 75 miles southwest of Palau, launched an aerial attack. Japanese defensive efforts were ineffective. Later that day, Koga learned that American transports were heading westward from the Admiralty Islands. He and Fukudome concluded that the attack was not intended against the Marianas but against the western Carolines, which would constitute the southern part of the area to which Koga referred as the line of defense. They believed the Americans intended a landing in western New Guinea. If this was the case, Koga did not desire to be isolated at Palau, and he decided to withdraw his headquarters the next night to Davao in the Philippines, 600 miles to the west.[6]

For this trip three planes were called from Saipan, the first two arriving just after the air raid on Palau had ended, the third being somewhat delayed. The first two planes left on the evening of the 31st. of March 1944 at around 9 o'clock. It was originally planned for the first and second planes to take off simultaneously and fly in formation. Just before taking off, there was an air raid alert, which later proved to be a false alarm, but that alert made the Japanese give up the idea of taking off together.[7]

The first plane carried Admiral Koga and his staff. For security reasons, Fukudome, accompanied by 14 staff officers, flew in a second plane. Fukudome carried the leather pouch with the complete set of the Z Plan documents (it was a bound copy, the red cover bearing a "Z"), an air staff study of carrier fleet operations, rules for code use, a place-name abbreviation list, and other signals information. The second plane left a little later than the first. The third aircraft, much delayed, took off at 3 a.m. on 1 April with communications and clerical staff with their top-secret codes aboard. The first two planes were supposed to arrive at Davao by midnight.

On the way to Davao Fukudome's plane encountered a low-pressure area which was avoided by going to the right. This detour in heavy weather cost a lot of fuel and Davao became unreachable. Fukudome suggested that the plane head north for Manila, as they had enough fuel to reach that city. Headwinds, however, impeded the plane's flight and forced greater consumption of fuel. Manila was now also out of the question. Then there was the pilot, who according to Fukudome's testimony after the war, was worn out because of the long flight from Saipan via Palau to where they were now. Another problem was, according to the admiral in his testimony, that the Navigation Air Staff Officer aboard had become somewhat groggy from lack of oxygen and overtiredness. There was no other choice than to head for Cebu Island which was, according to the pilot, only six miles away.[8]

When Fukudome received the warning that an emergency landing would have to be made, he went forward in the plane and stated that he thought this was not Cebu. The pilot, however, insisted that he was approaching Cebu. The exhausted pilot put the plane in a steep approach to land but misjudged the altitude. Fukudome, fearing the plane would crash, grabbed the controls from the pilot to gain altitude. The plane overresponded, and within seconds it hit the water and settled into the Bohol Strait, about two and a half miles from shore. It was about 2:30 a.m.[9]

When the plane crashed, the remaining fuel in the wing tanks exploded, and flaming aviation fuel spread across the sea, encircling the wreckage. As the plane started sinking, Fukudome, with an injured leg, freed himself from the wreckage. He grabbed a seat cushion as a float and tried to get as far away as he could from the plane and the flames on the surface, not bothering to look for the leather pouch with the Z Plan documents. He thought it would sink anyway. Floating around him were 12 survivors. Twelve others must have died. As the plane sank, Fukudome believed the Z Plan documents must have gone down with the plane. His immediate concern was survival. He swam for about eight and a half hours before being picked up. The others saved with him were Staff Officer Captain Yamamoto, one warrant officer and eight petty officers and sailors. Apart from the eleven Japanese that were picked up by Filipino fishermen there was one dead body brought ashore.

Pedro Gantuangko had difficulty sleeping as he suffered from a *bonol* (gout) on his left foot. In the middle of the night of that fateful 1 April 1944 he heard the roar of engines of a low-flying plane. He heard people on the beach talking for whatever reason. He did not go to the beach because his leg hurt too much. Once the sun was up and most people had disappeared he got up and looked, from his unfinished kitchen, over the sea to the returning fishermen. He did that every morning if the weather was good, and then his neighbors told him about the plane crash.

Sipping his coffee he saw something floating in the sea. He called his neighbor Rufo "Opoy" Wamar and pointed out the object. It might be something from the plane wreck. Rufo waded into the sea to take a look. It was a wooden box blackened by oil from the plane. He looked through a crack in the wood and saw something like a *maleta*, a bag or wrapping that looked like leather. Rufo put the box in his baroto boat, covered it with an old rice bag and anchored his baroto a little bit outside from the place where all the other barotos were anchored. Opoy thought to have a better look once it was dark.[10]

Japanese soldiers patrolled the beach the whole day, apparently looking for parts of the crashed airplane. That night Opoy picked up the box and brought it to his own house since in Pedro's house, actually a sari-sari store, there were too many people around. Carefully they opened the box. The first thing they took out was a thick leather pouch; it was full of bundles of papers written with Japanese characters. After they took out the bundles of paper they saw a silk pouch containing a small bag with six condoms inside. Then there was a red silk pouch holding a handful of what looked like white pieces of gold the size of corn grains.[11]

It took two days for the items to dry. By that time more and more Japanese soldiers were starting to search the area. Pedro began to get a feeling that they were looking for the papers. He put all the items, except the portfolio, in a bag and buried it in the ground under his house. He wrapped the still wet portfolio in a cloth and hid it in his mother's house in the hills.

On 3 April some 200 Japanese soldiers searched the area again. They checked all houses and interrogated everybody. They were looking for Japanese papers they said. The next day the Japanese returned but they still found nothing. And so it went on day after day. Pedro got extremely worried so he sent word to guerrilla Corporal Norberto "Berting" Varga that he might have something important. He showed the portfolio to Berting and told him to pick up the remaining papers at his mother's house in the mountains. After a few days Berting delivered the portfolio and the papers to Jim Cushing in the mountains. Jim was busy with the Japanese prisoners, including the "general" who had survived the crash, and while fending off Japanese attacks had no time to look at it.[12]

After the agreement was made to hand over his prisoners to Colonel Ohnisi, it took Jim and his fellow officers a few days to recover. Col. Ohnisi refrained from activities for three days, after which he renewed his hunt for the guerrillas as ferociously as before. As Jim pondered what to do next he remembered that they still had some maps and papers they had found on the Japanese prisoners. They appeared to be field orders and Jim was sure that headquarters in Australia would be interested in these items. He prepared a long coded message and dispatched it via Col. Andrews in southern Negros. The message was as follows:

TO: GENERAL MACARTHUR
FROM: CUSHING
NR 6: 13 APRIL
WE HAVE TWO JAPANESE OPERATIONS MAPS PRESUM-
ABLY OF 1942 TO 1944 SHOWING AIRBASES NAVAL BASES
WIRELESS STATIONS, EMERGENCY LANDING FIELDS, TRI-
ANGULATION POINTS, HEIGHTS AND OTHER CONTROL
SYMBOLS IN THE LEGEND. THESE MAPS COVER PALAO,
PHILIPPINES, MOST OF FRENCH-INDO-CHINA, HAINAN
AND SOUTHERN CHINA. FOUR UNIDENTIFIED TRANS-
PORTS LANDED LILOAN NIGHT OF APRIL 11 UNLOADING
WITH LANDING LIGHTS. FROM PRISONERS WE STILL

HAVE PAPERS AND FIELD ORDERS WHICH WE ARE SEND-
ING TOGETHER WITH MAPS TO COL. ANDREWS HEAD-
QUARTERS, SOUTHERN NEGROS AND SHOULD ARRIVE
THERE IN APPROXIMATELY TWO WEEKS[13]

On 18 April 1944, the following radio message NR 9 from MacArthur
arrived:

FROM: MACARTHUR
TO: CUSHING
NR 9: 16 APRIL 1944
DOCUMENTS DESCRIBED IN YOUR NUMBER SIX MAY BE
OF EXTREME VALUE PD TAKE EVERY POSSIBLE PRECAU-
TION TO INSURE SAFE ARRIVAL AT SOUTHERN NEGROS
FOR DISPATCH HERE AT EARLIEST OPPORTUNITY PD AD-
VISE WHEN DELIVERY IS EFFECTED[14]

Whitney's memo simply noted that the documents in question "will be
available for dispatch by ABCEDE on supply trip of USS *Narwhal* about
end of June unless desired earlier by G-2." General Charles Willoughby (the
G-2) added a note as the memorandum crossed his desk the next day: *"De-
scription of documents indicates they . . . may be of extreme value. Suggest they
be brought here at earliest opportunity."* However, for three weeks nothing happened.[15]

While waiting for an answer from Australia Jim remembered the package recovered from the sea by Pedro Gantuangko. The hectic events that had
occured around the Japanese prisoners and their exchange had taken up all
his time. Most probably Berting, the guerrilla who had promised to deliver
the papers to Jim, was just lying low. If Jim was in the possession of these
papers, certainly with an eye on the volume, it might have leaked out to the
prisoner General Furomei. The captured officer never gave any hint that he
had told Col. Ohnisi that Jim might have the papers, and the Japanese never
acted as if they thought he had them.

Once Jim saw what he had he realized the find was extraordinary. A red
leather pouch with large Japanese characters printed in gold on the cover,
plus sealed envelopes and documents. It was a real treasure. He realized that
Australia needed these items as soon as possible.

Jim pondered how to send the documents to Australia. He knew that MacArthur had ordered the repatriation of all Americans that were still stranded in the Philippines. He knew too that submarines were regularly visiting southern Negros. He discussed the matter with his closest commanders and with the three American servicemen, Snell, Dyer and Joseph, who had come over with him from Negros. They decided to pack as many documents as possible in two empty mortar shells. He selected Snell and Dyer for the trip; they had to be repatriated anyway. He gave them an escort of a few experienced guerrillas and sent them on the 15th of April on their way to Col. Andrews' headquarters in Southern Negros. They crossed Cebu and then the Tañon Strait, and on 28 April arrived at Andrews' headquarters in the hills behind the village of Culipapa, on the southwestern coast of Negros. They turned over to Andrews the mortar shells containing the documents.[16]

Most probably Jim did not get all the papers from the plane wreck in one time. Pedro Gantuangko had hidden part under his house, but another part in the house of his mother in the mountains. Apart from this the complete box might have been too much to carry at one time. With all the Japanese patrols searching for papers it could have been suspicious to bring too much at once. It is in this light that message NR 19 should be seen, sent on 27 April 1944 to SWPA:

TO: MACARTHUR
FROM: CUSHING
NR 19: 27 APRIL

THROUGH HELP OF FISHERMEN WE HAVE RECOVERED A LARGE QUANTITY DOCUMENTS AND TOOK WHAT WE BELIEVE TO BE LANDING FLARES FROM THE CRASHED SEAPLANE OFF SAN FERNANDO. ALL NOW ENROUTE TO ANDREWS HEADQUARTERS.[17]

He was sending these papers also to south Negros for Andrews to forward on. Meanwhile the Japanese, having given up their search for the still missing Commander-in-Chief Admiral Koga, were still concerned about the missing documents they believed were on Cebu. They even offered a reward of 50,000 pesos (about $25,000).[18]

But Jim still had another problem. He was informed that there were supplies for the Cebu Area Command on their way by submarine to Nasipit, at the western end of Butuan Bay. Apart from this he still had many more documents that might be useful for SWPA, documents concerning the defense of Cebu Island such as fortifications protecting Lahug Airport, drawings of the airstrip at Opon, Mactan, and remaining documents from the plane crash. He pondered who would be the best person to take charge of such a difficult mission. He chose Captain Celso C. Enriquez.

Captain Enriquez was an experienced soldier. At the beginning of the war he was with the 2nd Battalion under 1st Lieutenant Luis B. Jakosalem. The battalion was detached from the regiment at Cebu and shipped to Davao in early December 1941. They landed in Cagayan de Oro, on Mindanao's northern coast and proceeded overland to Davao. In Davao their job was the defense of the Matina Beach when the Japanese landed. They were routed and many of his friends died. He was taken prisoner by the Japanese and severly maltreated, but after being brought to Malaybalay in Central Mindanao he managed to escape. After a long, arduous trip he reached Cebu again and reported for duty at Tabunan Headquarters.

Col. Jim Cushing's nipa headquarters, looking like any hut in the area, was on the west slope of the ridge facing Barrio Tagba-o to the west. When Enriquez entered the hut he saw the guerrilla leader in khaki shorts and bare feet with the ever present .45 caliber pistol weighing down his belt. The safety grip was tied down by a dirty white tape wound around the handle. As usual he had a cigar clamped between his teeth as he watched the captain approach. Enriquez saluted as he reported to the commander of the Cebu Area Command. Jim returned the salute and moved forward to shake hands with the captain. He invited him for a cup of strong hot coffee spiked with some native alcohol.

Jim explained to the captain what he wanted him to do. He was to bring a collection of important papers through the island of Bohol and across the Mindanao Sea to Nasipit, Agusan. The papers were placed in five empty tubular carton casings used for 81mm mortar shells. The covers were securely taped to minimize the seepage of moisture during the long trip.

Apart from the papers he would bring along a German prisoner of war, a certain Herbert Ritter, who while on a ship to Yokohama had jumped ship in Cebu. According to Lieutenant Irving Joseph, who had gained the German's confidence because he spoke a little German, Ritter had substantial information about German ships sailing to Japan, minefields in East Asia, and the huge Japanese submarine base at Penang, in Malaya. Irving was one of the three Americans who had come with Jim from Negros after his visit to Villamor.[19]

With Jim Cushing's blessings and wishes of good luck, Captain Enriquez took the trail to Yuta-on, site of the headquarters of his Regimental Commander, then Major Albinda. The party then proceeded to the coastal barrio of Cotcot, Lilo-an where they secured a banca that could accommodate all members of the party. From there they sailed to northern Bohol, and then to Ubay and successively across the Mindanao Sea to Camiguin Island. After a short stop in Agoho they proceeded to Balingoan. Here they were told that it was impossible to go to Nasipit as the town had been taken by the Japanese Army. There was no other choice than to return to Camiguin. Here they were informed that there was a submarine on its way to Tolong Bay in southern Negros.

After lengthy discussions Captain Enriquez decided to sail first back to Bohol and from there to Sumilon Island, just off the Cebu coast near Oslob and then to Dumaguete City in Negros. From there it was not very far to Tolong Bay. After a few days, on 19 June 1944, the American submarine USS *Nautilus* surfaced at Balatong Point, not far from the place where Enriquez was camping. As soon as the submarine was secured he went on board and handed over all his documents to Commander George Arthur Sharp.[20]

The submarine carried almost 100 tons of supplies, 20 percent intended for Cebu, 80 percent for Negros. To bring back 20 tons of supplies to Cebu, in the middle of a war-zone, was an enormous task. Enriquez had a few sleepless nights over this. He hired in Tolong Bay many *kargadores* (hands) to load his bancas. In crossing Tañon Strait, the waterway between Negros and Cebu, one of the bancas sank near Sumilon Island. A *Manok-manok* wind struck the craft while it was negotiating a whirlpool. This aberration of the sea comes to life when the current from Tañon Strait meets that from Mindanao Sea and when the *Manok-manok* wind blows. Fortunately no lives were lost. Finally, on 12 September 1944, Enriquez and his party arrived back in Tabunan. They were just in time to witness the first American bombing of Cebu City. Enriquez's mission had taken almost four and a half months.[21,22]

When Whitney, Willoughby and SWPA Chief of Staff Lt. Gen. Richard Sutherland heard about the reward and the additional documents, they concluded they might be high importance. Whitney immediately sent a message to Andrews telling him that the documents "may be of considerable value"[23] and asked about the advisability of sending them via regular or special pickup.

Cushing on 1 May sent a message to SWPA that he was sending more documents to Col. Wendell Fertig's headquarters. Fertig commanded all guerrillas on Mindanao. From there, apparently, Cushing believed they could be forwarded to Negros. "We are," Cushing added to his message, "attempting interception to meet your carriage."[24]

The next day, 2 May 1944, Cushing notified SWPA that the most important documents had made it to Andrews and that more documents were on their way. This message was received at SWPA on May 4.[25] Immediately Whitney notified Sutherland about the message and indicated they would not be able to pick them up on a regular supply mission until about the middle of the next month due to an unexpected delay in the USS *Narwhal* refitting.[26]

He asked Sutherland if he should try to arrange an earlier special pickup, and the next day Willoughby recommended to Whitney that the documents be picked up as soon as possible. But the following day, in a message to Sutherland, Willoughby cautioned that while a special pickup may be warranted, they should "avoid blowing up their importance any more than is absolutely necessary to assure security, to minimize the danger of the enemy acquiring knowledge that we have actually recovered them. The value of the documents may well largely depend upon our ability to keep such information from the enemy."[27]

On 3 May American intelligence decrypted a message to high-level officers confirming the death of Admiral Mineichi Koga, "in performance of his duties," and appointing Admiral Soemu Toyoda as his replacement. The signal stressed the need to keep the news secret until a public announcement was made.[28] The public announcement followed on 5 May. It indicated that Koga had been killed in action in March while directing naval operations from a plane.

Whitney began connecting the dots between the public announcement of Koga's loss, Cushing's past messages, and the intercepts regarding the "Otsu incident," the documents, and the high reward for the documents. He immediately wrote to Sutherland, urging that the documents with Andrews may be of such great importance that there should be a special pickup. Sutherland agreed, and the Navy informed SWPA that the USS *Crevalle*, patrolling off the coast of northern Borneo, was the nearest submarine. At 1130 on 7 May, it received top-secret orders to proceed north to the eastern part of Sulu Sea and to be prepared for a special mission on 11 May.[29]

Whitney became apparently quite nervous. On the 7th of May he sent a message to Col. Abcede on Negros:

DOCUMENTS DESIRED THIS HEADQUARTERS EARLIEST DATE POSSIBLE. ADVISE SITE AT WHICH DOCUMENTS AND EVACUEES CAN BE PICKED UP ON ELEVENTH THIS MONTH. EXERCISE GREATEST CAUTION IN THE EXECUTION OF THIS MISSION. PRESERVE UTMOST SECRECY CONCERNING DOCUMENTS.[30]

Late on the afternoon of 8 May, instructions were radioed to the USS *Crevalle* to proceed to a position just north of Basay, Negros, and at sunset on 11 May, after observing security signals, surface and receive from native sailboats about 25 passengers and important documents.[31] To make sure that there was no misunderstanding whatsoever, two days later Whitney sent another message to Abcede:

HAVE ARRANGED FOR SUB TO RENDEZVOUS ELEVENTH SUNSET OFF BALATONG POINT UPON SIGHTING SECURITY SIGNALS TWO WHITE PANELS FIFTY YARDS APART. CONFIRM IMMEDIATELY THAT SITE IS SECURE BAND AVAILABLE TO YOU FOR DISPATCHING DOCUMENTS AND EVACUEES.[32]

Abcede confirmed that all arrangements were made and that he could guarantee the safety of the evacuees. But Whitney was still not sure that nothing could go wrong, on 10 May he sent another message to Abcede:

WHEN VESSEL SURFACES BE PREPARED SEND DOCUMENTS AND EVACUEES ALONGSIDE IMMEDIATELY TO PERMIT VESSEL TO CLEAR WITHIN THIRTY MINUTES IF POSSIBLE. IF VESSEL DOES NOT ARRIVE ON ELEVENTH CONTINUE SIGNALS AND VIGILANCE UNTIL CONTACT MADE. WHEN MISSION COMPLETE ADVICE AT ONCE.[33]

But it was still not enough. On 11 May 1944, the day the submarine was supposed to arrive; Whitney sent one last message to stress his point:

IMPERATIVE THAT POSITIVE OR NEGATIVE REPORT ON
RENDEZVOUS BE RECEIVED HERE BY FOURTEEN HUN-
DRED ELEVEN MAY. KAZ WILL GUARD YOUR REGULAR
FREQUENCY UNTIL REPLY. LAZ WILL STAND BY UNTIL
MISSION ACCOMPLISHED.[34]

In Brisbane everybody, Whitney, Sutherland, and even MacArthur, were waiting on the edge of their seat for confirmation from Abcede that all went according to plan. The failure to keep the prisoners was forgotten; the papers seemed suddenly far more important than anything else. If one had a prisoner, it remained to be seen if he was willing to talk. And could you trust or believe whatever he said? Papers, and certainly a whole set, especially if carried around by a Chief of Staff of the Imperial Japanese Navy, might be worth far more than the simple story of an admiral.

Lieutenant Colonel James M. Cushing, leader of the Filipino guerrillas on the island of Cebu. This picture was probably taken sometime in 1943. James would have been around 33 years old.

Admiral Shiguru Fukudome, the Chief-of-Staff of the Imperial Japanese Navy, who ended up in the hands of Col. James Cushing.

Fort Drum with the battleship USS *New Jersey* and the island of Corregidor in the background. The concrete fortress was built by the US in 1909 as one of the harbor defenses of Manila Bay. It kept on firing with its 14-inch guns until five minutes before the American surrender on Corregidor on 6 May 1942. The fort was constructed on top of El Fraile island.

Battery Crocket with heavy mortar on Corregidor. There were 23 batteries on the island, consisting of 56 coastal guns and mortars. The main armaments of Battery Crocket were the 12-inch mortars, which needed a crew of 30 men to hurl a 900-pound projectile more than 16 miles. Unfortunately the guns were faced the wrong way to be of any use against the Japanese so were never fired during the defense of Bataan and Corregidor. On 24 April 1942 a 240mm Japanese howitzer scored a direct hit on Battery Crocket and knocked out both of the guns.

Japanese soldiers celebrating victory after the fall of Manila and most of the Philippines in April 1942.

Japanese victory parade in Manila, May 1942. The parade was in Luneta Park after the final American surrender on 6 May 1942.

Generals Wainwright (left) and MacArthur. General MacArthur was the commander of the American forces in the Philippines at the start of World War II. After his departure in early 1942, General Wainwright took over the command.

Lieutenant General Masaharu Homma, commander of the Japanese 14th Army. With 43,110 men of the 14th Army, Homma led the most intense battle in the invasion of the Philippines, the Battle of Bataan. He was considered responsible for the Bataan Death March in 1942 and was executed by firing squad after the war.

Marshall Admiral Isoroku Yamamoto was the architect of the attack on Pearl Harbor in 1941. He was assassinated by an American squadron of Lockheed P-38 Lightnings in April 1943 after a security breach.

Admiral Mineichi Koga took command of the Imperial Japanese Navy after Yamamoto's death; however, he died in a plane crash soon after, and his invaluable strategy documents, "Plan Z," fell into American hands.

Kawanishi H8K Flying Boat, "Emily," used by the IJN for maritime patrol and transport. It was a plane of this kind that crashed, killing Admiral Koga, while his Chief of Staff, Admiral Fukudome, survived the crash of a separate plane off Cebu.

SS *Doña Nati*, one of the two vessels which successfully ran the Japanese blockade from Australia to Cebu City. The *Doña Nati* was one of three sizable merchant ships that were successful blockade runners, bringing various supplies and materiel from Australian ports to major islands of the Philippines south of Luzon.

The Cebu railway in the 1930s. Cebu used to have its own railway, a narrow gauge system running from Danao in the north to Argao in the south, built in the late 19th and early 20th century. The Japanese made extensive use of the system during their occupation. For the Cebu guerrillas it was an easy target.

Cebu Normal School, headquarters of the notorious Japanese Kempetai in World War II. Established in 1902, it is one of the oldest educational institutions in Cebu. In 1998 the institute became a university.

Japanese troops attacking with a flamethrower. This picture was taken somewhere on Cebu Island, probably in 1943 during the attacks on Cushing's headquarters in Tabunan. It shows the ferocity of the battles going on in Cebu.

Japanese soldiers in an unknown location in the Philippines. It was toops of this kind that undertook the desperate search for Admiral Fukudome and the captured Japanese strategy document, "Plan Z."

The USS *Haddo* on patrol. A Gato-class submarine. During her fifth patrol she was close by Cebu and was kept in reserve to pick up James Cushing's Japanese prisoners. She was decommissioned in 1946.

Aichi D3A, or "Val," a carrier-borne dive bomber of the Imperial Japanese Navy. It participated in almost all IJN actions, including the attack on Pearl Harbor. In 1944/45 it was replaced by the Yokosuka D4Y Susei and the Val ended up with land-based units.

The Japanese battleship *Yamato*, which along with its sister ship, *Musashi*, was the world's largest battleship ever built (72,000 tons) with nine 18-inch main guns. The *Musashi* was the flagship of the Japanese Imperial Navy during the command of Admiral Koga and was sunk in October 1944 during the battle in the Philippine Sea. The *Yamato* was sunk on 7 April 1945 by American carrier-based bombers and torpedo bombers, with the loss of most of her crew.

Lt. Col. Russell W. Volckmann, a West Point graduate and US Army officer who became the guerilla commander of Northern Luzon. After the fall of Bataan he escaped the Death March and went to northern Luzon to continue resistance against the Japanese. He became the major guerilla commander in the Northern Philippines.

Col. Wendell Fertig, guerilla commander on Mindanao. Like Col. Cushing, Fertig was an American mining engineer when Japan attacked the Philippines. After the war he returned to mining.

General McArthur decorates Jesus Antonio Villamor, a Filipino American pilot who fought the Japanese in World War II. After his squadron was destroyed he escaped to Australia to rejoin the Allied forces. On 27 December 1942 he was part of a team inserted by the submarine USS *Gudgeon* into the Philippines, making contact with Roy Bell on Negros.

Chief Justice Jose Abad Santos, shortly before he became the first Filipino politician to be arrested and executed by the Japanese.

Manuel Quezon (left) and Sergio Osmeña, President and Vice President of the Philippines at the start of World War II. Both followed MacArthur to the Island of Corregidor and both were later evacuated by submarine.

Admiral Takeo Kurita, one of the key Japanese admirals in the Battle of the Philippine Sea.

Admiral Soemu Toyoda was the successor of Admiral Koga after the latter died in a plane crash off Cebu.

Fleet Admiral William ("Bull") Halsey, Jr., one of the leading US Navy officers of World War II. In 1943 he was made commander of the Third Fleet which operated around the Solomon Islands, the Philippines, Taiwan and Japan. Initially his flagship was the USS *New Jersey*, later the USS *Missouri*.

A Mitsubishi Zero (A6M3 Model 22) patrolling over Cebu. In the first
years of the war the Zero was considered the most capable carrier-based
fighter in the world. More than 11,000 aircraft were built in Japan.

The Vought F4LT-1 Corsair was the pride of the Jungle Air force on Cebu.
A successful fighter-bomber, after World War II the Corsair also saw service
in the Korean War. More than 12,000 were built over the years.

Troops of the Americal Division landing on the beaches of Talisay.
Finally the Americans are back in Cebu.

Picture taken in the US 132nd Regiment's sector of the beach in Talisay,
looking towards the 182nd's sector. Note the tracked landing vehicles
parked at the beach; due to mines they could not move forward.

Cebu port under attack. This picture dates from September 1945 when American planes had begun to bomb Cebu on a daily basis.

General MacArthur wades ashore on the beaches of Leyte, fulfilling his vow to return to the Philippines.

A photograph found on the body of a Japanese officer showing an execution through beheading. The Allied soldier in the picture was Australian POW Sergeant Leonard Sifleet. He was executed with a shin gunto sword in Papua New Guinea, in 1943. The picture was discovered near Hollandia (New Guinea) by American troops. It is believed to be the only surviving depiction of a Western prisoner of war being executed by a Japanese soldier.

General Tomoyuki Yamashita is removed from the courtroom by MPs after hearing the verdict of death by hanging. Yamashita had defeated the British in Malaya and Singapore, gaining from his victories the nickname "The Tiger of Malaya." His attitude toward prisoners gained him the nickname "The Beast of Bataan." He was hanged as a war criminal for his part in the Bataan Death March.

Above: General Douglas MacArthur signing the Instrument of Surrender on behalf of the Allies on board the USS *Missouri* on September 2, 1945.

Left: The flag of the United States is lowered while the flag of the Philippines is raised during the Independence Day ceremonies on July 4, 1946. Finally independence for the Philippine people.

CHAPTER **18**

PLAN Z IN AMERICAN HANDS

T HE DROPPING OF Major Jesus A. Villamor on the shores of the island of Negros, on 14 January 1943, by Lieutenant Commander William S. Stovall Jr., Captain of USS *Gudgeon*, was only the beginning. That first landing was the realization of a dream long held by General MacArthur. From the very beginning MacArthur thought that guerrilla warfare in the Philippines was the road for his return someday. Since then many submarines had visited the Philippines secretly, either to pick-up stranded Americans or to bring supplies for the guerrillas. Initially the submarines used were so-called fleet-type boats. These were not very efficient because their loading capacity was too small. Gradually the navy went over to using supersubs, submarines with a loading capacity of close to 100 tons. These submarines, with a length of about 370 feet and beams of about 33 feet, were quite large. Most of the work in the Philippines was done by either the USS *Narwhal* or the USS *Nautilus*.[1]

In case of emergency, however, fleet-type submarines were also used. The USS *Crevalle* left the submarine base in Fremantle, Australia, on 4 April 1944.[2] The *Crevalle* was a Balao-class submarine with an overall length of 312 feet, a displacement of 1,500 tons and it was armed with a 40mm Bofors cannon, a 20mm Oerlikon machinegun and 24 torpedoes. The crew was composed of 10 officers and 70 enlisted men. Captain of the boat was Lieutenant Commander Francis David Walker, Jr.[3]

On 11 April, the *Crevalle* reached Darwin in Australia's Northern Territories. A few hours later the boat left for her assigned patrol waters in the Sulu Sea near the Philippines. On Saturday morning of 6 May Captain

Walker received a message from Rear-Admiral Ralph Waldo Christie, Commander Submarines Southwest Pacific:

TOP SECRET. YOUR PATROL TERMINATED. PROCEED EASTERN PART SULU SEA. BE PREPARED SPECIAL MISSION ABOUT ELEVEN MAY.

He was sailing at the moment along the northern coast of the Indonesian island of Borneo. He would have to pass through the Balabac Strait to enter the Sulu Sea. Apparently the special mission had something to do with the Philippines. Late in the afternoon of Monday, 8 May, another urgent message came through. The *Crevalle* was ordered to rendezvous three days hence off Balatong Point, on the southwestern coast of Negros Island in the Philippines. The mission: to pick up passengers and documents.[4]

In the meantime Colonel Abcede, the guerrilla commander of Negros, and his number two, Colonel Placido Ausejo, were rounding up the passengers for embarkation on the *Crevalle*, among them Russell Snell and Jimmy Dyer. They had left Cebu on 14 April with the first batch of papers, sealed in empty mortar shells. After a slow and perilous journey they had reached Lieutenant Colonel Edwin Andrews' camp in the hills behind the small coastal town of Culipapa, close to Tolong Bay. Andrews, an American-Filipino mestizo, had replaced Major Jesus Villamor as the key Allied Intelligence Bureau operative in the Philippines. His main job was to funnel intelligence down to SWPA GHQ in Brisbane. Snell and Dyer arrived in Andrews' camp on 28 April. They were to proceed the following night to a beach above Basay, about five miles south of Andrews' headquarters, for immediate evacuation.[5]

Early in the morning of 11 May 1944, Captain Walker arrived near Balatong Point, southern Negros.[6] About 0430 the *Crevalle* was in position for the pickup. Through its periscope, the captain saw boats and people on the beach, and at 0500 he saw two large boats and some small outriggers heading to the pickup point. Walker waited until exactly 0530 to surface. His crew was ready, fully armed as they stormed to the watery deck as soon as the *Crevalle* surfaced. The Bofors and the Oerlikon gun were manned before any Filipino could board the submarine. Safety first, was Walker's attitude. You never knew, perhaps the Japanese had infiltrated the ranks of the guerrillas.[7]

Abcede approached the submarine at 0557, and identified himself properly to Walker. Salvador Abcede had a lot at stake ensuring that *Crevalle's* brief call was trouble-free. The aftermath of *Narwhal's* previous visit had caused concern at GHQ in Brisbane about sending another submarine to Basay. Off Balatong Point on 7 February *Narwhal* had successfully unloaded a shipment of supplies badly needed by the guerrillas. She then evacuated two dozen refugees, most of them civilians. But within hours the Japanese had learned, in detail, of her exploit. Five days later the enemy launched a punitive action against Abcede's district that left eighty-nine people dead.[8]

Abcede told Walker that there were 41 people, all American citizens (including 21 children and 8 women) to pick up, not 25, and asked if Walker could take that many. Walker, answering affirmatively, suggested they be hurried aboard. At 0559, 40 evacuees (a minister decided to stay behind), including Snell and Dyer, began boarding the submarine. Abcede gave Walker a small wooden box and told him that it contained extremely important documents captured from the Japanese on Cebu and that MacArthur was most anxious to see them. At 0637 p.m. the submarine got under way.[9]

By dawn the next day (12 May) the *Crevalle* was two hundred miles away from Balatong Point and cruising south-southeast at fourteen knots towards the Sibutu Passage. Walker intended to stay as long as possible on the surface where he could make much better speed than below. At 2126 they cleared the Sibutu Passage and headed for Bangka Passage.[10] Several times they had to submerge as they were sighted and attacked by Japanese aircraft and ships. On Sunday, 14 May, just after clearing the Banka Passage, they were spotted by a Japanese twin-engine Betty bomber. They had to crash dive to avoid being hit by depth charges. That morning it became a matter of alternately diving and surfacing. Planes and destroyers tried to catch them, but fortunately they managed to stay out of reach. It was a narrow escape, but the boat was severely damaged. The guns on the deck were disabled, the periscope and the radar were destroyed, and the sonar crippled. She was still afloat and could still get safely down to Australia; another attack, however, had to be avoided at all costs.[11]

While the USS *Crevalle* was making its way to Australia, Cushing on 14 May sent a message to SWPA reporting that the second batch of documents from the crash of the Japanese plane had arrived too late to be included with the first batch of documents already on their way to Brisbane. He indicated that the second batch had been sent to Mindanao. On 17 May Whitney informed Sutherland that the first batch of documents should arrive in two days, and from them Willoughby should be able to determine the desirability of arranging a second special pickup or leaving it to a regular supply run.[12]

Shortly after midnight on Tuesday, 16 May, near the western tip of Lifumatule, the *Crevalle* finally crossed the equator.[13] Early on 19 May, the submarine neared the Australian coast, and two small Australian navy boats headed toward it. The *Crevalle* stopped, and Comdr. X.M. Smith, commander of the American base at Darwin, came aboard and informed Walker that he was there to pick up the "mail" brought from Negros. Smith took the wooden box, signed a receipt, and his boat immediately headed to Darwin. Smith gave the box to a courier, an army officer, who rushed it to the nearby airport, where a special courier plane, the fastest long-range fighter, a Lockheed P-38 Lightning, was waiting. Some six hours and 1,800 miles later, the plane landed at Brisbane. By midday the box of Japanese secrets was in the hands of General Charles A. Willoughby.[14]

Expectations were very high at GHQ. Though Willoughby and his people had no idea what was in the box, they had arranged a complete welcome party with coders, translators and material experts. When the box was opened and the documents laid out, the American intelligence personnel were shocked to see they were in plain language, not code. The leather portfolio with its gold-embossed seal of the Imperial Japanese Navy made quite some impression. When the flap was opened, the examiners could see sheaves of paper tied together with silk ribbons, and others bound in red. High-level stuff, no question, the observers concluded. The Japanese used red covers only for the most important papers. Very quickly, it was apparent that its contents were extremely sensitive. The portfolio and the red covers on some of the documents were sure signs of highly classified material.[15]

On 21 May, Whitney sent the documents to Willoughby, who forwarded them to Col. Sidney F. Mashbir, the head of the Allied Translation and Interpreter Section (ATIS), for the highest priority translation and interpretation. Mashbir's unit provided language services to MacArthur's entire organization. His unit would now tackle the initial work on the Koga papers, probably the most important cache ever to come their way.

That morning, at ATIS headquarters at Indooroopilly, a Brisbane suburb, photostatic copies of the documents were made and given to Mashbir's top five translators. They quickly identified one document as copy six of 550 copies of *"Secret Combined Fleet Order No. 73."* It had been issued on 8 March 1944 from the flagship *Musashi* at Palau and was signed personally by Koga, the Commander in Chief of the Japanese Combined Fleet. The preamble greatly excited them, as it stated:

> The Combined Fleet is for the time being directing its main operations to the Pacific Area where, in the event of an attack by an enemy Fleet Occupation Force, it will bring to bear the combined maximum strength of all our forces to meet and destroy the enemy, and to maintain our hold on vital areas. These operations will be called "Z Operations."[16]

They labored over the rest of the document, for not only did it contain Japanese place names for islands (e.g. Wake was Otori), but it contained many naval terms whose meaning was not always clear to Army men. All day and night on 21 May and the next day the translators worked.

Slowly the Z-Plan began to be revealed. The operations, painted in broad strokes, outlined a plan capable of devastating the American army, navy and air forces:

> All forces will concentrate to attack the enemy transport convoy and endeavor to annihilate it.
>
> Attack and annihilate the enemy using full strength, and cooperating closely with Base Air Forces.

Koga's papers illuminated Japanese naval thinking in a way no one had ever imagined possible. It was an unprecedented intelligence find.[17]

While the translation was under way, on 22 May Jim Cushing radioed SWPA to report that the Japanese knew his men had found more documents.[18] Takeshi Watanabe, the Japanese naval commander in Cebu, had an airplane drop leaflets, dated 17 May and addressed specifically to Cushing, across the island instructing that all documents, bags and clothing either picked up from the airplane that had made a forced landing off San Fernando, Cebu, on April 1 or robbed of the passengers and the crew be returned unconditionally by noon on 30 May to the mayor of San Fernando for safekeeping. If Cushing did not comply, the Japanese navy would resort to "drastically severe" methods against them.[19]

Whitney sent a copy of Cushing's message to Sutherland on 23 May, adding that it showed the value of the documents in Japanese eyes. He informed Sutherland that ATIS was translating the documents and that they appeared to contain a file of Japanese Combined Fleet operational orders and a file of naval dispatches. He added that other documents from the same recovery arrived too late for the 11 May pickup and that the Navy was arranging a special pickup for them.

Japanese Naval Headquarter, Cebu / May 17, 1944

Mr. James Cushing:
I, as the commander of the Imperial Japanese Naval Garrison of Cebu, am sending you the following important message to you.
    1. The Imperial Japanese Navy is taking the serious consideration against you in view of the guerrilla-like and inhuman treatment by your men of the passengers and the crew of our seaplane which made a forced landing off San Fernando, Cebu on April 1, 1944. Therefore, we strongly demand that you immediately carry out the following:
    2. Return unconditionally until the noon of May 30, 1944, all documents, bags, and clothings either picked up from the said airplane or robbed of the passengers and the crew to the Mayor of San Fernando for safekeeping.
    3. We notify you that in case when you fail to fulfill our demand stated in the second clause, the Imperial Japanese Navy will resort to drastically severe method against you.

TAKESHI WATANABE
Commander of the Imperial Japanese
Naval Garrison of Cebu

When Willoughby saw the translation on 22 May, he was excited at having the Japanese navy plans in his hands. Either that night or the next morning, Mashbir operated a hand-cranked mimeograph machine to run off 20 copies of the 22-page translation, and on May 23 ATIS issued Limited Distribution Translation No. 4, *"Z Operation Orders."* The Limited Distribution Translation No. 4 gave American commanders their first look at Japan's "Plan Z." The first copy went by officer courier to Gen. George C. Marshall, chief of staff of the U.S. Army in Washington. The second copy went to MacArthur in Brisbane, Australia.

Next the translators attacked a packet of papers with the provocative title "A Study of the Main Features of Decisive Air Operations in the Central Pacific."[20] On 25 May the ATIS team sent Mashbir its 29-page translation of this document as well as collateral notes and other documents from the packet. These documents were published on 28 May as ATIS Limited Distribution Translation No. 5.

After reading the two publications, Willoughby, Sutherland and MacArthur were impressed with the high-level strategy put forth in the documents, but were not completely sure what it all meant. Capt. Arthur McCollum, the Seventh Fleet's director of intelligence and Navy liaison with Whitney's Philippine Regional Section, however, did. McCollum had trained early in his naval career as a Japanese-language specialist. He immediately saw the importance of the translations and realized that Admiral Chester Nimitz, commander in chief of the Pacific Fleet, needed to see them as soon as possible.

Two copies were flown by officer courier for hand delivery to the Joint Intelligence Center, Pacific Ocean Area (JICPOA) at Pearl Harbor, there to be studied by Admiral Nimitz's people. General Sutherland agreed and arranged for copies of the published translations to be sent to JICPOA. An Army bomber flew nearly 5,000 miles in 48 hours, stopping at various islands to refuel, to deliver the copies to Pearl Harbor. By the end of the week the courier had safely delivered his top-secret package into the hands of Nimitz's Fleet Intelligence officer, Captain Edwin T. Layton.[21,22]

Layton saw the bold stamp on the translations:

Top Secret. Not to be copied or reproduced without permission of General MacArthur.

Immediately, under Nimitz's signature, Layton sent a message to SWPA asking MacArthur's approval to distribute the translations. Although he recognized that the translations had been made by someone unfamiliar with Japanese naval terminology, it was evident that the captured documents were the Japanese Combined Fleet's operational plans for concentrating its total sea and air strength against the next American advance into the Japanese island defense system.

As the Fifth Fleet and the Marianas invasion forces were already assembling at Eniwetok, Layton believed quick action was needed and that a retranslation had to be as correct as possible before it was distributed. He radioed Mashbir and asked for photostats of the original Japanese documents. Two days later, with the photostats in hand, Layton and a small group of JICPOA translators retranslated the entire Z Plan. When finished, Layton believed that ATIS had gotten it mostly right.[23]

The same day the ATIS completed translation of the Z Plan, Jim Cushing radioed GHQ with a message reporting that the Japanese had not given up trying to recover Koga's papers. After receiving the leaflet dated 17 May 1944, Jim had written to Commander Takeshi Watanabe, the Japanese commander, that he did not know anything about documents from the crashed seaplane. The Japanese did not accept this answer. Apparently the Japanese had learned via their undercovers that the guerrilla movement had found documents. Japanese planes again dropped leaflets. Jim sent another letter to the Japanese commander in which he stated that he had investigated the claim of Commander Watanabe and was told, by some fishermen, that they saw a *banca* (small boat) pick up what looked like a small *maleta* (suitcase) and proceed towards the island of Bohol.[24]

Soon after this letter was delivered, a Japanese expeditionary force estimated to be 3,000 troops left for Bohol in the last week of June 1944. The maneuver took much of the pressure off the Cebu Area Command, but it disrupted severely the Bohol Area Command. Their radio station, their only link to SWPA, was taken by the Japanese troops. Some of their officers fled to eastern Cebu. All these things strengthened everybody in the believe that the Koga papers were extremely important.[25]

May 30, 1944
Mr. James Cushing:
We are again sending you the following important message.
1. Although we received your reply at 4:00 P.M. in the afternoon of May 28, as it is not satisfactory to us, we have decided to resort to the firm and drastic measure against you. Our offensive, from now on, will increase extremely in its vigor and fierceness.
2. Our imperial forces, however, are merciful as well as being righteous and powerful. We are determined to exercise our uncompromising might and crush any enemy that resists. Yet we are liberal and magnanimous enough to pardon all those who surrender.
3. If you show your sincerity in repenting your misdeeds in the past

and surrender to the Imperial forces, we swear to God that not only shall we guarantee the safety of your life as well as those of your relations, but also shall we accord you the favorable treatment in every sense. Therefore, we advise you to come to the position of the Japanese forces with a white flag until the evening of the 30th of May, 1944.

We are hoping that you will take the decisive steps concerning this matter.

> Supreme Commander
> The Imperial Japanese Army Garrison in Cebu
> Supreme Commander
> The Imperial Japanese Naval Garrison in Cebu[29]

SWPA was most concerned about the rest of the documents recovered from the crash site of the Japanese plane. Through radio exchanges, Whitney knew there was at least one more load of papers, but he was unsure where they were or who had them. On 23 May he sent a message to Cushing:

HAVE ALL ENEMY DOCUMENTS ARRIVED AT ANDREWS HEADQUARTERS? IF NOT DISPATCH REMAINDER IMME-DIATELY AND ADVISE WHEN THEY MAY BE EXPECTED TO ARRIVE THERE. PRESERVE UTMOST SECRECY.[26]

In response Col. Salvador Abcede wired back on the 25th to say that the papers had not yet arrived from Cushing. Four days later he radioed that some documents did arrive, and Cushing had informed him that there were more on the way. SWPA became busy arranging the pick-up of the last ship-ment of the documents, assigning the USS *Nautilus* to the mission. Whitney sent a warning to Abcede:

EXPECT SUPPLY SHIPMENT ARRIVE YOUR AREA AROUND 20 JUNE. BE PREPARED TO UNLOAD FULL CARGO 100 TONS DURING ONE NIGHT. SHIPMENT WILL BE 4/5THS FOR YOU. 1/5TH FOR CUSHING. PUT ALL ENEMY DOCUMENTS FROM CUSHING ON THIS VESSEL.[27]

On 26 May 1944, Lt. Irving Joseph, the last of the three American servicemen operating in Cebu, left Cushing's headquarters with the last batch of the documents. He took with him, on his way to Andrews in southern Negros, only two experienced trail men in order to keep the party as inconspicuous as possible. He was in a hurry because he wanted to be in Tolong no later than 5 June 1944 in order not to miss the rendezvous with the submarine. Joseph made it on time.

The Japanese continued to look for the documents on Cebu. Near the end of May, even before the 30 May ultimatum expired, the Japanese stepped up their bombing and strafing. On 3 June Cushing radioed SWPA that the Japanese had taken his headquarters by surprise on 30 May and that his forces had sustained several casualties in their escape. He also noted that the Japanese were burning many homes on Cebu. Later that day, Cushing radioed SWPA that all additional documents were then at Andrews' headquarters and that the Japanese were using nine planes in the current drive against his forces. He noted that he might be forced off the air as the Japanese were then 13 hours away from him.

On June 4 Whitney informed Sutherland that all of the remaining documents had been delivered to southern Negros, and plans called for the pickup of the documents in about 10 days.

While the submarine pickup plans were being developed, Cushing's forces were continually under Japanese fire. On 16 June, Cushing informed SWPA that the bombing and strafing continued until 12 June, and since then there was day and night plane activity over Cebu. Apparently the Japanese had not given up on finding any captured documents the guerrillas had recovered.

Eventually the second batch of documents was picked up and delivered to MacArthur's headquarters in Australia. The documents consisted of two volumes of typewritten and penciled radio messages that had been received and decoded. The messages were between various naval units from the end of 1943 to 29 March 1944, with code symbols on the messages. The messages were primarily about the change of codes of Japanese fleet units and radio broadcasts, and appeared to be of primary value to the Central Bureau, the Allies' code-breaking unit in SWPA.[28]

It was clear to Layton that the Japanese planned to hurl everything they had against the American fleet. Layton immediately presented his findings and the documents to Admiral Chester Nimitz. He had copies mimeographed and sent at once, with a cover letter, to every flag officer associated with the planned Marianas invasion. A flying boat rushed copies of Layton's translation with Nimitz's final instructions out to the task force at Eniwetok. It arrived on 8 June and was delivered to Admiral Raymond A. Spruance, commander of the Fifth Fleet, aboard his flagship the USS *Indianapolis*. The translations arrived too late to reach Task Force 58, under Vice Admiral Marc A. Mitscher, before it departed Majuro in the Marshall Islands, but copies were air-dropped to his flagship USS *Lexington* on the high seas. Spruance and Mitscher were therefore well aware of the enemy strategy when they set course north across the Philippine Sea for the Marianas.[29]

Admiral Koga's plan was inherited by Admiral Soemu Toyoda, who had been appointed on May 1 as the new Commander in Chief of the Combined Fleet. Within a week after he took command, he modified the old Z-Plan slightly to provide for a battle area in the western Carolines or Marianas, renaming it the "A Operation" (or *A-Go*). His plan provided for concentrating Japanese shore-based air forces and to operate his carrier planes from shore bases when the Americans attacked the Philippines, Palau or the Marianas. He also planned to use his empty carrier forces as a diversionary attack force to draw off American carriers while the Japanese surface fleet fell upon and destroyed the Americans.

The Japanese knew about the American forces steaming their way toward the Marianas, but there was nothing they could do about it. The American force consisted of 535 ships (including 15 carriers with 900 planes) and 127,571 troops, making Operation Forager the largest amphibious assault yet mounted in the Pacific. It began with an air strike on Saipan on 15 June. To meet the American threat, Admiral Toyoda, who had six carriers and some 450 airplanes, intended to use airfields on Tinian and Guam while he rushed in his reserve of land-based planes from Japan, using the Bonin Islands as way stations.

An elaborate decoy operation was supposed to lure U.S. forces westward, but Spruance did not take the bait. His primary task was to protect the Saipan beachhead. He knew from the captured documents that if he went full tilt after the Japanese fleet some 600 miles west of Guam, the enemy carrier planes would be able to multiply their effectiveness by using the other airfields in the Marianas for shuttle-bombing runs. It would also expose him to attacks from land-based planes flying south from Japan. Instead he waited for the Japanese to come for him, and they did. The major battle, the greatest carrier battle of the war, took place on 19–20 June in the Philippine Sea, west of the Marianas. The American fleet dealt a major defeat to the A-Go operation during the so-called "Marianas Turkey Shoot," downing some 550 to 645 Japanese planes and forcing the Japanese fleet to flee westward.[30] The Japanese also lost three fleet carriers (*Taihu, Hiyu, Shukaku*), two oilers, and six ships damaged, among which were the fleet carriers *Zuikaku, Jinyu* and *Chiyoda*. The American losses were limited to a damagaed battleship (USS *South Dakota*) and 125 fighter aircraft.[31]

The losses to the Japanese fleet air arm were irreplaceable. The Japanese had spent the better part of a year reconstituting their carrier air groups, and the U.S. Fast Carrier Task Force had destroyed 90% of it in two days. The Japanese only had enough pilots left to form an air group for one of their light carriers.

Without the knowledge of Plan Z the outcome of this battle might have been very different. At that point in time the most important part, the main report, of the captured Z-Plan had been translated and distributed. It was delivered to Admiral Spruance and airdropped to other commanders such as Admiral Mitscher, commander of Task Force 58. It gave these commanders insight into the thinking, planning and behavior of their adversary. This was an enormous advantage that saved precious men and material for the Allied forces and delivered a fatal blow to Admiral Toyoda's fleet air arm. An important step in the final defeat of Japan was accomplished. Admiral Spruance's chief of staff, Carl Moore, said the following about this after the war:

> I think the thing encompassed heavy ships as well, with the whole idea being that if they could draw the ships to an attack in the center, and heavy ships or carriers could make an end run and get in behind, they could do the damage they wanted to do. The report indicated that this sort of action might be taken. His experience with the Japanese influenced his [Spruance] actions right through the operations.[32]

Hard Times for Cebu

For the Cebu Area Command and Jim Cushing, the months of April, May and June 1944 were an extremely hectic period. In the early months of 1944 they were recovering from the Fenton-Cushing controversy, ending in the execution of Harry Fenton as well as Estrella, the one who ordered Fenton's execution. From a double command the Cebu Area Command went over to a single command, with Jim Cushing firmly in the driver's seat. Although initially recognition by SWPA in Australia was denied, in January 1944 the Cebu Area Command was finally recognized.

The crash of Admiral Fukudome's plane, followed by the prisoner exchange, and the issue of the highly classified papers from the plane kept Jim and his men extremely busy for months. Jim was not able to keep the prisoners, but the papers were safely delivered to Australia. In hindsight nobody doubted that the papers were far more valuable than the prisoners. It took a long time before the Japanese understood that the papers were out of reach, as either they were never recovered from the crash or the guerrilla movement was able to hide them. After Jim was able to get the Japanese believe the papers might be on the island of Bohol, Cebu was able to get some rest.

The pressure was off, but the damage was great. Again the guerrilla headquarters in Tabunan was in Japanese hands and they lost a considerable number of experienced fighters. The difference between Cebu and the other islands, as far as guerrilla actions was concerned, is quite clear in ADVATIS TRANSLATION NO 45, a report from the Japanese intelligence services concerning mid-1944. According to the report, "Cebu is the center of guerrilla spy activities in the Visayan Islands." The report also states that there was almost no guerrilla activity on any of the neighboring islands.[33]

During the following months Cebu kept a low profile. Again the organization had to be rebuilt from scratch. Experienced people had either been killed, wounded or simply disappeared.

There was some assistance from neighboring islands, but that was not enough. Fortunately they were informed that a submarine with supplies was on its way to Cebu. This was an important issue to get supplies straight from Australia. Until then the Cebu Area Command had only gotten supplies via either Southern Negros or via Bohol/Mindanao.

ADVATIS TRANSLATION NO. 45

Extracts from mimeographed file of intelligence reports issued 31 July 44 to 20 Sep 44 by I Batsu and Batsu (Iloilo) and held by 63 Indep MT Bn. Dahagan, Leyte—20 Dec 44

BATSU STAFF INTELLIGENCE REPORTS 31 JUL 44 TO 20 SEP 44 / BATSU STAFF INTELLIGENCE REPORT NO. 8 31 JUL 44 / INTELLIGENCE RECORD (B) No. 3 Guerrilla Activities

1. CEBU

Cebu is the center of guerrilla spy activities in the Visayan Islands. The recent Onishi Force's punitive expedition paralysed the activities of Lt. Col. Cushing for a time and destroyed his headquarters, but information received from the Cebu MP Section (obtained from examination of a surrendered guerrilla officer who was attached to headquarters) is to the effect that it was subsequently reestablished at Kamungayan (three kilometers east of Tabunan) and that guerrillas have been coming in from Leyte, Negros and Bohol to build up strength again. The present figures are:

Men: 3,500

Equipment: 2 mortars (Hakugekiho);10 MG; 15 automatic Rifles, 150 carbines: 1,500 rifles

The guerrillas are still expanding and are moving their headquarters to Mit-ol. Besides Cushing, the Americans, 1st Lt Daniel and 1st Lt Joseph, are in the area. They are in close contact with Maj. Gen. Fertig on Mindanao and are also sending liaison officers there to arrange fort supplies. Recently, in April and May, the following were obtained:

1st batch: 100 carbines and large quantities am, many pistols, clothes, etc.

2nd batch: 50 carbines and large quantities pistol am, propaganda material

The captured Z-Plan had an enormous influence on the Battle of the Philippine Sea. For Admiral Toyoda this battle was planned to be the *Kantai Kessen*, or Decisive Battle, as outlined in the plan. The outcome of the battle, the total destruction of Toyoda's fleet air arm, was unforeseen. The Battle of the Philippine Sea was a carrier battle, however, where the big battleships such as the *Musashi* and the *Yamato* did not participate. The Japanese Imperial Navy was thus severely beaten, but not yet destroyed.

Then there was the question of MacArthur's return to the Philippines. The destruction of Toyoda's fleet air arm made the Japanese carrier fleet practically useless. It also took away the air cover for the battleships. In other words it made any landing in the Philippines less risky. Were the captured documents also going to have any influence on MacArthur's timeline for his return to the Philippines?

CHAPTER 19
GENERAL DOUGLAS MACARTHUR
AND THE PHILIPPINES

Douglas MacArthur: Assignment in the Philippines

D OUGLAS MACARTHUR, THE youngest of three brothers, was born in 1880 in Little Rock, Arkansas, where at the time of his birth his parents were stationed. His father was Lt. General Arthur McArthur (at the time a captain), and his mother Mary Pinkney Hardy MacArthur of Norfolk, Virginia. Douglas was the grandson of jurist and politician Arthur McArthur, Sr., a Scottish immigrant, and his father had won the Medal of Honor in the Civil War.[1]

After two rejections, MacArthur entered the United States Military Academy at West Point in 1898. He was an outstanding cadet and graduated first in his 93-man class in June 1903, and was awarded the title of "First Captain of the Corps of Cadets."[2] Upon graduation he was commissioned as a second lieutenant in the U.S. Army Corps of Engineers.

A few months later the young second lieutenant boarded the liner SS *Sherman* with the 3rd Engineer Battalion for a 38-day voyage to the country where he would become a legend: the Philippines.[3] He arrived just after his father had left. Landing in Manila, MacArthur immediately fell in love with the country.[4]

He was posted first to the Visayas, where he was almost ambushed by guerrillas, but managed to kill two of them and escape. In October 1904 he returned to San Francisco. MacArthur fought in World War I and during the conflict he received two Distinguished Service Crosses, seven Silver Stars, a Distinguished Service Medal and two Purple Hearts.

In 1919 MacArthur became superintendent of the U.S. Military Academy at West Point, and in 1924 he returned as a Major General to the Philippines. From 1930 until 1935 he served as Chief of Staff of the United States Army.

Back in the Philippines
When the Commonwealth of the Philippines achieved semi-independent status in 1935, President of the Philippines Manuel Quezon asked MacArthur to supervise the creation of a Philippine Army. MacArthur chose not to retire but to remain on the active list as a major general, and with President Roosevelt's approval he accepted the assignment.

MacArthur took his job very seriously. By 1946, when the commonwealth would become independent, the nation would have a trained military force of forty divisions, comprising about 400,000 men."[5]

Japan became concerned about these developments in the Philippines, and its propaganda went into high gear to discredit the Quezon-MacArthur team. To quote from a staff report of the period: "The Philippines are overrun with Japanese political spies—businessmen, sidewalk photographers and bicycle salesmen in every small town and hamlet. One is sure to see them."[6]

But nothing was forthcoming. The quota of trainees was cut in half, the budget dropped considerably, and promised equipment did not show up. Relations with Japan deteriorated fast and became threatening. In July 1941 Roosevelt recalled Douglas MacArthur to active duty in the U.S. Army as a major general. He appointed him as commander of United States Armed Forces in the Far East (USAFFE), promoting him to lieutenant general the following day.

An eleventh-hour struggle in the Philippines developed to build up enough force to repel an enemy. The ten-year period so essential for the successful completion of MacArthur's basic plan was evidently going to be cut in half. Too late, Washington had come to realize the danger. Men and munitions were finally being shipped to the Pacific, but the crucial question was, would they arrive in time and in sufficient strength?[7]

MacArthur's forces were grouped into four major commands. The *North Luzon Force*, under command of General Jonathan Wainwright, the *South Luzon Force*, under General George Parker, Jr., the *Visayan Force*, under General Bradford Chynoweth, and the *Mindanao Force*, under General William F. Sharp.[8,9,10]

On 21 November 1941 the Bombardment Group of B-17s was moved from Clark Field (Fort Stotsenburg) to Delmonte Field in Mindanao, in order to place it beyond the range of attack from Japanese planes based on the island of Formosa. As tension in Washington rose to a climax the pursuit interceptor planes from Clark began night patrols on December 4th in territorial waters well out to sea. Each night they located Japanese bombers from 20 to 50 miles out, but these presumed enemy planes turned back before the international line was reached. The last of these night flights was intercepted and turned back at the exact time of the attack on Pearl Harbor. Whatever might come, they were as ready as they possibly could be in their inadequate defenses, on the night of the 7th of December 1941. Every disposition had been made, and every man, gun and plane was on the alert.[11]

On 7 December 1941 the Japanese surprised the world with their attack on Pearl Harbor. As was expected the Philippines was pulled into this war. MacArthur pulled his main force back to the Bataan Peninsula. The fight on Bataan lasted another four months. On 9 April 1942, Gen. King and the remaining weary, starving and emaciated American and Filipino defenders on the battle-swept Bataan peninsula surrendered. The island fortress of Corregidor still held out, and after the fall of Bataan it took almost a month before General Wainwright realized that it was hopeless. On 6 May 1942, at about 0130 he finally surrendered the Corregidor garrison. The initial fight for the Philippines was over.

"I shall return"

General Douglas MacArthur did not wait in Corregidor until the end. On the specific orders of President Roosevelt he left the Philippines on 13 March 1942 for Australia. Upon arrival there MacArthur issued the following famous statement when he spoke at Terowie of the beleagured Philippines:

> The president of the United States ordered me to break through the Japanese lines and proceed from Corregidor to Australia for the purpose, as I understand it, of organizing the American offensive against Japan, a primary object of which is the relief of the Philippines. I came through and I shall return.[12]

This promise to return to the Philippines became MacArthur's *leitmotif*, his guiding goal for the war against Japan. Nothing could change his mind; every move he made or planned was with the ultimate aim to return to the

Philippines. That was his promise to the Philippine people.

A month later, on 18 April 1942, MacArthur was appointed Supreme Commander of Allied Forces in the Southwest Pacific Area (SWPA).[13,14] He initially located his General Headquarters (GHQ) in Melbourne, and then in July 1942 moved to Brisbane, the northernmost city in Australia with the necessary communications facilities.[15]

In the months following the attack on Pearl Harbor in December 1941, the Japanese drove the Americans out of the Philippines, the British out of Malaya, and the Dutch out of the East Indies. The Japanese then began to expand into the Western Pacific, occupying many islands in an attempt to build a defensive ring around their conquests and threaten the lines of communication from the United States to Australia and New Zealand. The Japanese reached Guadalcanal in May 1942.[16]

Guadalcanal (native name: Isatabu) is a tropical island in the southwestern Pacific. It is the largest island in the Solomon Group. In the eyes of the Allied Forces, this was the place to stop the Japanese advancements. If Guadalcanal was lost the way to Australia and New Zealand lay wide open. And so the United States, as a matter of urgency, despite not being adequately prepared, conducted the first amphibious landing of the war.[17,18]

Surprised by the Allied offensive, the Japanese made several attempts between August and November 1942 to retake the airfield that was the key to the island, Henderson Field. Three major land battles, seven large naval battles (five nighttime surface actions and two carrier battles), and almost daily aerial battles culminated in the decisive Naval Battle of Guadalcanal in early November 1942, in which the last Japanese attempt to bombard Henderson Field from the sea and land with enough troops to retake it was defeated. In December 1942, the Japanese abandoned further efforts to retake Guadalcanal.[19]

On 9 February, U.S. Army Major General Alexander Patch, who just had replaced U.S. Marine Major General Alexander Vandegrift as commander of Allied forces on Guadalcanal, which by January totaled just over 50,000 men,[20] realized that the Japanese were gone and declared Guadalcanal secure for Allied forces, ending the six months long campaign.[21]

The Guadalcanal campaign was a significant strategic combined arms victory by Allied forces over the Japanese in the Pacific theatre. The Japanese had reached the high-water mark of their conquests in the Pacific, and Guadalcanal marked the transition by the Allies from defensive operations to the strategic offensive in that theatre and the beginning of further operations, including the Solomon Islands, New Guinea and Central Pacific campaigns.[22]

The Guadalcanal campaign was costly to Japan strategically and in material losses and manpower. Roughly 25,000 experienced ground troops were killed during the campaign. The drain on resources also directly contributed to Japan's failure to achieve its objectives in New Guinea. Japan also lost control of the southern Solomons and the ability to interdict Allied shipping to Australia. Japan's major base at Rabaul was now further directly threatened by Allied air power. Most importantly, scarce Japanese land, air and naval forces had disappeared forever into the Guadalcanal jungle and surrounding sea. The Japanese could not replace the aircraft and ships destroyed and sunk in this campaign, as well as their highly trained and veteran crews, especially the naval aircrews, nearly as quickly as the Allies.[23]

In the meantime MacArthur already planned and worked on the next steps to fulfill his promise to return to the Philippines.

Back to the Philippines

While the Imperial Japanese Navy had the element of surprise at Pearl Harbor, Allied code breakers had now turned the tables. Their first success was discovering that an attack was planned against Port Moresby, which if lost would allow Japan to control the seas to the north and west of Australia and isolate the country. The carrier USS *Lexington* under Admiral Fletcher joined USS *Yorktown* and an American-Australian task force to stop the Japanese advance. The resulting Battle of the Coral Sea, fought in May 1942, was the first naval battle in which ships involved never sighted each other and only aircraft were used to attack opposing forces.

A few weeks later, in June 1942, the code-breakers were able to determine the date and location of the planned Japanese attack against the Island of Midway, enabling the forewarned U.S. Navy to set up an ambush of its own. The ensuing Battle of Midway was a decisive victory for the U.S. Navy and a solid check to Japanese aspirations in the Pacific.[24,25,26,27]

The Battle of the Coral Sea was for the Japanese Imperial Navy the end of its move southward. The Battle of Midway was the end of its move eastward in the Pacific. They were the turning points in the war. From then on the Allied forces were able to crawl back to the Philippines and, eventually, Japan.

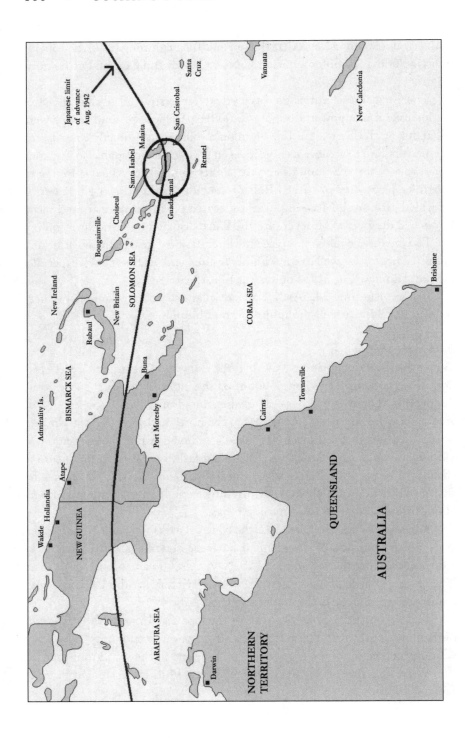

General MacArthur's forces were rolling back General Adachi's Eigh-teenth Army at an accelerating pace all along the coast of New Guinea. On his right flank, the capture of Arawe and Gloucester Bay had placed the south-ern end of New Britain in his hands. Farther to the east, the Allies controlled the entire stretch of the Solomon Islands and the waters of the Solomon Sea.[28]

Rabaul had no air support left whatsoever. In spite of replacements and reinforcements, the once-powerful Japanese air force in this area had been driven to the point of extinction.[29] The gradual decimation of the enemy's land-based air power by the Fifth and Thirteenth Air Forces sharply de-creased his ability to defend his vital sea lanes and opened the way for Allied naval craft to advance in increasing strength.[30,31]

As supplies for the Allies kept coming into the Southwest Pacific Area, and the shortages which initially shackled every plan were gradually being removed, General MacArthur prepared to launch heavier blows against the Japanese.

At the same time, Japan fell further and further behind. In strategic terms the Allies began a long movement across the Pacific, seizing one island base after another. Not every Japanese stronghold had to be captured; some, like Truk, Rabaul and Formosa, were neutralized by air attack and bypassed. The goal was to get close to Japan itself, then launch massive strategic air attacks, improve the submarine blockade, and finally (only if necessary) execute an invasion.[32]

In November 1943 U.S. Marines sustained high casualties when they overwhelmed the 4,500-strong garrison at Tarawa. This helped the Allies to improve their techniques of amphibious landings, learning from their mis-takes and implementing changes such as thorough pre-emptive bombings and bombardment, more careful planning regarding tides and landing craft schedules, and better overall coordination.[33]

The U.S. Navy did not seek out the Japanese fleet for a decisive battle, as Mahanian Doctrine would suggest (and as Japan hoped); instead the Allied advance could only be stopped by a Japanese naval attack, which oil shortages (induced by submarine attack) made impossible.[34]

Mahanian Doctrine
Mahanian Doctrine is a concept of seapower based on the idea that countries with greater naval power will have greater worldwide impact. This idea was presented by Alfred Thayer Mahan (1840–1914) a United States Navy flag

officer, geostrategist and historian, who has been called the most important American strategist of the nineteenth century.[35] His concept of "sea power" was most famously presented in *The Influence of Sea Power Upon History 1660–1783*.[36] The concept had enormous influence in shaping the strategic thought of navies across the world, especially in the United States, Germany, Japan and Britain, ultimately causing a European naval arms race in the 1890s, which included the United States.

Mahan's views were shaped by the 17th-century conflicts between Holland, England, France and Spain, and by the 19th-century naval wars between France and Britain, where British naval superiority eventually defeated France, consistently preventing invasion and blockade. The Royal Navy's blockade of Imperial Germany during World War I was a critical direct and indirect factor in the eventual German collapse; Mahan's theories were thought to be vindicated by the First World War.[37]

The Influence of Seapower Upon History, 1660–1783 was translated into Japanese[38] and used as a textbook in the Imperial Japanese Navy (IJN). This strongly affected the IJN's doctrine on stopping Russian naval expansion in the Far East, which culminated in the Russo-Japanese War of 1904–1905.

The IJN's pursuit of the "decisive battle" was such that it contributed to Imperial Japan's defeat in World War II,[39,40] and so rendered obsolete the doctrine of the decisive battle between fleets, because of the development of the submarine and the aircraft carrier.[41] However, one could argue that the IJN did not adhere entirely to Mahan's doctrine, as they did divide their main force from time to time, particularly the extensive division of warships in a complicated battle plan that led to the disaster at Midway, and as such sealed their own defeat.

The route of General MacArthur's return to the Philippines lay straight before him—westward along the coast of New Guinea to the Vogelkop Peninsula and the Moluccas. The successive Allied blows in New Guinea, New Britain and the Solomons had seriously breached the Japanese outer wall of island defenses. General MacArthur was still about 1,600 miles from the Philippines and 2,100 miles from Manila, but he was now in a position to carry out with increasing speed the massive strokes against the enemy which he had envisioned since the beginning of his campaigns in the Southwest Pacific Area.[42]

With the Japanese confused and thrown off balance by the recent series of Allied successes, a clear and direct result of the capture of the "Plan Z" documents, General MacArthur urged that the situation be exploited immediately:

> There are now large forces available in the Pacific which, with accretions scheduled for the current year, would permit the execution of an offensive which would place us in the Philippines in December if the forces were employed in effective combination. . . . All available ground, air, and assault forces in the Pacific should be combined in a drive along the New Guinea-Mindanao axis supported by the main fleet based at Manus Island [planned for a later operation] and other facilities readily available in these waters. I propose that on completion of operations in the Marshalls, the maximum force from all sources in the Pacific be concentrated in my drive up the New Guinea coast, to be coordinated with a Central Pacific operation against the Palaus and the support by combatant elements of the Pacific Fleet with orders to contain or destroy the Japanese Fleet. Time presses. . . ."[43]

CHAPTER **20**
PLANNING THE RETURN

THE PHILIPPINE ISLANDS constituted the main objective of General MacArthur's planning from the time of his departure from Corregidor in March 1942 until his dramatic return to Leyte two and a half years later. From the very outset, this strategic archipelago formed the keystone of Japan's captured island empire and therefore became the ultimate goal of Allied operations in the Southwest Pacific. After the Philippines were liberated, they would form the main base for the final assault against the Japanese homeland. Whoever controlled the air and naval bases in the Philippine Islands logically controlled the main artery of supply to Japan's war industry.

First there was the *Reno Plan* and then there were *Musketeer I* and *II*, based on the idea to land somewhere in Mindanao in the southern Philippines. Initial lodgements were to be made at Sarangani Bay in southern Mindanao on 15 November and at Leyte Gulf on 20 December.

The Japanese were obsessed by the prospect of losing the Philippines. Lt. Gen. Seizo Arisue, Chief of G-2, General Staff Headquarters, made the following comment: "To shatter American war plans, the Japanese Army held it necessary to maintain the Philippines to the end and to fight a decisive battle with the Americans who planned to recapture the Philippines. Furthermore, the Philippines were of absolute necessity for the security of traffic between Japan Proper and the southern areas."[1]

The capture of Admiral Fukudome and the translations of the Z-Plan documents captured in Cebu changed everything. Now every detail of the enemy's plans in regard to the Decisive Battle was clear. This knowledge played a crucial role in the defeat of the Japanese Imperial Fleet in the Battle of the Philippine Sea from 19–20 June 1944. However. the Imperial Fleet was beaten but not destroyed. The Japanese carriers had lost almost all their planes, but the huge battleships were still there.

When carrier task groups of the U.S. Third Fleet, with Plan Z in hand, sortied carefully northward, on 12 and 13 September 1944, to hit Mindanao and the Visayas, enemy air reaction was surprisingly meager and heavy loss was inflicted upon Japanese planes and ground installations. The island of Leyte was almost without defences. This sudden change in the battle picture of the Pacific Theater made a drastic revision of Allied strategy, as set forth in the "Musketeer" plans, necessary.

Immediate orders were issued to capitalize on the enemy's apparent aerial weakness. It became more and more apparent that a considerable part of the once mighty Japanese Air Force had not only been destroyed in the costly war of attrition incidental to the New Guinea operations,[2] but also in the Battle of the Philippine Sea. The disclosure of such great vulnerability in the enemy's air shield over the Philippines caused an immediate reassessment of the situation to ascertain whether an acceleration of the existing schedule would be possible by omitting certain previously planned operations designed mainly for air support. Intelligence sources indicated that the Japanese had been increasing their ground forces in the Philippines:

> An appraisal of information, over the period 15 May to 15 June, discloses a contemporary trend of events, indicating definitely that the Japanese are massing troops, bolstering dispositions, and shifting units in the Philippine area. This trend was not indicated prior to 1 April.[3]

With the enemy thus strengthening his ground positions to meet the anticipated Allied assaults, each month or week that could be cut from the Allied timetable for the Philippines would accordingly reduce the overall cost of the campaign and help ensure its rapid accomplishment. The fact that the enemy at the same time had lost most of his carrier aircraft made advancing the timetable even more attractive.

On 13 September Admiral Halsey advised Admiral Nimitz and General MacArthur that he believed the seizure of the western Carolines, including Palau, was no longer essential to the occupation of the Philippines.[4] He suggested that Leyte could be seized immediately if all projected operations in the Carolines, with the exception of Ulithi, were cancelled and the landings were covered by carrier aircraft. Admiral Nimitz concurred in the proposal to bypass Yap, but directed that the Palau and Ulithi operations be carried out as scheduled, the former being needed as an air base and the latter as a fleet anchorage.[5] Admiral Halsey's recommendation was relayed to the Joint Chiefs of Staff who were then participating in the Quebec Conference between President Roosevelt and Prime Minister Churchill. General MacArthur's views were requested on the proposed change of the invasion date for Leyte and the reply came back as follows:

> In view of COM3rdFLT's latest report on carrier operations in the Philippines Islands area, I am prepared to move immediately to execution of King II (Leyte) with target date of 20 Oct 44.[6]

General Marshall described this dramatic sequence of events leading up to the orders for the Leyte invasion in his report to the Secretary of War:[7] ". . . General MacArthur's views were requested and 2 days later he advised us that he was already to shift his plans to land on Leyte 20 October, instead of 20 December, as previously intended. It was a remarkable administrative achievement."

> The message from MacArthur arrived at Quebec at night and Admiral Leahy (Chief of Staff to the President), Admiral King, General Arnold, and I were being entertained at a formal dinner by Canadian officers. It was read by the appropriate staff officers who suggested an immediate affirmative answer. The message, with their recommendations, was rushed to us and we left the table for a conference. Having the utmost confidence in General MacArthur, Admiral Nimitz, and Admiral Halsey, it was not a difficult decision to make. Within 60 minutes after the signal had been received in Quebec, General MacArthur and Admiral Nimitz had received their instructions to execute the Leyte operation on 20 October, abandoning the three previously approved intermediary landings.[8]

In his State of the Union Message on 6 January 1945, President Roosevelt commented on the advanced date for the invasion of the Philippines as follows:

Within the space of twenty-four hours, a major change of plans was accomplished which involved Army and Navy forces from two different theaters of operations—a change which hastened the liberation of the Philippines and the final day of victory—a change which saved lives which would have been expended in the capture of islands which are now neutralized far behind our lines.[9]

The advance planning and preparation of alternative solutions, which were standard operational procedure for General MacArthur's staff, permitted the necessary flexibility for rapid change. Accordingly, with the assurance that the SWPA forces could conform to the proposed change in schedule, the target date for the Leyte landing was advanced fully two months ahead of the original schedule.[10]

Cebu Resupplied

It took a while before the Cebu Area Command needed additional supplies from outside. Initially they were lucky to have the shipments from the *Doña Nati* and the *Anhui*. As time went on these supplies dwindled, however, and other sources had to be found. But there were also things that were simply not around, such as spare parts for certain weapons, modern weapons such as submachine guns, automatic rifles, radio spare parts, medical supplies and so on. These had to be brought in from Australia. During the first years of the war, certainly as long as the Cebu Area Command was not recognized, Cebu did not get any direct shipment from Australia. Items had to be brought in came from Mindanao, Bohol, Negros or Panay. These were long, difficult and dangerous roads, and not everybody returned safe and sound. Notwithstanding, there were always volunteers to do the dirty and dangerous work.

Sometimes it went completely wrong. One of those cases was the trip of Private Gabuya and Captain Eusebio Habacon. They went on a mission to get arms, ammunition and supplies in Mindanao. On their way back they were intercepted at sea by a Japanese patrol boat. Unfortunately they did not manage to throw their American supplies overboard and they were caught redhanded. They were taken to Nasipit, a few kilometers east of Butuan in Misamis Oriental, where they were interrogated and tortured. When the Japanese interrogators got tired of that exercise they bayoneted the two and buried them on the beach. Habacon, still alive, was buried up to his neck near an anthill, Gabuya in a shallow grave. Gabuya pretended to be dead under the earth shoveled over him. After their work the Japanese stayed for a while making jokes over Habacon who tried to keep the aggressive ants from his face. After a while they gave up and left. Gabuya was not dead, just pretending to be, and he had a little bit of air near his mouth and could keep breathing a little. When he thought the Japanese were gone he slowly tried to get out of his grave. He managed to do so. Once he was out he saw that Habacon was already dead, the ants had completely eaten his face. Gabuya was lucky; he returned to Cebu, but without Habacon and without supplies.[11]

Another case was the mission of Major Jesus Ybañez. He went in charge of a six-man mission to get arms and ammunition through Bohol from Mindanao. He went to Carmen, Bohol in the central plateau of the island, which was very close to the headquarters of Major Ingeniero, the island's commander, in the forest fastnesses of Ma-itom.

Upon receiving the supplies Ybañez had to find a way to get them to Cebu. He used *caromatas* (carts) and *balsas* (sleds) drawn by carabao or horse. They made their way down to the seacoast town of Inabanga. Here, at the mouth of a small river, he hired bancas for the crossing of Bohol Strait to Cebu. Ybañez knew that the best place to land the stuff on Cebu was the area between Cebu City and Minglanilla. From there to Tabunan was not too far. They left Inabanga at around two o'clock in the afternoon and set sail for Cogon, close to Pardo on the western edge of Cebu City. On this route they passed close to Kawit Island where a small Japanese garrison was located. Close to Kawit the wind died down and left them floating still. They drifted close to Kawit, and at one point they were not further than 300 meters away. Fortunately the Japanese guards were not watching closely. Nothing happened and they managed in the end to reach the beach in Cogon. Major Ybañez quickly organized transport to bring the goods as fast as possible to the interior. That night they reached Cantipla, the next morning Tupas and Tabunan. The success of their trip soon leaked out and as a result many Filipinos in the Cogon area were rounded up and brought to the Kempetai headquarters in Cebu Normal School building. Many were never seen again.[12]

The first signs that the Americans intended to be back soon occured on 12 September, 1944, and it was the day nearly all Cebuanos had been waiting for. A few minutes past eight in the morning there were planes in the air above Cebu. That was not in fact unusual since the airport in Lahug, in the northern part of Cebu City, was used by Japanese fighter and reconnaissance planes. But this morning the sound was different. The planes were not Japanese. Suddenly people saw the San Carlos University building on P. del Rosario being bombed to rubble. It was the place where the Japanese *Subu Tai*, or Fighting Unit of the Japanese Occupation Forces, was housed. There were many casualties among the soldiers. A huge fuel depot was also hit and would burn for many days. From this time onwards the Americans were overhead daily.[13]

Destination Cebu

In September 1944 Jim Cushing was informed that finally the Cebu Area Command would get its own submarine with supplies. The USS *Nautilus* could be expected at the end of September. The message brought tears to the eyes of many old veteran guerrillas. The Americans had not forgotten them.

For the *Nautilus*, under the command of Commander George Arthur Sharp, USN, it was war patrol number 12. For Commander Sharp it was his fourth war patrol, a mission pursuant to CTF Top Secret Operation Order S55-44.[14]

The *Nautilus* left Port Darwin in Northern Australia on 17 September 1944 at 1056 hours. It had loaded 106 tons of supply and had on board two army officers who had to be dropped off somewhere in the southern Philippines. At 2345 on 24 September they passed the Philippine island of Siquijor at the entrance of the Cebu Strait. Two hours later, at around 0147 on 25 September, they spotted the submarine USS *Mingo*, which was on its sixth war patrol.[15]

As the ship's patrol report describes:

> At 0613 the *Nautilus* made a dawn dive five miles south of Iuisan Point on the eastern coast of Cebu Island, halfway between Oslob and Boljoon. While submerged the boat quietly conducted reconnaissance of Spot 1.[16]
>
> At 0714 the proper security signals were sighted. A little later they spotted a Japanese reconnaissance plane. The plane did not notice the American submarine. It stayed submerged during the day.
>
> At 1838 a small sailing boat was sighted, standing out from the beach and waving a small American flag. Occupants of the boat displayed length of hair to demonstrate their nationality.[17]
>
> At 1908 the *Nautilus* surfaced.

At 1911 Lt. Col. Cushing came aboard.

At 1913 Opened deck hatches and commenced striking cargo top-
side. Maneuvering to keep about 600 yards off beach.

At 1924 First of small boats alongside to receive cargo.[18]

Jim was informed about the arrival of the submarine at the beginning of
September 1944. The scheduled time of arrival was 25 September 1944. The
place where the submarine was to surface was Nueva Caceres, near Boljoon
on the southeast coast of Cebu island. To get there on time he would need
approximately two weeks marching though difficult terrain.

Jim selected 20 Cebu patriots to accompany him. As deputy commander
he selected Major Bernard Hale, former commander of the 88th Infantry Reg-
iment, and just like him a former mining engineer. Jim Cushing and Bernard
Hale had a lot in common. Their skin colour, only slightly lighter than a
Filipino, betrayed the fact that both had a non-white mother. Both smoked
cigars. The difference was in their stature. Jim was two heads taller than
Bernard. Another important member of the group was Staff Sergeant Alfredo
Marigomen, Jim's trusted clerk. Wherever Jim went, so did Marigomen.[19]

The men initially followed the trail to Cantipla, passing the headquarters
of Captain Plaicido Abasolo's unit. From here on the trail became worse and
worse, slippery and full of hidden holes and tree roots. Among the leaves on
each side of the trail lurked those toothpick-sized bloodsucking *alimatok*
(leeches) that sprang upon their unsuspecting prey and fastened their suckers
on the skin. They would soon grow the size of a finger, gorged with their victim's blood. They would work their way inside shoes, boots and socks so that
when the tired traveler bared his feet he would recoil in surprise on seeing
those rubbery parasites between his toes ballooned with his own blood. But
while the leeches were a nuisance, far more dangerous was the Philippine
cobra, the *Naja philippinensis*, since a bite from this meter-long snake could
mean death within 20 minutes.

At the trail fork they took the path on the right leading towards Tungkay.
The other trail led to Sudlon. They passed through the rather open lands of
the Valley of Malubog, in January 1943 the site of one of the most ferocious
battles between guerrillas and the Japanese Army.[20]

Crossing the Tabunok-Toledo road, they started up the hills and continued on towards the south until they reached Duangan, Pinamungajan. From
here they traveled in the dark to avoid detection. They wanted to keep their

mission as secret as possible. It was pitch dark when they reached the Nailon Ridge in Barrio Valencia, Carcar. Suddenly the lead guerrilla was stopped by a voice that shouted "JC kami!" (We are Japanese Constabulary.) The guerrillas immediately opened fire with their carbines. Jim joined them with his Thompson submachinegun. It seemed only moments before the firing stopped and Jim's familiar Texas-drawl broke the silence, "All clear!"

Nobody was hurt in the encounter. Two of the JC's were captured and taken along to the camp of Captain Llanos. They then took the trail to Argao town. Hours later they passed the famous Argao Church, one of the oldest churches in the Philippines, and boarded, as was pre-arranged, a banca which brought them to a Boljoon barrio. Here, only two kilometers away from Nueva Carceres, they disembarked.

At Nueva Carceres, Boljoon, the prearranged security signals were put in place at the designated landing place. Jim searched the horizon with his binoculars for any sign of the submarine. He was excited and nervous at the same time. He had not seen an American from outside in more than three years. Hour after hour passed with the sea like a mirror, no ripple, no periscope, simply nothing.

Then suddenly there she was! He watched the small line of the periscope come closer and closer. Radio contact was established and proper identification was made. Commander Sharp informed Jim that he would surface at seven o'clock that evening.[21]

For Jim it was a historic moment when he shook hands with Commander Sharp. He felt the arrival of the American submarine as the greatest achievement in his career as a guerrilla commander. For years he had said that the Americans would not let them down and that it was only a matter of time before they would be back. And there they were. And not only a submarine—since 12 September American fighters and bombers had strafed and bombed Cebu on a daily basis. The return of the American Army was only a matter of time.

The visit of the submarine was not only to bring supplies, as there were still American families living in Cebu. General MacArthur had ordered all Americans to repatriate to Australia. Lt. Col. Abel Trazo had rounded up a total of 15 Americans, many with children. The submarine could accommodate 11 of them.[22]

At 2206 the *Nautilus* was ready to leave. Three minutes later, however, the submarine ran aground on the Iuisan Shoal. There was only 18 feet of water forward and Commander Sharp tried to back off. It didn't work. He blew all the main ballast tanks and the variable ballast and let the crew rally[23] on deck. All efforts were futile, the submarine was firmly aground.

Commander Sharp knew very well that he was only safe as long as it was dark. Around 05:00 it would start getting light. Then the Japanese reconnaissance planes would spot him right away. Japanese patrol boats would finish him off in no time, or they would try to capture the submarine and its crew. He was in a difficult position. Jim and his men could defend him for a while, but in the long run the submarine's fate was sealed. Sharp sent an urgent message to Australia explaining his situation. He suggested that, worst case scenario, he would take the crew ashore and destroy the submarine using her built-in demolition charges. Australia acknowledged the message and wished him good luck.[24]

But Commander Sharp did not give up his submarine so easy. He knew that the next high tide was at 0400 hours.

At 0300 hours: Captain started blowing all ballast tanks, and decided to lighten the ship as much as possible in order to try at all costs to get off the reef at the next high water. He sent all evacuees back to the shore as well as all mail and captured documents. He burnt all secret and confidential papers, blew all reserve fuel ballast tanks dry blew all variable ballast overboard and jettisoned 190 rounds of 6-inch .53 caliber ammunition. Gasoline tanks were blown dry of ballast and flooded forward and middle groups to hold ship on bottom as tide came in.[25]

At 0330 hours: Secured lightening ship. Tide has actually gone out instead of coming in. Ship is up by the bow 1½° and has 12° starboard list. Coral heads and sandy bottom clearly visible on port side abreast of No. 1 gun even as dark as it is. Blew all main ballast tanks. Gradually built up to all back emergencies.

At 0336 hours: Ship began to go astern rapidly, clearing reef.
At 0400 hours: In deep water and clear of the reef.
At 0542 hours: Passed Siquijor, distance 6 nautical miles.[26]

The *Nautilus* was saved in the nick of time, as one hour later it would have been light enough for Japanese spotter planes to see it. From Cebu the submarine proceeded to Panay to discharge its remaining cargo. The USS *Nautilus* arrived on 6 October safely back in Darwin, Australia.

Cebu was lucky, as it got far more of the cargo than it was supposed to get. Volunteer guards and civilians worked the whole night through to disperse the shipment, and the next morning there was no remaining trace of the submarine's visit. Japanese patrols, hearing rumors about the American submarine's appearance, came but found nothing. But the poor evacuees were left behind.[27] Cebu was ready for the last phase of the war: its liberation. The island did not know that its liberation came months earlier than planned because of the heroic actions of its own guerrillas.

CHAPTER 21
"I HAVE RETURNED"

T
HE LEYTE OPERATION was to be the crucial battle of the war in the Pacific. On its outcome depended the fate of the Philippines as well as the future course of the war against Japan. Located in the heart of the archipelago, Leyte was the focal point where the Southwest Pacific forces of General MacArthur were to converge with the Central Pacific forces of Admiral Nimitz in a mighty assault to wrest the Philippines from the hands of the enemy. With Leyte under General MacArthur's control, the other islands would be within effective striking distance of his ground and air forces.[1,2]

On 20 October 1944, the largest mass of naval assault craft and warships ever concentrated in the Pacific sailed into Leyte Gulf. The landing beaches had already been softened by a continuous two-day ship and plane bombardment.

The severity of this bombardment accounted in great measure for the initial ease of the Allied landings. In addition to forcing the enemy from many of his beach entrenchments, it seriously disrupted his entire communication system," General Yoshiharu Tomochika, deputy chief of staff of Japan's 35th Army stated later during his interrogation after the war.[3] "The positions of the 16th Division Artillery Regiment along the first line of defense were subjected to a severe pre-landing naval bombardment which resulted in the destruction of a great number of its field pieces. Regimental radio-telegraphic communications were disrupted by this bombardment, and direct communications with the 35th Army and with the 14th Area

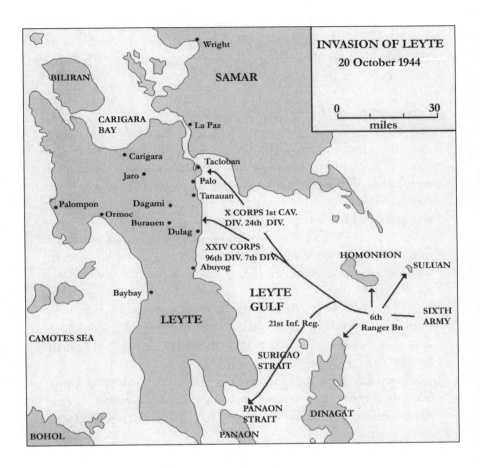

Army Headquarters in Manila were never re-established. Direct liaison between regiments and smaller units of the division could no longer be carried out effectively.

The main assault on the east coast of Leyte began at ten o'clock in the morning with landings along an 18-mile front between the two small villages of Dulag and San Jose. X Corps covered the right flank of the landings, to the north; XXIV Corps secured the left flank. Both shores of Panaon Strait at the southern tip of the island were seized by a single regimental combat team of the 21st Infantry which had gone ashore an hour prior to the main assault.

General MacArthur's promise to return to the Philippines was fulfilled shortly after the main landings. In a drenching rain he strode ashore on the muddy beachhead near Palo. Speaking to millions of waiting Filipinos over a portable radio set, he declared:[4]

> This is the Voice of Freedom, General MacArthur speaking. People of the Philippines: I have returned. By the grace of Almighty God our forces stand again on Philippine soil-soil consecrated in the blood of our two peoples. We have come, dedicated and committed to the task of destroying every vestige of enemy control over your daily lives, and of restoring, upon a foundation of indestructible strength, the liberties of your people.
>
> At my side is your President, Sergio Osmeña, worthy successor of that great patriot, Manuel Quezon, with members of his cabinet. The seat of your government is now therefore firmly re-established on Philippine soil.
>
> The hour of your redemption is here. Your patriots have demonstrated an unswerving and resolute devotion to the principles of freedom that challenges the best that is written on the pages of human history.
>
> I now call upon your supreme effort that the enemy may know from the temper of an aroused and outraged people within that he has a force there to contend with no less violent than is the force committed from without.
>
> Rally to me. Let the indomitable spirit of Bataan and Corregidor lead on. As the lines of battle roll forward to bring you within the zone of operations, rise and strike! For future generations of your sons and daughters, strike!
>
> In the name of your sacred dead, strike! Let no heart be faint. Let every arm be steeled. The guidance of Divine God points the way. Follow in His name to the Holy Grail of righteous victory!

Opposition at the landing beaches was negligible and casualties were low. By midafternoon the 1st Cavalry Division, supported by tanks, had secured Tacloban Airfield, the most important early objective.

Although the Japanese had anticipated the landings at Dulag, they were not prepared for a direct assault on Tacloban and had even located their division headquarters there, thinking it would be well behind the battlefront. "We had misestimated the location of the initial enemy landings," said General Tomochika when interrogated after the war, "and consequently our defense in the area was very weak. We had estimated that there was a greater possibility of an enemy landing in the Dulag area since it was at the entrance to Leyte Gulf, instead of at Tacloban which was almost at the upper extreme end of the Gulf. The strategy employed by the enemy in landing at our weak spots can be attributed to the splendid intelligence system of the enemy, aided at times by the guerrilla agents who had infiltrated into our lines and had sent out vital information concerning our troop dispositions."[5]

The 24th Division pressed forward, fighting its way inland in the area of the Palo-Tacloban Highway. In the Dulag sector the 96th Division advanced against stiffening resistance. Dulag aerodrome was secured on 21 October. The airfield, however, situated as it was in the flat, flood plain of the Marabang River, was not suitable for immediate use.

Naval Threat to Leyte Gulf

While the Allies were fighting to improve their beachheads on Leyte, the Japanese were preparing to stake their remaining striking power on a gigantic gamble to maintain their position in the Philippines. The role of the Combined Fleet in this critical battle was vital. Brilliantly conceived and immense in scope, the Japanese plan was to deliver a crippling attack against the US Navy and, with the strategic situation in their favor, to destroy in the same stroke General MacArthur's invasion at the beaches. The Japanese were willing to risk the loss of their entire mobile fleet for the one opportunity of maneuvering their cruisers and battleships to within target range of the troop and supply transports in Leyte Gulf.[6]

The decision to risk their most valuable military assets in an attempt to repel General MacArthur's invasion of Leyte emphasized again the importance which the Japanese attached to the Philippines. Admiral Soemu Toyoda, Commander in Chief of the Combined Fleet, was fully conscious of the hazards involved: "Since without the participation of our Combined Fleet there was no possibility of the land-based forces in the Philippines having any chance against your forces at all, it was decided to send the whole fleet, taking the gamble. If things went well we might obtain unexpectedly good results, but if the worst should happen, there was a chance that we would lose the entire fleet; but I felt that that chance had to be taken. . . . Should we lose in the Philippines operations, even though the fleet should be left, the shipping lane to the south would be completely cut off so that the fleet, if it should come back to Japanese waters, could not obtain its fuel supply. If it should remain in southern waters, it could not receive supplies of ammunition and arms. There would be no sense in saving the fleet at the expense of the loss of the Philippines."[7]

Based on similar strategic speculation and aided by the knowledge obtained from the Z-Plan, the Allied intelligence services assumed that the Japanese would employ the mass of their fleet to defend the Philippines. The logical conclusion was that if the Japanese used their fleet against General MacArthur's landing forces in the Philippines they would probably converge from two areas, with the stronger elements coming up from the south.

In a report of 10 January 1945, Admiral Kinkaid commented on the background for the assumption that the Japanese surface fleet would come out in force in case the Philippines were attacked: [8,9]

> The reconstruction of the Japanese fleet, after the sweeping U.S. air victory over Truk on February 17th, into a strong task force organization termed the First Mobile Fleet; the capture of the 'Z' Operations Orders issued by the Combined Fleet Staff on April 8th, detailing the circumstances in which that fleet would be used to counter the U.S. offensives; the fact that the striking force was brought out by the Japanese in mid-June to engage our forces in defense of the Marianas—all these factors, and many others combined to provide the background of subsequent intelligence bearing more directly on probable Japanese reactions to Blue landings in the Philippines. By September it was clear that the striking force . . . had been readied for use in the immediate future. The 7th Fleet Intelligence Officer, in a Staff memo on 24 September, estimated that the 2 diversion attack forces comprising the tactical organization of the First Mobile Fleet would be utilized for the defense of the Philippines.

The Battle of Leyte Gulf was a huge naval engagement that was fought, at the same time, all over Philippine waters. In reality it consisted of four separate engagements between the opposing forces, forces that were hundreds of nautical miles apart from each other: (1) the Battle of the Sibuyan Sea, (2) the Battle of Surigao Strait, (3) the Battle of Cape Engaño; and (4) the Battle off Samar, as well as other actions. It was the first battle in which Japanese aircraft carried out organized kamikaze attacks.[10,11] By the time of the battle, Japan had fewer aircraft than the Allied Forces had sea vessels, demonstrating the difference in power between the two sides at this point of the war.[12]

Approach of Enemy Naval Forces

Definite indications that the enemy was approaching the Philippines in force came from sightings of powerful enemy naval units by U.S. picket submarines previously assigned to search the waters off Borneo and Palawan.[13,14] Admiral Shima was nearing Coron Bay. Admiral Ozawa's task force was prowling the waters of the Formosa-Philippine Sea area, although he had not yet been located. The fourth unit of the Japanese naval forces converging on the Philippines, Vice Adm. Shoji Nishimura's Southern Force, had also not been sighted by midnight of 23 October.

On 24 October, however, the various pieces of the Japanese naval puzzle were gradually pieced together.[15] Early in the morning US carrier planes reported that the Japanese Central Force, consisting of five fast battleships including the mysterious and dangerous 72,000-ton monsters *Yamato* and *Musashi*, 12 accompanying cruisers, and 15 destroyers were moving towards Tablas Strait.[16] The Southern Force, consisting of several battleships and cruisers, under Admiral Nishimura, was sighted off Cagayan Islands.[17,18] In the meantime Admiral Shima, with a small force of three cruisers and four destroyers, sailed southward from Coron Bay.[19]

The Americans could avail of the 7th Fleet commanded by Vice Admiral Thomas C. Kinkaid,[20] and the 3rd Fleet, commanded by Admiral William F. Halsey, Jr. A fundamental defect in the American plan was there would be no single American admiral in overall command. By coincidence, the Japanese plan, using three separate fleets, also lacked an overall commander.

The Center Force (Adm. Kurita) was spotted around 0800 on 24 October, entering the Sibuyan Sea and was attacked by carrier aircraft from USS *Enterprise* of Halsey's 3rd Fleet. Despite its great strength, 3rd Fleet was not well placed to deal with the threat. On the morning of 24 October, only three groups were available to strike Kurita's force.[21] They did this with remarkable success. After some of his battleships were hit and damaged by carrier planes, Kurita turned his fleet around to get out of range of the aircraft. For the huge battleship *Musashi,* the pride of the Japanese Imperial Fleet, it would be the last performance in the war. After being struck by at least 17 bombs and 19 torpedoes *Musashi* finally capsized and sank at about 1930, 24 October 1944. She sank in deep water about seven nautical miles west of Bontoc Point in the Sibuyan Sea.[22,23]

In the meantime, Admiral Nishimura's Southern Force sailed on into the Mindanao Sea and passed the south coast of Bohol despite the fact that it had been sighted and attacked off Cagayan Island.[24] Admiral Kinkaid had dispatched Rear Adm. Jesse B. Oldendorf to intercept and destroy the approaching Japanese warships.[25] Admiral Oldendorf took full advantage of both the geography of the battle area and his foreknowledge to form the classic horizontal bar to a "T" of vast firepower which the enemy would be forced to approach vertically as he moved forward.[26] The ambush worked perfectly.[27] Admiral Nishimura's force was mortally crippled, virtually every unit in the formation either sunk or badly damaged. Only a lone destroyer, the *Shigure*, managed to survive the incredible carnage.[28]

After brief blinker contact with the single surviving destroyer of Admiral Nishimura's fleet, Admiral Shima retired southeastward into the Mindanao Sea and headed for Coron Bay. With the destruction of the Japanese Southern Force, the southern entrance to Leyte Gulf had been successfully closed and General MacArthur no longer had to fear a Japanese naval threat from the south. However, Admiral Halsey misinterpreted the situation.[29] Based on (faulty) reports from aviators, Admiral Halsey believed the Kurita's Central Force was neutralized by the 3rd Fleet's airstrikes. He decided to move his entire force northward as a unit to intercept the Japanese carriers and leave Admiral Kinkaid to deal with the Southern Force. Admiral Kinkaid and his staff, however, assumed that Vice Admiral Lee was guarding San Bernardino Strait. But Lee's battleships were on their way northwards with the 3rd Fleet's carriers. Halsey had consciously and deliberately left San Bernardino Strait absolutely unguarded.[30, 31]

Kurita's Center Force therefore emerged unopposed from San Bernardino Strait at 0300 on 25 October 1944 and steamed southward along the coast of Samar Island. Admiral Kurita's Central Force had suffered considerable damage in its course across the Sibuyan Sea, losing for instance the enormous *Musashi*, but it was still a formidable fleet when it broke through San Bernardino Strait and headed for Leyte Gulf.[32] In Kurita's path stood only three groups of escort carriers with a total of 16 small, very slow, and unarmored escort carriers. In command was Admiral Thomas L. Sprague.[33] Kurita's force caught the escort carriers entirely by surprise. The light carriers

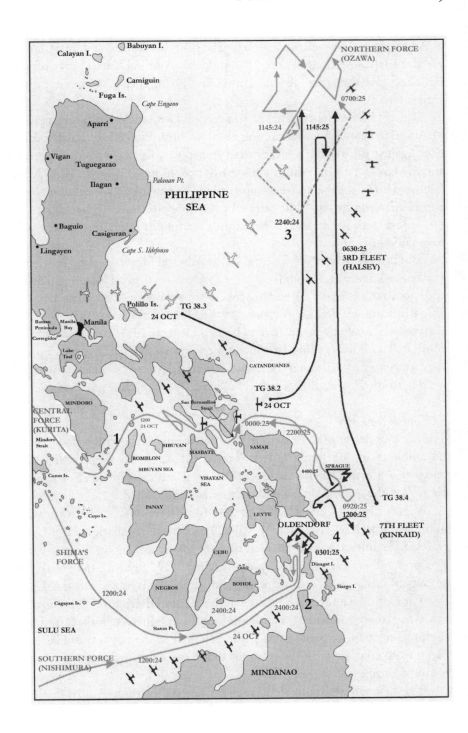

of Admiral Sprague were no match for the giant battleships and heavy cruisers of the Japanese Central Force. But suddenly Admiral Kurita broke off the fight and gave the order "all ships, my course north, speed 20," apparently to regroup his fleet.

Kurita's battle report stated he had received a message indicating a group of American carriers was steaming north of him. Preferring to expend his fleet against capital ships rather than transports, Kurita set out in pursuit and thereby lost his opportunity to destroy the shipping in Leyte Gulf. After failing to intercept the non-existent carriers, Kurita finally retreated towards San Bernardino Strait.[34] The retreat of Kurita was a total surprise. If he had pressed on with his attacks, MacArthur's landing in Leyte might very well have ended in a disaster.

But it was not over yet. There still was Admiral Ozawa and his Northern Force to take care of. Around dawn on 25 October, Ozawa launched 75 aircraft to attack the 3rd Fleet. Most were shot down by American combat air patrols, and no damage was done to the US ships. A few Japanese planes survived and made their way to land bases on Luzon. In return, US air strikes continued until the evening, by which time they had flown 527 sorties against the Northern Force, sinking three carriers and a destroyer. Ozawa transferred his flag to the light cruiser *Kyodo*. The battle of Leyte Gulf was over.[35]

The Battle for Leyte

The decisive defeat of the enemy fleet in the waters of the Philippines meant the failure of only one phase of Japan's threefold plan for disrupting the Allied invasion of Leyte. Despite the loss of the naval battle, Japanese efforts in the air and on the ground intensified rather than diminished.

Vigorous enemy air assaults began in the afternoon of 24 October with numerous low-level attacks upon Allied beachhead installations. But General MacArthur's troops continued to drive inland and along the coast in a two-pronged attack and envelopment. After heavy fighting they took the key city of Carigara. The strategic consequences of this move were described by Major Chuji Kaneko, staff officer of the 102nd Division:[36] "This surprise maneuver caught us off guard and upset the Thirty-fifth Army's plans to recapture Tacloban, since our units advancing on Tacloban by way of Carigara had now to contend with these troops that had established positions to the south of Carigara."

The Japanese were unable to retake Carigara. In the words of General

Tomochika, "The loss of Carigara was a stunning blow to Japanese defense plans, especially to the 16th Division, whose main force was in the Dagami area, because Carigara was a key center of supply and communication to the entire Leyte Valley. Furthermore Carigara was important as a port for direct supplies by sea from Luzon. . . ."[37]

According to the interrogation after the war of Col. Junkichi Okabayashi,[38] Chief of Staff, Japanese 1st Division, the Japanese planned to use two newly arrived divisions in a drive northwestward to secure the Carigara-Jaro sector. It did not work out properly, and step by step MacArthur's forces drove them back. Organized enemy resistance in Leyte was finally brought to an end. On 25 December, the last connecting road between the enemy's chief remaining port of entry for reinforcements and his troops inland was severed.[39] General MacArthur now controlled all major supply and communication routes of the enemy, and on Christmas Day, albeit somewhat prematurely, he declared Leyte secure.

Aftermath

The campaign for Leyte proved the first and most decisive operation in the American reconquest of the Philippines, and it cost American forces a total of 15,584 casualties, of which 3,504 were killed in action. Australian casualties included 30 dead and 64 wounded when a *kamikaze* plane crashed into the heavy cruiser HMAS *Australia* during the Gulf Battle.

The Japanese lost an estimated 49,000 combat troops in their failed defense of Leyte. Their losses at Leyte were heavy, with the army losing four full divisions and several separate combat units, while the navy lost 26 major warships and 46 large transports and hundreds of merchantmen in the campaign.

The struggle also reduced Japanese land-based air capability in the Philippines by more than 50%, forcing them to depend on *kamikaze* pilots. Some 250,000 troops still remained on Luzon, but the loss of air and naval support at Leyte so narrowed Gen. Yamashita's options that he now had to fight a defensive, almost passive battle of attrition on Luzon, the largest and most important island in the Philippines. In effect, once the decisive battle of Leyte was lost, the Japanese gave up hope of retaining the Philippines, conceding to the Allies in the process a critical bastion from which Japan could be easily cut off from outside resources, and from which the final assaults on the Japanese home islands could be launched.[40]

CHAPTER 22
THE LIBERATION OF CEBU

T HE SUDDEN ADVANCEMENT of the date for the Leyte invasion, as a result of the capture of Japan's "Plan Z," had necessitated certain revisions in General MacArthur's original scheme. A final MUSKETEER III plan was prepared on 26 September, covering operations to take place as soon as the seizure of Leyte was successfully accomplished.[1]

Under the new plan the first operation scheduled to follow the initial entry into the Philippines was the seizure of southwest Mindoro, contemplated for 5 December 1944. The full-scale invasion of Luzon, with landings along Lingayen Gulf, was projected for 20 December, when it was expected that the airfields on Mindoro would be ready for use. A preliminary attack at Aparri, in northern Luzon, was also tentatively outlined. This last operation, however, would take place only if carrier-borne aircraft could insure uninterrupted transit of naval assault shipping around northern Luzon should such an alternate route be chosen.

Concurrent with these operations, all other available Southwest Pacific forces were to undertake the consolidation of the Visayas, Mindanao, Palawan and the Sulu Archipelago. It was planned that the Eighth Army would conduct these mop-up campaigns with such assistance as could be obtained from guerrilla units organized throughout the central and southern Philippines.[2]

Due to stiff resistance on Leyte, MacArthur's troops landed ten days later, on 15 December, on the southwest corner of the Island of Mindoro. The postponement of the Mindoro operation to 15 December caused a corresponding delay in the Lingayen Gulf landing, originally set for 20 December. A new target date, 9 January 1945, was chosen to give time for the reorganization of forces and for the establishment of airfields on Mindoro.

The Jungle Air Force

The American landings in Leyte caused an outburst of joy in Cebu. Finally they would be freed from the hated Japanese. While the fight on Leyte continued, the Cebu Area Command was still on the job. The air warning net of coastal watchers was especially active in spotting Japanese reinforcements on their way to Leyte.

Later Colonel Jim Cushing was called to Leyte. Still unaware of the developments in Australia prompted by the captured documents, and burdened by the thought that he might be facing at least a serious reprimand, if not court martial, for releasing the Japanese prisoners, Jim plodded on to face the music. He, and many others, was not sure if he had really been reduced in rank to a private. If it was true what would be the value of a private to General MacArthur? Why was he then summoned to Leyte? Jim did not know what to think. He made his way over the rugged hills, the plains and the sea to the Island of Leyte. It was a difficult, long and hazardous journey.

In the absence of their leader and in the face of so many unsolved doubts, the guerrilla activities in Cebu came virtually to a standstill. The men sat on hillsides, leaned against trees and smoked in silence. What were they? Bandits? What was the status of the recognition accorded them by General MacArthur, a recognition that came too uncertainly and so late? After Leyte, when the Allied fight for liberation reached Cebu, what of the Cebu guerrillas?

When Jim returned the doubts soon disappeared. He was still wearing his shoulder insignias as a colonel and his grin was wider than usual. He had little to say, which was his nature anyway, but what he said counted. What he got from Leyte, other than the business of war, was possibly the greatest surprise of his life—it was one terse but clear statement, straight from General Douglas MacArthur:

> Had the Cebu Area Command done nothing else but turn in the documents that would have been more than enough reason for its existence!

This sentence, carried by word of mouth, soon swept across the bloodied hills of Cebu into the hearts and minds of every Cebu guerrilla and became transfixed there like a gold medal. Their sacrifices in blood and lives, their trials and supreme efforts, had hastened the liberation of the Philippines from the Japanese.

They finally also were told the real identity of the Japanese officer they had captured on the beaches of San Fernando. It was not General or Admiral Furomei, Commander of Japanese Land and Sea Forces at Makassar, but in reality Vice-Admiral Shigeru Fukudome, Chief of Staff of the Imperial Combined Fleet of Japan, next in line to the Fleet Commander, Admiral Mineichi Koga. But in Cebu there was still doubt over the dead body on the beach in San Fernando. Why did the surviving crew of the ill-fated Japanese seaplane treat the body with such honor?[3] Could it have been Admiral Koga after all?

It was a great disappointment when they heard from their commander that it might take months before they would be liberated. General MacArthur was sticking to his island-hopping principle. After Leyte, Mindoro would be the next destination, than on to Lingayen Gulf on Luzon Island and southward to Manila, then northward to the northern point of Luzon Island. The Visayan Islands were last on the list. It might be March or even later when their turn would come. In the meantime their work would not change; as long as there were Japanese to be fought there would be war. It was the job of the resistance movement to harass the enemy as much as possible, and that was what they were going to do. But there was something new and completely unexpected. The guerrillas were going to get their own secret air force. The men were shocked and flabbergasted at the same time. Cebu Area Command its own air force? How was that possible? Jim Cushing had a lot to explain.[4]

Jim explained to his men that there was an old airstrip in Tuburan, on Cebu's northwest coast. That strip could be used for fighter planes of the US Thirteenth Air Force (13 AF) a special air force for command, control, delivering and assessing air, space, and information operations in the Visayas region. The 13th Airforce was nicknamed the *Jungle Air Force*. The main unit worked from Tacloban airport, Leyte, but for fast and immediate action the use of the old Tuburan airstrip might be very handy. Jim's men were listening open-mouthed; nobody had ever thought about this. Only very few of Jim's men knew there was an airstrip in Tuburan. Marine Fighter Attack Squadron 115 was going to be the unit to use Tuburan. The planned date for arrival of the Air Support Party was set for 15 February 1945. There was a lot of work to do to make the strip ready for the first plane. It was work that had to be done in secrecy because the Japanese had eyes everywhere.[5]

With hundreds of volunteers they went to work on the airstrip in Tuburan. The strip had not been used for many years; it was overgrown with scrub and there were many holes to be filled. But by the end of the first week of February Jim was satisfied. The first plane could land.

From the air, Cebu held no inviting charms for the 11-man Air Support Party circling Tuburan strip. To begin with, the rugged strip, two-thirds of the way up the west coast of the pollywog-shaped island, had been hastily readied by the guerrillas. It looked like something out of *Terry and the Pirates*. The inland area of the island, as they saw from the air, was dominated by ridges rising to 3,500 feet and full of uninviting jungle. A main road girdled the lowlands along the shore with occasional dead-end tributaries to the foothills. Nearly all the towns were along the main road, but most of them looked as if they were full of Japs.

When the support party of the 13th Air Force landed safely in two fully loaded C-47s on the rough airstrip, guerrillas hurried to unload the equipment. It wasn't much, just a jeep-mounted radio control system and a trailer of supplies. After a very short stop the C-47s took off again and the party was on its own.

Commander of the support party was Captain Edward M. Thomson, who was accompanied by 1st Lieutenant Thomas Muldoon from Jersey City, 1st Lieutenant Thomas Larkin from New York City, and eight operators and drivers. Their job was to guide US warplanes to specific targets on the ground. The support party's operator used air photos of the target area and/or descriptions of the target from actual ground observation. This was supplemented with other information from the guerrilla officers and observers familiar with the target. The radio jeeps were brought as close to the target as possible. The eleven Americans were the first new US faces to be seen on Cebu in three years. It was 15 February 1945.[6]

"We shall never forget that welcome," the detachment leader, Capt. Thompson, recalls. "People cheered us all along our route. When the jeep stopped they offered us their food—eggs, chickens, bananas, pork, tuba—and with tears of joy in their eyes, crowded around to touch us. They walked for miles to see Americans."[7]

Jim Cushing explained the ground situation, which was ripe for action. A strong force of Japanese was in the area north of an east-west road slicing the neck of the island. Other forces held the east coast, with their main body in Cebu City. The Americans were quite surprised that Colonel Cushing, they found out, had a tattered but well-trained guerrilla army, its equipment limited to small arms. In earlier days they had made shotguns with pipe barrels—using almost anything that could be fired as ammunition. Later they added rifles supplied by the 8th Army and 4,000 pieces captured from the Japs. There were a few .50 calibers with homemade mounts, salvaged from crashed planes. Hundreds of guerrillas formed the Volunteer Guard service group. They hauled supplies to the front with a few pre-war trucks fueled with Japanese gas or alcohol distilled from tuba, the juice of the palm tree.

The Americans were also surprised to see how Jim's organization worked. In every town, womens' groups fostered by Mrs. Cushing functioned as volunteer auxiliaries. They fed the army, sewed their ragged uniforms, and nursed the injured. Food and quarters were obtained in house-to-house fashion. Nothing was denied the soldiers; no questions were asked concerning payment. Colonel Cushing's ground strategy was to let the Japanese take any specific objective they wanted, then harass them by hemming them in, picking off expeditions and severing communication lines. It was quite effective. Compared to neighboring islands the guerrilla activities in Cebu were substantial. Thousands of Japanese soldiers had died in the skirmishes; it was a real war that was being fought on Cebu.[8]

With the arrival of the Air Support Party, the concentration of Japanese troops in the north was given first priority. "You're going close to the Jap lines," Colonel Cushing told the team. "But don't worry, Major Hale's MP battalion is assigned to you for security, and every man will fight to the last ditch to protect you and your equipment."

On the first night, 300 Volunteer Guards built a road and hauled the jeep and trailer up the hills to a summit overlooking the Tabuelan-Lugo Road. On the morning of 16 February radio contact with the Leyte headquarters of the 13th Air Force was accomplished. Everything was ready for the start of the operations.

Home and workshop for the control team was a grass shack topping a hill overlooking the target area. Gathered around a bamboo table were the controller, guerrilla intelligence and operations officers, and skilled technicians. Equipment, besides the radio jeep, consisted of an LS-3 speaker, grid maps from headquarters intelligence, penciled maps drawn by residents of the target area, photo reconnaissance pictures, and a pair of 7x50 field glasses.

Four F4U Corsairs of Marine Group 12 came over the first day and their flight leader called in to the station. After the flight was authenticated, the controller flipped one earphone for the guerrilla liaison to hear, and clarified the target for the pilots. Checking back, the flight leader described the target as he saw it—an estimated 500 Japs in Lugo, Liki and surrounding palm groves. Guerrilla liaison satisfied, the flight was sent in to bomb and strafe.[9]

The next day four flights of four Corsairs peppered concentrations in Lugo, Liki and Sogod. On 19 February an operator standing by on the telephone system rigged of barbed wire received a message: "The advance guard of a Jap column will be at the Carmen-Sogod Bridge at 1420." The operations officer glanced at his watch. It was 1400. He handed the message to the controller. Three flights were expected that day; only two had appeared. A longshot, blind message went out over VHF.

"Hello. Hello. Any flights in area needed at once. Report to controller. Report to controller. Over."

An answering voice came from the third scheduled flight—from over the Camotes.

"Hello, controller. Hello, controller. Will be with you in 15 minutes. Over."

At 1420 on the button, the four Corsairs bombed and strafed Carmen-Sogod Bridge and the land around it. Twenty minutes later, the telephone monitor handed another message to the operations officer: "Jap advance guard wiped out by planes at bridge. Main body turned back into Rough Riders ambush. Thank you."

Timing had been perfect, the Jap attempt to reinforce Lugo prevented. Four days later, the guerrilla 88th Regiment under Col. Alexandro Almendras took Lugo with but one casualty. He sent back a runner with the report that the town's approaches were dotted with fresh graves, blood and a pile of burning bodies. North Cebu was under control. Cebu City was next on Colonel Cushing's list.

When guerrilla forces formed their pressure block against Cebu City from the west, the fighter control team and its equipment had to be moved 50 mountainous miles to Dacit Ridge, four miles north of the capital city. Almost like magic, 1,000 Volunteer Guards materialized and the trek was started. Most of the way there had been no road, but the guards had built one. In some places there was too much mountain. The guards harnessed jeep and trailer with ropes, bodily hoisted them up the side of cliffs, and lowered them down mud-slithering walls. They made the trip in the almost incredible time of 30 hours. Behind was a barbed wire telephone line of 35 miles. Aerial pummeling of Cebu installations began at once. Indicating a healthy respect for American bombing, the Japs disposed troops around unlikely targets, like Guadalupe church.

Their stores were in tunnels and caves. The controller called for 1,000-pound GP and jellied fire bombs. Installations were burned and mauled, and then the target shifted to dispositions facing guerrilla lines. For the safety of the guerrillas, ground markers came into play. Panel sheets were laid out to designate both friendly positions and the Japanese. When the enemy imitated the panels to confuse the pilots, the guerrillas outfoxed them with a variety of symbols. As an added precaution to assure precision bombing, the controller often had pilots drop one test bomb. With any corrections necessary, the next run delivered the works. At times, close-in strafing was controlled by a guerrilla observer in a P-61 Black Widow. It worked well. The Lightnings or Corsairs would track on behind the Black Widow and head on the target.[10]

During February, 402 combat missions and 1,116 total hours were flown, most of which were for ground support or escort flights over Cebu, with some sorties using napalm bombs. A number of new pilots joined the squadron, as veterans were rotated back to the United States.

A unique mission occurred on 23 February. Major Eldon H. Railsback, executive officer of VMF-115; First Lieutenant Paul Chambers; Second Lieutenant Robert O. Bunce; and Second Lieutenant Charles B. Collin spotted two small Japanese submarines on the surface while on a bombing and strafing mission at Cebu City.

Missing the submarines on their first attack, they returned to base and received permission to go back for a second try. Fully rearmed, they attacked in runs at a 20–25 foot altitude, skip-bombing their 1,000-pound bombs. One submarine was hit, "probably the first submarine sunk by a Corsair," the squadron war diary noted. The next day, on a sortie to bomb Japanese antiaircraft positions near the airstrip at Cebu City, the plane of Second Lieutenant John E. Dixon was hit. His report gave a firsthand account:

"When advised by a wingman that my Corsair was smoking, I looked at my oil pressure. It read zero. The plane began to stall. I suppose I had been hit somewhere by Jap 12.7's. I ascertained that all switches were on so that the plane would blow up on crashing, and promptly prepared to bail out. To prevent banging my leg on the tail assembly, I grasped the trailing edge of my right wing, suspended myself from there by my hands, and from the cockpit by my toes, and pushed myself down. The tail assembly went a good six feet over my head. I bailed out at 1,200 feet, and the chute opened at 500 feet. The wind blew me from my position over Jap lines 100 yards into guerrilla territory. I landed among bamboo trees and dangled twelve feet above the ground. The straps unfastened easily, and I dropped to the ground and ran like hell toward the guerrilla lines, while the other three Corsairs continued strafing the enemy, keeping them down. Unarmed volunteer guards [guerrillas] met me and escorted me to guerrilla headquarters." Lieutenant Dixon returned to his squadron four days later.[11]

By 12 March the Japanese command had apparently decided something must be done about the accuracy of the fighter-bombers. One way was to choke off Tuburan strip—both a supply funnel and emergency landing field—and maybe corral the support team in the hills. The move to Tuburan would also relieve pressure on Cebu City. A message reached the air support team from Colonel Cushing: "Proceed at once to Tuburan strip; 1,500 Japs with 500 reserves are attacking."

When the team arrived, the Japs were four miles away and the field socked in. Leyte had planes, but it, too, was weathered in. On the field were two F4Us which had flown dusk patrol the night before and set down at Tuburan on bad weather reports from Leyte. The pilot's decision to stay over was influenced somewhat by the prospect of guerrilla-cooked chicken and steak.

With a ceiling under 1,000 feet, their planes rearmed with ammunition from crash-landed aircraft, they made one pass on the Jap lines. That was that—they had no more starting cartridges to get up again. The Nips had been scattered but they were reforming for another assault. Even the guerrilla regimental commander—outnumbered and outgunned—was ready to admit the strip was doomed. Suddenly two lone P-38s of the Jungle Air Force Ringmaster Group winged over, heading home after a cover mission. Just on a chance, the controller contacted them.[12]

"Have you gas and ammunition enough to handle an emergency mission for us?"

"Roger!"

Orbiting the battleline, the pilots were briefed on the most difficult target there is—a zig-zag line, something like this:

"See that bridge and tall tree beside it?"

"From there to the schoolhouse. See?"

"School house. Roger."

"Then to where the third creek empties into the river."

"Roger."

"Now back to a point crossing the road at the bridge by the crossroads."

Finally the jigsaw was traced. The steeplechase was on. On the second pass, a pilot's jubilant voice came in.

"Hey! There's a whole mob of guys running down the road headed north."

The controller: "It can only be Japs—go get 'em!"

The pilot, a moment later: "Whoopie! Look at 'em go."

When the pilots came back, one called, "I'm on my return run and they're still lying all over the road."

Those two pilots saved the strip. What was left of 2,000 Japs were scattered so badly the guerrillas took a two-day rest. From then on, there was no peace for the Japanese; they were herded back to their enclaves by fighter planes and heel-sniping guerrillas.[13]

On 21 March 1945 Guerrilla Team No. 1 received its final communication from headquarters:

Have your team at Tuburan 0830, 23 March, to be lifted up this headquarters.

There was no doubt of the mission's success, despite being one of the first of its kind, in the face of adverse weather and terrain and against a better armed, numerically stronger ground force. Reasons boiled down to radio equipment, which was operational the entire 37 days, guerrilla liaison, which was fast and accurate on vital targets, and pilot savvy.[14]

Before the the Jungle Air Force left, arrangements were made to construct an extra airstrip in Lusaran Valley, a place close to Cebu City that was fed by two small rivers. The purpose of this strip was to serve small spotter planes for the big guns, the 105s and 155s, or Long Toms, and the guns on the Navy ships that were going to cover the landing of the Americal Division at Talisay beach on 26 March 1945. These L-4 spotter planes had only a limited range and for them Tuburan was too far.[15]

Preparing Cebu's Liberation

General Robert L. Eichelberger's Eighth Army was tasked with the recapture of the Visayan Islands, including Cebu.[16] Prior to the war, Cebu had been the Philippines' second-most important industrial centre, and it offered the Allies a harbor for future operations.[17] The second purpose of the Cebu operation was therefore to secure an additional staging base for an eventual assault on Japan, adequate to mount a corps of three reinforced divisions: the Americal Division, and, upon their redeployment from Europe, the 44th and 97th Infantry Divisions.[18] Airfield development on Cebu would be limited to that required to provide a small base for transport and evacuation aircraft.

Two areas of operation were suggested to divide the entire Visyas region: *Victor I* and *Victor II*. Operation Victor I concerned the recapture of the island of Panay, Operation Victor II the seizure of Cebu and Bohol. The Americal Division under Maj. Gen. William Arnold was tasked by Gen. Eichelberger for the operation.

The Americal Division numbered nearly 14,900 men. The division proper was understrength; it lacked one Regimental Combat Team (RCT). Already tired from arduous mopping-up operations on Leyte, the division received only the rest that its hurried loading operations afforded. General Arnold, commanding the Americal, expected considerable help from Cebu guerrillas under Colonel Jim Cushing, who had about 8,500 men available in his Cebu Area Command.

The Japanese Defenses of Cebu

There was good reason for Arnold to hope for guerrilla aid. He expected to encounter around 12,250 Japanese on Cebu, an estimate close to the actual strength—14,500—of the Japanese garrison.[19]

Roughly 12,500 Japanese were deployed in and near Cebu City, while another 2,000, under Maj. Gen. Takeo Manjome, held positions in far northern Cebu. Trained ground combat strength was low. At Cebu City there were less than 1,500 Army ground combat troops, most of them members of the reinforced 173d IIB, 102d Division. Naval ground combat strength at Cebu City totaled 300 men, all from the 36th Naval Guard Unit, 33d Naval Special Base Force. In northern Cebu the combat element numbered about 750 men of the 1st Division, who had recently arrived from Leyte. Finally, the 14,500 Japanese on Cebu included about 1,700 noncombatant civilians. The Japanese commander of Cebu was General Sosaku Suzuki, commander of the 35th Army.

General Suzuki, when he reached Cebu from Leyte on 24 March, immediately took steps to centralize the command. Assuming control of all forces on Cebu, Suzuki made General Manjome *de jure* commander in the Cebu City region and left General Kataoka in control in the north. At the end of the month Suzuki went north to prepare for his ill-fated attempt to escape to Mindanao, leaving Manjome complete discretion in the Cebu City sector. Manjome's command also embraced Japanese forces on Bohol Island and southern Negros.

Manjome designed his defenses so as to control—not hold—the coastal plains around Cebu City, and for this purpose set up defenses in-depth north and northwest of the city. The inner defense lines were a system of mutually supporting machinegun positions in caves, pillboxes and bunkers. Many of these positions had been completed for months and had acquired natural camouflage. Manjome's troops had an ample supply of small arms and machineguns, and employed remounted aircraft and antiaircraft weapons. Manjome had some light and heavy mortars, but only a few pieces of light (70-mm. and 75-mm.) artillery.[20]

Before the landing the Allies, in mid-March 1945, could have the assistance in Cebu of the following units: the 85th, 86th, 87th and 88th Infantry Regiments, the MP Battalion and the Rough Riders Company of the Cebu Area Command. These guerrilla units had control over most of the land area and were eager to get into full-scale action with the American forces for the recapture of their island. The Cebu Area Command was redesignated the 82nd Infantry Division, Philippine Army, with Colonel Jim Cushing as its commander.

The 87th Inf. Regt. was given the mission to clear southern Cebu Island of the enemy. The regiment made a sweep northward to the Talisay-Toledo boundary. The timetable required that the regiment be in the vicinity of Barrio Buhisan, Cebu City, by the 25th of March 1945. Lt. Col. Abel Trazo, who commanded the regiment, was handicapped by the absence of his 3rd Battalion under Major Llanos, which was still mopping up in the southeastern Cebu area in the vicinity of Sibonga, and his 2nd Battalion under Captain Ricardo Mascariñas, which was attached to the 88th Inf. Regt. operating in the north. This left him with the 1st Battalion under Captain Eutiquio Acebes as well as the headquarters battalion. Barrio Buhisan was important because of the location of the Cebu City water supply system.[21] There were rumors that the Japanese intended to poison the water reservoir in Buhisan. This had to be prevented.

Landing at the Beaches of Talisay

After an hour's bombardment by three light cruisers and six destroyers of Admiral Berkey's Task Force 74, leading waves of the 132d and 182d Infantry Regiments, aboard LVT's, landed unopposed on beaches just north of Talisay at 0830 on 26 March 1944. Within minutes confusion began to pervade what had started out to resemble an administrative landing. Japanese mines, only a few yards beyond the surf line, knocked out ten of the leading fifteen LVT's. Troops in the first two waves halted after about 5 men were killed and 15 wounded from mine explosions, and as subsequent waves came ashore men and vehicles began jamming the beaches.[22]

Colonel Cushing had warned about the existence of minefields at Talisay, and the American Division had sent engineer mine disposal teams ashore with the first waves. The minefields proved quite a problem; they were much more extensive than anticipated. The Japanese had placed 50-kilogram (111-pound) aerial bombs under most of the mines and when these blew they tore LVT's apart and left huge holes in the beach. Appalled by the nature of the explosions, the leading troops were also surprised at how thickly the Japanese had sown the mines, as well as by the fact that the pre-assault naval bombardment had not detonated the bulk of them. The effect was the more serious because the troops had had no previous experience with an extensive and closely planted minefield. Another element of surprise that helped, paradoxically, to halt the troops on the beaches was the complete absence of Japanese resistance. Had a single Japanese machinegun opened fire, it is probable that the leading troops would have struck inland immediately, mines or no mines.[23]

Brig. Gen. Eugene W. Ridings, Assistant Division Commander, found movement at a complete standstill when he came ashore with the second wave. Feeling that commanders already ashore had failed to employ the means available to them to clear the minefields or to find a way through them, General Ridings set men of the 132d Infantry to work probing for and taping routes through the obstacles. This work was under way by the time the last boats of the third wave reached the beach, but it was nearly 1000 before beach traffic was completely unjammed and the advance inland had fully developed.

The air and naval pre-assault bombardments had not destroyed all the Japanese defensive installations in the Talisay area. Had Japanese manned the positions that remained intact, American Division casualties, given the stoppage on the beaches, might well have been disastrous. Luckily for the division, Japanese tactical doctrine at this stage of the war called for withdrawal from the beaches to inland defenses. The few outposts left in the Talisay area evidenced no stomach for sitting through the naval bombardment and had fled when Task Force 74 opened fire. The Japanese had missed an almost unparalleled opportunity to throw an American invasion force back into the sea.[24]

Once past the beach minefields, the American Division's leading units probed cautiously through abandoned defenses as they advanced inland to the main highway to Cebu City. Encountering only one delaying force during the day, the main bodies of the 132d and 182d Infantry Regiments nevertheless halted for the night about a mile and a half south of the city. Patrols entered the city before dark but did not remain for the night. However, the guerrillas of the Cebu Area Command managed to establish that night their headquarters at the Aznar Compound at Urgello Street in downtown Cebu City. The Japanese were in the mountains, the guerrillas were in the city![25] The next day the infantry secured Cebu City against no opposition and on the 28th moved to clear Lahug Airfield, two miles to the northeast.[26]

While maneuvering to take Lahug airfield, the American Division encountered its first strong, organized resistance. Initially, this took the form of machinegun and mortar fire directed against the left of troops moving toward the airfield, but during the afternoon forward elements discovered that Hill 30 and Go Chan Hill, close together a mile north of Cebu City, were infested with Japanese. The 182d Infantry seized Hill 30 after a sharp fight on 28 March and on the next morning launched an attack to clear Go Chan Hill, half a mile to the east.[27] The Japanese, by remote control, blew an ammunition dump located in caves along an eastern spur of the hill. In the resulting explosions Company A, 182d Infantry, lost 20 men killed and 30 wounded; Company B, 716th Tank Battalion, lost one tank and crew and suffered damage to two more tanks. The infantry company, already understrength as the result of long service on Leyte, ceased to exist, and the regiment distributed its survivors among Companies B and C.[28]

In a revengeful mood, almost the entire 182d Infantry returned to the attack on 30 March. All available tanks, artillery, and mortars provided support, and the 40mm weapons of the 478th Antiaircraft Automatic Weapons Battalion joined in. By dusk the 182d had cleared all of Go Chan Hill.[29]

The American forces were assisted by Col. Jim Cushing's guerrilla forces, some 8,500 local Cebuano guerrilla and irregular forces, and Filipino troops

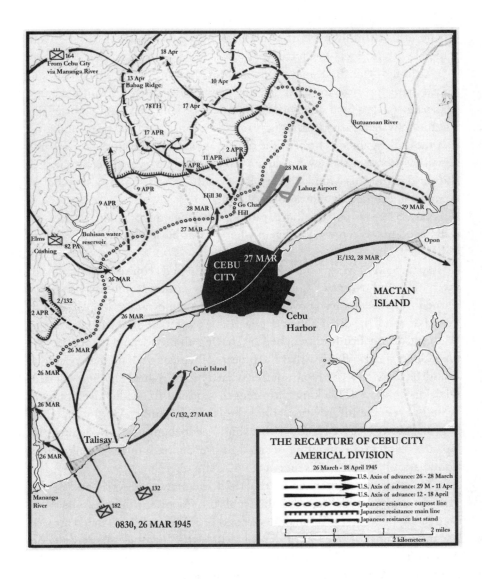

THE RECAPTURE OF CEBU CITY
AMERICAL DIVISION
26 March - 18 April 1945

of the Philippine Commonwealth Army's 3rd, 8th, 81st, 82nd, 85th, 86th and 87th Infantery Divisions and the Philippine Constabulary's 8th Infantery Regiment. Units fought on the outskirts of Cebu, capturing Pari-an on 29 March and liberating T. Padilla on 7 April. As Allied morale heightened and Japanese forces withdrew to the ports, the U.S. naval commander, Ferdinand Ernest Zuellig, directed naval bombardments on the ports, prompting the

Japanese to withdraw to Fort San Pedro. Many did not make it and were trapped within Piers One and Two.[30,31]

Although the final operations around the ports were successful and forced many Japanese to surrender, the Japanese headquarters unit in charge of the area made a final stand near the border of Mandaue City. Led by Major Rijome Kawahara, after further fighting these forces were defeated, and after that the Allies gained control of the remaining areas of the city as Kawahara's remaining troops withdrew. Kawahara was killed while trying to cross a make-shift bridge towards Mandaue City. Reportedly, he was shot by a sniper after being incapacitated by mortar or tank fire.

Kawahara was posthumously promoted to the rank of colonel. After the war, his body was returned to Japan where it was buried in Sapporo, the city of his birth.[32]

By the end of March the Americal Division had acquired a good idea of the nature and extent of General Manjome's principal defenses, and had learned that it had already overrun some of his important strongpoints. On the other hand, the division had not been able to pinpoint the Japanese flanks. With the enemy firmly entrenched and having all the advantages of observation, General Arnold knew that the process of reducing Manjome's positions would be slow and costly no matter what type of maneuver the Americal Division employed. Lacking the strength required for wide envelopments as well as specific information about the Japanese flanks, Arnold hoped he might achieve decisive results with a single sledgehammer blow against the Japanese center. He therefore decided to use the bulk of his strength in a frontal assault into the hills due north of Cebu City.[33,34]

The attack was launched by the 182d Infantry on 1 April, and by the 11th the regiment had reduced almost all the important defensive installations along the center of Manjome's second line. Meanwhile, General Arnold had moved most of the 132d Infantry against the Japanese left. Striking up the west bank of the Butuanoan River and then west from that stream, the 132d, by 11 April, actually turned the Japanese left and reached a point on the extreme left of Manjome's last-stand positions. But the Americal Division, still lacking information on Japanese dispositions in the hinterland, did not recognize the significance of the 132d Infantry's gains and made no immediate provision to exploit the success.[35]

Casualties during the attacks between 1 and 12 April were quite heavy, and as early as the 3rd General Arnold had concluded that he was not going to realize his hopes for quick breakthrough in the Japanese center. He decided that success at a reasonable cost and within a reasonable time required a wide envelopment—as opposed to the 132d Infantry's more or less frontal attack on the Japanese left—and for this purpose he asked General Eichelberger to release the 164th RCT from Eighth Army Reserve and dispatch it to Cebu.

Arnold planned to have the 164th Infantry envelop the Japanese right and right rear via the Mananga River valley. Guerrillas would screen the regiment's movement with operations off the east bank of the Mananga while the 132d and 182d Infantry Regiments would concentrate on the Japanese left, undertaking maneuvers the Japanese would interpret as presaging a major attack from the Butuanoan River. (The 132d Infantry's attack up that river had in large measure been tied to this deception plan.) Finally, Arnold directed the 182d Infantry to employ part of its strength in a holding attack against the Japanese center.[36]

The 164th Infantry, less one battalion, reached Cebu on the 9th and started up the Mananga Valley during the night of 11–12 April. Halting throughout the 12th, the regiment then swung northeast and during the night of 12–13 April moved into position about a mile northwest of the major strongpoint on the right rear of Manjome's last-stand area. Hoping to achieve surprise, the 164th attacked on the morning of 13 April without preliminary artillery bombardment. The Japanese, however, reacted quickly and strongly. The American unit soon lost the element of surprise, and by the end of the day found its outflanking thrust evolving into another frontal assault.[37]

Meanwhile, the 132d and 182d Infantry Regiments had resumed their attacks. The 182d succeeded in overrunning the last strongpoint along the Japanese second line, but the 132d Infantry had made no significant gains by 13 April. All three regiments of the Americal Division now settled down to a series of costly, small unit attacks during which they gained ground painfully, yard by yard, behind close artillery and air support. Finally, on 17 April, organized resistance in the Japanese last-stand area began to collapse, and by evening that day the division had reduced all of Manjome's major strongpoints. The end of organized resistance in the hills north of Cebu City came on the 18th of April 1945.[38]

On 16 April the Americal Division had estimated that Manjome could hold out in his last-stand area for at least another two weeks, and the sudden collapse of organized opposition came as something of a surprise. Unknown to the Americal Division, Manjome had decided about 12 April that further resistance would be futile and had directed a general withdrawal northward to begin during the night of 16–17 April. By the morning of the 17th the withdrawal was well underway, and some 7,500 men managed to extricate themselves in fairly good order. Manjome left behind large stores of ammunition, weapons, and food, and also lost a good many troops as they ran through a gauntlet of 132d Infantry outposts.[39]

Mass Suicide

At some point during the campaign, some 2,000 Japanese women from Palau and the Marianas arrived in a transport and were brought up to Babag. They were civilians, nurses, civilian staff, and many prostitutes. Before Manjome left he told the civilians that they should not allow themselves to be caught alive as they would be abused and brutalized. The next morning they were seen on a fairly level spot on Babag ridge. They were holding bottles of poison. As the sun rose over the eastern skies, they shouted: *"Teno kika, wari wari wa senda aisimas!"* (Emperor Hirohito, we will die in your name!) They all drank from the bottles, but there was not enough poison for all of them. Some 100 survived the ordeal.

Manjome then ordered the non-combatants, some 500 Taiwanese quartermaster soldiers, to surrender. They had no weapons, only sharpened bamboo poles. The remaining 4,000 or 5,000 followed Manjome in the hills.[40]

A pursuit operation was quickly set in motion. The 85th and 86th Infantry Regiments (Philippine Army) were advised of the Japanese withdrawal. On 20 April the 2nd Battalion, 87th Inf. Regt., was picked up in Talisay, to where it had been moved from Sibonga in the south and shipped in small boats to Danao to act as blocking force. The move forestalled Manjome's attempt to join forces with the Japanese 1st Division's remnants in northern Cebu. General Manjome's retreating group was overtaken on the plateau of Danasan, Danao. But he managed to move even farther north. Isolated small Japanese units started to surrender, but the main units kept fighting on and off. Apparently the Japanese did not want to surrender to guerrilla units. Finally they realized they could not escape and surrender feelers were sent out. Col. Almendras was the one who attended. He relayed the messages to Colonel Baura, Chief of Staff of the 82nd Infantry Division, who passed it on to Colonel Jim Cushing, who informed the American Army. Arrangements were finalized and the first field surrender of the Japanese in World

War II, involving altogether some 10,000 troops, took place in the vicinity of Kilometer 82 in northeastern Cebu to Major General William H. Arnold on 28 August, 1945.[41,42] This was 13 days after the surrender of Imperial Japan on 15 August, 1945!

Casualties

The Americal Division estimated that it killed nearly 9,000 Japanese on Cebu from 26 March to 20 June. This figure seems exaggerated, for after the surrender in August 1945 over 8,500 Japanese turned up alive on Cebu.[43] It therefore appears that roughly 5,500 Japanese lost their lives on Cebu from 26 March to the end of the war. The Americal Division, defeating a military force of approximately its own size—the division was considerably outnumbered by the Japanese until the 164th RCT reached Cebu on 9 April—suffered battle casualties totaling roughly 410 men killed and 1,700 wounded. In addition, the division had incurred over 8,000 nonbattle casualties, most resulting from an epidemic of infectious hepatitis. Other tropical diseases also took a toll, and toward the end of the operation, according to the Eighth Army's surgeon, relaxed discipline on Cebu led to an increase in malaria and venereal diseases.[44]

For Cebu the war was over, but the city was in ruins. It would take many years to recover the old glory of Cebu City.

PART FOUR

EPILOGUE

CHAPTER 23

THE END OF WORLD WAR II

The End of the Philippines Campaign

AFTER THE LANDINGS on the beaches of Mindoro and Lingayen Gulf, at the end of 1944 and beginning of 1945, two more major landings followed. One was to cut off the Bataan Peninsula, and another, which included a parachute drop, south of Manila. Pincers closed on the city and, on 3 February 1945, elements of the 1st Cavalry Division pushed into the northern outskirts and the 8th Cavalry passed through the northern suburbs and into the city itself. On 16 February paratroopers and amphibious units assaulted the island fortress of Corregidor, and resistance ended there on 27 February.[1]

The battle for Manila was a costly one. Some 100,000 civilians were killed in February 1945 alone. Its fate was comparable to that of Warsaw during the Second World War, and at the end of the war almost all of the structures in the city, especially in Intramuros, were destroyed.[2]

In all, ten U.S. divisions and five independent regiments battled on Luzon, making it the largest campaign of the Pacific war, involving more troops than the United States had used in North Africa, Italy or southern France. Of the 250,000 Japanese troops defending Luzon, 80 percent died.[3]

Palawan Island was invaded on 28 February with landings of the U.S. Eighth Army at Puerta Princesa. The Eighth Army then moved on to its first landing on Mindanao (17 April), the last of the major Philippine Islands to be taken. Throughout the Philippines, U.S. forces were aided by Filipino guerrillas to find and dispatch the holdouts.

The End of World War II in the Pacific

The Italian dictator Benito Mussolini was killed by Italian partisans on 28

April, 1945.[4] Two days later Hitler committed suicide, and was succeeded by Grand Admiral Karl Dönitz.[5] A few days later World War II in Europe ended. German forces surrendered in Italy on 29 April, and then total and unconditional surrender was signed on 7 May 1945 to be effective by the end of 8 May. But the war in the Pacific went on.[6]

The first step to bringing an end to World War II in the Pacific occurred on 3 February 1945 when the Soviet Union agreed to enter the Pacific conflict. It promised to act 90 days after the war ended in Europe and did so exactly on schedule, on 9 August, by invading Manchuria. A battle-hardened, million-strong Soviet force, transferred from Europe, attacked Japanese forces in Manchuria and quickly defeated the Japanese Kwantung Army Group.[7]

The second step happened on 6 August 1945, when the B-29 Enola Gay dropped an atomic bomb on the Japanese city of Hiroshima, in the first nuclear attack in the history of mankind. On 9 August another was dropped on Nagasaki. More than 240,000 people died as a direct result of these two bombings.[8] The effects of the "Twin Shocks"—the Soviet entry and the atomic bombing—were profound. At noon on 15 August 1945 Emperor Hirohito spoke directly to his subjects for the first time in his reign. His announcement would shock Japan but it would also transform it, altering in a few short minutes the entire mission of the Japanese nation in ways that it, and the world, still feel today. The Emperor told his people that he had accepted the terms of unconditional surrender,[9, 10] ending the Second World War.

Hirohito was more than Japan's head of state. He was its divine monarch and the personification of both the nation and its spiritual imperative for imperial expansion, the literal living embodiment of Japan past and present, a paradigm of moral excellence. Hirohito both embodied and galvanized imperial Japan's race-based nationalism, and the radical militarist ideology that had led it to sow war and much worse across Asia.[11]

The formal end to hostilities in the Pacific came while fighting was still underway in the Philippines. On 15 August 1945, almost 115,000 Japanese—including noncombatant civilians—were still at large on Luzon and the central and southern islands. One Japanese force, the *Shobu Group* in northern Luzon, was still occupying the energies of major portions of three U.S. Army infantry divisions and the USAFIP(NL) as well. Indeed, on 15 August the equivalent of three and two-thirds Army divisions were engaged in active combat against Japanese forces on Luzon, while the equivalent of another reinforced division was in contact with Japanese forces on the central and southern islands. On Luzon the 21,000 guerrillas of the USAFIP(NL) were still in action, and some 22,000 other Luzon guerrillas were engaged in patrolling and mopping-up activities. At least another 75,000 guerrillas were mopping up on the central and southern islands.[12]

The cost had not been light. Excluding the earlier campaign for the seizure of Leyte and Samar, the ground combat forces of the Sixth and Eighth Armies had suffered almost 47,000 battle casualties—10,380 killed and 36,550 wounded—during their operations on Luzon and in the southern Philippines. Nonbattle casualties had been even heavier. From 9 January through 30 June 1945 Sixth Army on Luzon suffered over 93,400 nonbattle casualties, losses that included 86,950 men hospitalized for various types of sickness, 6,200 men injured in various ways, and 260 troops dead of sickness of injury. The bulk of the battle casualties occurred, of course, on Luzon, where the heaviest fighting took place and where the opposing forces had their greatest concentration of strength.[13]

Philippine Guerrillas

One phenomenon of the reconquest of the Philippines was certainly far different from any other experience of the war in the Pacific. That was the presence of a large, organized guerrilla force backed by a generally loyal population waiting only for the chance to make its contribution to the defeat of Japan. It is debatable whether American headquarters was adequately prepared to make the most effective use of the guerrilla forces that existed on Luzon and in the Southern Philippines; it is also questionable whether American forces made the best possible use of the guerrillas after the campaign began. From GHQ SWPA on down through infantry divisions in the field, the orders and plans concerning the guerrillas, as well as the machinery set up at various echelons to control and supply them, indicate that before the invasion of Luzon U.S. forces expected little more of the guerrillas than the acquisition of tactical intelligence and certain types of service support. It appears that in many instances American commanders were reluctant to assign guerrilla units specific combat missions of even the most innocuous sort. Sometimes guerrilla units acquired a combat mission only after they had launched an operation themselves; sometimes, as seems to have been the case with Sixth Army vis-à-vis USAFIP(NL), the combat mission came only after American headquarters realized that they did not have sufficient regular forces to undertake assigned tasks. In any case, it is certain that both the Sixth and the Eighth Army ultimately made more extensive use of guerrillas than was originally contemplated.[14]

It is unfortunately impossible to measure in concrete terms the contribution of guerrilla forces to the outcome of the campaigns. Some units were good; some were not. An occasional guerrilla force, with political aims or under a leader with delusions of grandeur, caused more trouble than it was worth. In the end, however, almost all served in one way or another to the limits of their capabilities. Beyond the shadow of a doubt the guerrillas saved many thousands of American lives.

The story of the Filipino contribution to the final triumph in the Philippines does not end with mention of guerrillas, for thousands of other Filipinos aided the U.S. Army in many capacities. Filipinos contributed services of all types, as railroad men, truck drivers, engineers, clerks, government officials and employees, guides, spies and carriers who often risked their lives hand-carrying supplies to the front lines. There is no doubt that the guerrillas and other Filipinos made the task of the U.S. Army infinitely less difficult. It is indeed difficult to imagine how the Southwest Pacific Area could have undertaken the reconquest of the Philippines in the time and manner it did without the predominately loyal and willing Filipino population.[15]

Philippine Independence

On 4 July 1946, representatives of the United States of America and of the Republic of the Philippines signed a treaty providing for the recognition of the independence of the Republic of the Philippines as of that day, and the relinquishment of American sovereignty.[16]

There were initially numerous strings attached to the independence, however. The U.S. not only retained dozens of military bases, including a few major ones, but also limited Filipino independence via the Bell Trade Act.[17] In 1955 though, nine years after passage of the Act, a revised United States-Philippine Trade Agreement was negotiated to replace it. This treaty abolished, among others, the United States authority to control the exchange rate of the peso. In 1992 the last US military base in the Philippines was closed.[18]

Many East Asian countries that were ruined by war used the rebuilding and reconstruction of their country as a starting point for progress and development. Japan, China, Korea and Taiwan, to name a few, became examples of economic power and success. The Philippines, notwithstanding that Manila was one of Asia's most destroyed cities of World War II, never lived up to its potential after its initial rebuilding. All ingredients for success were and are available. The country has more mineral resources than any of its neighbors, and the population is well educated and English speaking. The problem is purely political, with power continued to be held by a handful of rich and influential families comprising less than 1% of the population. However, signs, as well as hopes, are increasing that eventually the Philippines will join the first rank of successful Pacific nations.

CHAPTER 24
THE OTSU INCIDENT IN HINDSIGHT

VICE ADMIRAL SHIGERU Fukudome was interrogated after the war by Rear Admiral R. A. Ofstie, USN on 9–12 December 1945. About his capture in Cebu he testified as follows[1]

Admiral Ofstie:

What directives were issued or what action was taken when the American Task Force was first picked up approaching PALAU near the end of March?

Admiral Fukudome:

The first information regarding the approach of the Task Force was brought by scouting planes from TRUK on the 28th and repeated on the 29th, but since the number of reconnaissance planes was small, we could not learn from that source whether they had seen the whole Task Force or only a part. By noon of the 29th, we estimated that the Task Force attack would begin on the 30th; so all the ships, including merchant ships, were moved out and the Second Fleet was ordered to stand by ready for action. As already stated, we could not judge on the basis of information at hand whether this would be a repetition of earlier brief air attacks or if it was the beginning of a massive-scale advance towards what we called the last line of defense; so the order was issued for each local commander to defend with such force as he had locally and to watch developments. Should the enemy thrust be concentrated in any one locality, the subsequent concentrations would be ordered.

Admiral Ofstie:

Briefly, what were the results and what were the effects of the Task Force strike on PALAU on 31 March?

Admiral Fukudome:

On the morning of the 30th, the situation suggested that we might have a Task Force attack on PALAU, and an air raid did take place on PALAU by part of the Task Force air force. Our scouting planes in the MARIANAS and West CAROLINES went out but reported that they saw nothing in the morning; but in the afternoon of that day, it was reported that a large transport group was proceeding westward from the ADMIRALTY Islands. We therefore estimated that no attack was intended against the MARIANAS, but rather against the Western CAROLINES, which would constitute the southern part of the area to which Admiral KOGA referred as the line of defence. In other words, that your Task Force might undertake a landing in Western NEW GUINEA. That estimate was furnished on the basis of two facts—that on the 30th a part of the Task Force which attacked PALAU kept on going westward, and that this large transport group was seen proceeding west from the ADMIRALTIES.

Admiral Ofstie:

What subsequently developed?

Admiral Fukudome:

The measures adopted by Admiral KOGA to meet this new development were as follows: first, most of the fighter planes in the MARIANAS were moved to PALAU, but the attack planes were left behind because an attack could be made from that position. Second, Admiral OZAWA's training fleet—air fleet in SINGAPORE, was ordered to proceed to DAVAO by 2 April, because these planes, although not sufficiently trained for effective use in support of fleet operations, could be used from land bases. It was intended that from DAVAO these planes should proceed further south to be used against the landing anticipated in the western part of NEW GUINEA. Admiral KOGA himself, in pursuance of his plan to command and guide the operations from a central position in the southern area in case the next American thrust should be directed southward, went to DAVAO on the evening of 31 March, leaving the command in the MARIANAS and Western CAROLINES to Vice Admiral NAGUMO, CinC Central PACIFIC Fleet. It was in the course of this flight to DAVAO on the evening of the 31st that he met death in the air accident. Regarding the air combat and results, the majority of the planes that participated in the air combat belonged to the First Air FLeet, and as those planes had been fairly well-trained, Admiral KOGA himself placed considerable reliance on them, but as it turned out the results did not come up to his expectations. The fighters that were sent out from PALAU were virtually wiped out. The other planes were hardly more successful, and the anticipated landing in the south did not materialize, so that the operations upon which Admiral KOGA had staked his very life ended in utter failure.

Admiral Ofstie:

Describe briefly the arrangements for the movement of the staff, and the result of those flights.

Admiral Fukudome:

The original plan was that Headquarters should be in SAIPAN in case the major American thrust should be in the region of the MARIANAS and Western CAROLINES, and in DAVAO in case of a thrust further south. Plans had been made as to where the planes and personnel should be obtained in both cases. Admiral KOGA decided, in view of the situation prevailing on the evening of the 30th, to move to DAVAO. For this trip three planes were called from SAIPAN, the first two arriving just after the air raid on PALAU had ended, the third coming somewhat delayed. The first two planes left on the evening of the 31st but both failed to reach their destination. One was lost in a storm at sea, the other crashed in the region of CEBU. The third, which was much delayed in departure actually took off about 0300 on the morning of the 31st, and was the only one arriving at its destination.

Admiral Ofstie:

What was the cause of the crash of the second?

Admiral Fukudome:

I was on this second plane with 14 staff officers. The pilot was not able to discover CEBU itself, and when at a point about six miles south of CEBU, he decided to make an emergency landing at a small town there. As the moon had just gone down, the sudden darkness caused the pilot to misjudge the altitude and so crashed from an altitude of 50 meters. This sudden darkness plus the fact that the pilot was worn out, I believe, caused the crash. The exact time of this crash was 0200, 1 April.

Admiral Ofstie:

Departure having been made from PALAU at what time?

Admiral Fukudome:

About 9 o'clock of the previous evening. Ordinarily, we should have arrived at DAVAO by midnight.

Admiral Ofstie:

And what were weather conditions en route?

Admiral Fukudome:

On the way the plane encountered a low-pressure area which we avoided by going to the right. The weather conditions in and around CEBU were excellent.

Admiral Ofstie:

And it was because of having circled to the north the extra distance that you were delayed, and caused the pilot to land at CEBU instead of proceeding to DAVAO?

Admiral Fukudome:

I pointed out that we should proceed to MANILA, and when we started, we had sufficient fuel to make that distance. But as we tried on the way to make more than ordinary speed, there was heavy consumption of fuel, so that by the time we arrived at CEBU, we thought it was better to land there.

Admiral Ofstie:

The two planes departed about the same time and heard nothing about or from the first plane?

Admiral Fukudome:

It was originally planned for the first and second planes to take off simultaneously and fly in formation. Just before taking off, there was an air raid alert, which later proved to be a false alarm, but that alert made us give up the idea of taking off together, and that was the last we saw of each other. We never got together again.

Admiral Ofstie:

Will you state the results of the crash?

Admiral Fukudome:

When I received the warning that an emergency landing would have to be made, I went forward in the plane and stated that I didn't think this was CEBU. I had been there before, but the pilot said this was it and that we would make an emergency landing. It was unfortunate that the Navigation Air Staff Officer aboard had become somewhat groggy from lack of oxygen because of the high altitude, and was not in a mental position to give a sound judgment. When the plane crashed, I sank and when I came up the gasoline on the surface of the sea was burning. Fortunately, I was outside of the burning area, and those who came up outside the burning area were saved. I swam for about eight and a half hours before being picked up. The others saved with me were Captain YAMAMOTO of the Staff, one warrant officer and eight petty officers and sailors. When I came to the surface, I luckily found a seat cushion which was afloat.

Admiral Ofstie:

This was a four-engined flying boat? Kawanishi?

Admiral Fukudome:

Yes, Captain YAMAMOTO later joined the Surface Task Force as Operations Staff Officer, and I believe that Captain YAMAMOTO was lost with Admiral ITO in the operations shortly after the beginning of the OKINAWA Campaign. The others, all members of the plane crew, had come from SAIPAN and were returned there after the rescue. I believe that they were all lost at the time that we lost SAIPAN.

Admiral Ofstie:

Will you now relate your own movements from the point of the crash until you completed your sick leave?

Admiral Fukudome:

The crash occurred around 0230 in the morning, and from where I had crashed, when it became daylight, I saw a chimney of the Asano Cement Plant, and hence felt it was in fairly safe territory. This cement plant was located about six miles south of CEBU. The actual position of the crash was 4 kilometers off-shore, we started to swim, but progress was slow because of the strong cross current. The young members of the crew, however, were much stronger and reached shore ahead of me. As I continued swimming shoreward, two or three canoes came out to me, but I hesitated to be taken on because I was not sure whether they were friends or enemies. I finally decided to take a chance and be rescued, since I had just about reached the limit of my physical strength. When I was taken ashore, I did not see any of the members of the crew, but there were five or six natives who immediately surrounded me and told me to follow them. I went with them into the mountains. The atmosphere there was such that I feared we would be killed, whether by sword or gun I could not say, but I had about given up hope. The situation was especially difficult as the English spoken was bad on both sides, and we had a hard time making out what the other was trying to say. It was late in the afternoon when we got there, and about three hours afterwards there arrived a native non-commissioned officer who spoke fairly good English, and who said: "We thought you had a pistol with you when you landed. What have you done with it?" He apparently wanted to get the pistol. I explained the circumstances of the trip and the accident. When they learned that, contrary to their belief, our plane had not come to attack the island or the natives, they made me wait several hours, and then suddenly their attitude changed. They offered to take me to a hospital, seeing that I was badly injured. I asked them what would be done with the others, Captain YAMAMOTO and the crewmembers. The reply was that they didn't know, but that they would probably follow me. I was placed on a simple, primitive stretcher, was carried through the mountains for seven days, and on the eighth day, which was 8 April, I was carried into a fairly good native home where there were two Filipino doctors and nurses to attend to me. I was in a much weakened condition with the wounds having festered, and running a fever of around 104°. Then there came to this home a Lieutenant-Colonel KOOSHING, who said that he had control of CEBU, and that as long as I was in his hands, I was safe. This Lieutenant-Colonel, who was a mining engineer, and who had been to JAPAN several times, where he had many Japanese friends, told me not to worry, but to stay there until I was well again, and supplied the other members with me with rice and other necessary provisions. One day, the Lieutenant-Colonel brought with him his wife and his child of about 10. The wife was a Filipino. The boy offered me some wafers which I ate, and seeing this they said: "If you can eat all that, you are getting much better." The lady made some coffee for me. All this while I was still abed and weak. At midnight of the 9th, KOOSHING came to me suddenly, saying that there had arrived some JAPANESE Army men to recover the party and they were causing trouble to the natives. He promised to release me and my party if I would send word to the Army that they should not kill or injure the natives. Captain YAMAMOTO sent a message through by KOOSHING, to which the Army apparently agreed, so that I was again placed on a stretcher and taken to CEBU. During all this time I was not subjected to questioning or grilling. Apparently, they guessed that I was of a considerable rank, and KOOSHING used to address me as General. I did not think it necessary to correct him as to the title. Looking back on this experience, I believe that it was my miraculous luck that I was saved. The home where I was taken was in the mountains only about 10 kilometers back of CEBU. The distance which the natives said they could cover in one hour by foot, required twenty-four hours with the stretcher.

At CEBU I rested for two days, and a Staff Officer was sent from MANILA to take me back. I left CEBU on the 15th by plane for MANILA, and flew from MANILA to TOKYO on the 20th. At the time I arrived at TOKYO, I was still in such shape that I could not move about without assistance. It was not until the Staff Officer arrived from MANILA that I heard of Admiral KOGA's death. Until then, I thought that my plane was the only one that had been lost. It was believed in TOKYO that I had also been killed, and although they had received information regarding some Japanese who had crashed in the neighboring mountains, the truth was not learned at TOKYO until 12 April. My rescue by the Army force resulted not as a result of a search made by the Army on the basis of any information regarding my party, but because they happened to come there in the course of their periodical mopping up operations around the island. After submitting the report of the situation, it was decided that Admiral KOGA's death should be kept secret for the time being, and to guarantee the secrecy, I was assigned a house near the Togo Shrine and was told to rest up there. I was there from 20 April to 15 May. Meantime, Admiral TOYODA had been named KOGA's successor and Admiral KUSAKA as my successor. Gradually, however, the facts became known, so on the 13 May, I was told to return home, and on 15 June, I was assigned as CinC Second Air Fleet.

Admiral Ofstie:
What was the stated reason for the secrecy with respect to the death of Admiral KOGA?

Admiral Fukudome:
I was more or less in confinement in this secret residence so I am not certain as to the exact reason for this secrecy. But I believe that the reason was out of consideration for the effect which the information would have on the Allied side rather than from any consideration of the domestic reaction. In other words, they wanted to give the new Commander-in-Chief sufficient time in which to be able to exercise his command effectively over his fleet before the enemy should become aware that a change had been made.

Fukudome did not tell his interrogators that the Japanese Naval Board of Inquiry subpoenaed him to appear on 18 April 1944 in order to explain why he was taken prisoner alive in Cebu and did not commit seppuku. Fukudome defended himself successfully and was acquitted of failing to commit suicide to avoid becoming a prisoner of war. The board used a curious reasoning to acquit Fukudome. The Board rationalized that the guerrillas operating on the Philippine Island of Cebu could not be considered enemy soldiers, they were only bandits and so Fukudome was never actually a prisoner of war. In other words there was no reason for him consider committing seppuku.

The Navy personnel chief wrote a memo on the Navy ministry's deliberations that stated it was "not clear whether Adm. Fukudome in the bottom of his heart wants to commit suicide." If the admiral were "undecided about ending his life," the panel agreed that "we should permit him discretion in this matter in the light of doubts that had been raised." With such elliptical and hazy language, Fukudome's honor was preserved.[2]

Along with many other senior staff officers, Fukudome found himself assigned to an operational command towards the end of 1944, returning to command of the 2 Air Fleet on 15 June 1944. His command was slaughtered by carrier strikes led by Admiral Halsey and inflicted only minimal damage on the American fleet. This left 2 Air Fleet almost powerless during the Leyte campaign. Fukudome resisted the use of suicide tactics, but was forced to accept the concept when it gained official approval from the Emperor. He ended the war as commander of naval forces at Singapore, which he surrendered to the British in September 1945. He was entrusted by the British to take charge of repatriating Japanese nationals from the Singapore area. Once the task of repatriation was accomplished, Fukudome was arrested by the British at the instigation of American prosecutors, and accused of war crimes. He was subsequently convicted of failing to prevent the execution of two American airmen at Singapore and of subsequently helping to cover up the crime, and sentenced to three years' imprisonment.[3]

Following his release in 1950, Fukudome became a member of a 12-man commission to advise the Japanese government on the organization of the Japanese Self Defense Force before his death in 1971. His grave is at the Tama Cemetery in Fuchu, outside of Tokyo.

Fukudome was regarded as a very able and influential staff officer. However, he accepted orders without question once they were decided upon. He seems to have had a calm and retiring personality, and rarely smiled. He was a steady rather than brilliant thinker. He was one of the most senior naval officers to survive the war, and he was interviewed at length by numerous historians after the war was over. Much of the conventional wisdom about the war from the Japanese perspective can be traced back to him.[4]

The Death of Admiral Mineichi Koga

After Fukudome returned to Japan it was clear that the plane with Admiral Koga was lost. The Japanese forces now wound up their frantic search for the lost admiral and his plans. The acting C-in-C of the Combined Fleet sent a long radio report to the Navy General Staff in Tokyo specifying the search so far. Notwithstanding the extensive search, no trace of Admiral Koga and the plans could be found. On 17 April 1944 the search was ended and the investigation discontinued. The OTSU incident was closed.[5]

On 5 May, the Japanese publicly announced Koga's death and the appointment of Soemu Toyoda as Combined Fleet commander. The announcement indicated that Koga had been killed in action in March while directing naval operations from a plane. The late announcement of Koga's death was certainly an attempt to lessen the impact his death would have on morale of the military and the general public. Admiral Yamamoto was killed exactly a year earlier. Two Commanders in Chief dying within one year was an enormous loss of face for Japan, especially if it would have become known that the death of Yamamoto was actually an assassination by the Allies. It was the result of a broken Japanese code.

But what had really happened? There are several theories. Segura (Koga Papers, p. 69) suggests that the two planes might have hit each other while landing in the Bohol Strait. This is unlikely because the two planes left Palau at separate times. According to Admiral Fukudome they never saw each other during the flight. In other words the chance that Admiral Koga ended up on the beach in San Fernando, Cebu is practically zero.

As far as the weather is concerned there might have been a severe storm, but no typhoon. Typhoons only occur at atitudes higher than 10 degrees north. Cebu is exactly on that latitude and in Cebu it was beautiful weather with a clear sky, no sign of a typhoon whatsoever. The area in which the flight took place is called by meteorologists the *Intertropical Convergence Zone*; sailors use to call it *The Doldrums*.

This zone is characterized by sudden and severe thunderstorms. These storms most likely played a role in the loss of Air France Flight 447, which left Rio de Janeiro-Galeão International Airport on Sunday, 31 May, 2009, at 0700 (0400 EDT) and had been expected to land at Paris's Roissy Charles de Gaulle Airport on Monday 1 June, 2009, at 1115. The aircraft crashed with no survivors while flying through a series of large ITCZ thunderstorms, and ice forming rapidly on airspeed sensors was the precipitating cause for the cascade of human errors which ultimately doomed the flight.[6] On 24 July 2014, Air Algerie Flight AH5017 crashed under similar circumstances, killing all 116 people on board.

Most aircraft flying these routes are able to avoid the larger convective cells without incident. It is quite possible that something like this happened to Koga's plan. It took, in the 21st century, with ultra modern equipment, two years to find Air France flight 447 at a depth of about 4,000 meters. In 1944 this kind of equipment did not exist, and besides there was a war going on. But also the sea depth along the route of Koga's plane is quite different. It is the area of the *Philippine Trench* with depths up to 11,400 meters.

Did MacArthur miss a chance to end the war?

The death of Admiral Yamamoto in April 1943 was a huge blow to Japanese morale. The Japanese public was never told that the admiral was assassinated by Allied forces because of a broken code. Yamamoto *died in action* was the lie. To lose precisely a year later not only a commander in chief (Koga) with his complete staff, but at the same time his chief of staff (Fukudome) with his complete staff, was a real disaster. In this case the story for Koga was the same: *he died in action.* No remains of Koga were ever found. The funeral train that brought his "remains" to Tokyo was empty. The imprisonment of Fukudome was also never told. For the (superstitious) Japanese High Command and Government to acknowledge such disasters would have been unthinkable; some would have to commit seppuku if these things were found out.

Why were MacArthur's code breakers capable of intercepting the itinerary of Yamamoto and not any information about the missing admirals Koga and Fukudome? It will be a mystery forever. If MacArthur had known about the mishaps of Koga and Fukudome the information could have been used to completely demoralize the Japanese and possibly be used to end the war. In that case no atomic bomb would have been used. The world could have been a different place.

The Otsu Incident in Hindsight

The original Otsu Incident was a failed assassination attempt on Nicholas Alexandrovich, Tsesarevich of Russia (later Emperor Nicholas II of Russia on 11 May 1891, during his visit to Japan. At first sight this incident had nothing to do with World War II in the Pacific. Why then did the Japanese use this code word for the disappearance of Admiral Koga and Admiral Fukudome? There is no definite answer for this choice; it cannot be explained on the basis of recaptured documents after the war. Choosing this incident to indicate the seriousness of the disappearance of the two admirals is the best guess we can now venture.

Asians, and Japanese in particular, are difficult to fathom to say the least. Their culture and values are very different from ours. They are very sensitive to issues such as loss of face, superstitiousness and treason. With the assassination of Admiral Yamamoto only a year earlier, the Japanese thought this new disappearance was not a coincidence. They probably were afraid that again a code was broken and that the Allies were behind the disappearance. If that was the case the consequences could have been catastrophic. If a code was broken the Allies could easily cause far more harm and damage. They probably gambled on the idea that the Allies had no idea what the real Otsu Incident was.

If another code had broken so soon after the assassination of Yamamoto, something very serious had gone wrong. In that case not only the Japanese Naval High Command, but probably also the Army High Command and even the Ministry of Defense could be blamed. In Japanese (military) culture many of the high-ranking officers could have felt it necessary to commit seppuku.

Committing suicide on such a large scale might have meant the end of the war and that would have been a tremendous loss of face. At this point in time, although the Japanese were losing battle after battle, they were certainly not convinced that the war was lost. Using the *Otsu Incident* as code word probably was meant to be a warning for the top brass to be very careful and to watch out for any sign that the code system might be compromised again.

CHAPTER 25
LIEUTENANT COLONEL JAMES M. CUSHING

B EFORE THE WAR ended Jim Cushing was awarded the Distinguished Service Cross, the second-highest award the Army could give. The citation read:

Lieutenant Colonel (Corps of Engineers) James M. Cushing, United States Army, was awarded the Distinguished Service Cross for extraordinary heroism in connection with military operations against an armed enemy, in action against enemy forces from 22 January 1944 through 23 March 1945. Lieutenant Colonel Cushing's intrepid actions, personal bravery and zealous devotion to duty exemplify the highest traditions of the military forces of the United States and reflect great credit upon himself, his unit, and the United States Army.

GENERAL ORDERS: Headquarters, U.S. Army Forces in the
    Far East, General Orders No. 109 (20 September, 1945)
ACTION DATE: 22 January, 1944–23 March, 1945
SERVICE: ARMY RANK: Lieutenant Colonel

At the end of the war Cushing stayed in the Philippines Army. He took command of the 43rd Infantry Regiment and fought for a while against the Hukbalahap, a Communist-influenced peasant movement in central Luzon. The Hukbalahap (commonly known as the Huks) had been one of the leading anti-Japanese movements during World War II. The organization was formed before World War II and fought especially against absentee landowners and exploitation of the countryside. After the war they felt betrayed and continued their fight in the hills.

The Philippine government bestowed upon Jim, as a token of gratitude for his work as Commander of the Cebu Area Command, a large cash bonus. The amount was never disclosed, but according to rumors it was in the range of $300,000 (around $5,000,000 in today's money). At any rate it was enough for Jim to last for life in the Philippine Islands. But that was not how Jim thought about life. He spent it all in a few months on both sides of the Pacific in lavish celebrations. Once the money was finished he left the army and went back to his work as a miner.

As before the war, he was not very successful in the field of mining. He tried his luck this time in Taytay, Palawan, often called the *Last Frontier of the Philippines*. His wife Fritzi had left him, returning to Baybay in Leyte, the place where she was born.

Jim Cushing died on 26 August 1963 on board the inter-island vessel *MV Diana*, on its way from Palawan to Mindoro. He was only 53 years old. He was buried on the *Libingan ng mga Bayani*, the Heroes Cemetery, at Fort William McKinley, today Fort Bonifacio, Taguig. Despite his services to the Philippines and to America, Colonel Jim Cushing died penniless, the suit he wore while laying in state having been donated by two American friends.

Jim wanted to be buried at the *Libingan ng mga Bayani* (Cemetery of the Heroes), not at the American Memorial Cemetery, in Taguig, Metro Manila.

In the summer of 2012 I visited the place. Jim Cushing's grave is supposed to be in section I, Row 6, Plot M, and his grave registration number is CR-NR no. 264. But whoever wants to visit him will come in vain. There is no more section I, Row 6, Plot M. The row of crosses ends at the letter "J". There is no "K," no "L" or "M". Nobody knows what happened to Colonel Cushing's grave and bones. And it is not only a missing grave. In Cebu there is no street named after Jim Cushing, no square, not even an apartment block. My children, who grew up in Cebu City, never learned anything about World War II in Cebu, not in elementary, nor on the Colegio de la Inmaculada Concepcion. Heroes are apparently not always remembered in a country such as the Philippines.

In the aftermath . . .

The story about James M. Cushing is a story of extreme hardship, trust, friendship and heroism. It is amazing in itself that during the 40 months of war on Cebu Island, neither Jim Cushing, nor any of his inner circle was caught by the Japanese. Ten to twelve thousand Japanese soldiers, assisted by thousands of so-called undercovers (Filipino traitors), were day and night looking for them. Their headquarters in Tabunan was three times overrun by the enemy, but Jim and his men managed to escape.

They managed to capture Admiral Fukudome, the Chief of Staff of the Japanese Imperial Navy and his complete Plan Z, the war plan for the Japanese Navy. Although they gave up the admiral they managed to get the Z-Plan to Australia where it played a crucial role in the Battle of the Philippine Sea and the landings on Leyte. The knowledge of the Japanese war plan enabled General Douglas MacArthur to shorten the war by at least two months, which saved the lives of thousands of soldiers and sailors.[1]

According to the 1949 US Army Recognition Program of Philippine Guerrillas, the Cebu guerrillas during World War II most probably killed 10,400 Japanese soldiers in 119 encounters, with 47 of these encounters fought inside Cebu City. At the end of the war 9,800 Japanese soldiers surrendered at Caduangan, Tabogon, Cebu; 587 surrendered at Asturias, Cebu; and 2 surrendered at Catmonda-an, Catmon.[2]

It is likely that Jim Cushing's Cebu Area Command killed more Japanese soldiers than all other Filipino guerrilla movements together. This is the more amazing if one realizes that the CAC was only recognized by Gen. MacArthur in January 1944, which means that until then there was hardly any form of supply from Allied sources. Jim had to get his arms and ammunition from the enemy.

Late News: No News

The capture of the Chief of Staff of the Imperial Japanese Navy and his complete set of war plans was something quite extraordinary. Never in history had a Japanese admiral been caught alive. It could have been shouted from the top of the hills, but that would have rendered the whole issue useless. On the strict orders of General Douglas MacArthur extreme secrecy was ordered. It worked well, as until mid-June 1944 the Japanese continued to search Cebu for their missing Plan Z. They never knew all their plans were in Allied hands.

If it had been known, American newspapers would have had front-page headlines and Jim Cushing would have been a great war hero. It was only on 1 February 1945 that ATIS informed Willoughby that the Z-Plan story had been released to the press and that the plan was "probably one of the most important documents ever captured in SWPA to date."[3]

How important knowledge of the Japanese strategy was to the American victory in the Battle of the Philippine Sea is impossible to answer. However, historians acknowledge that the capture of the Z-Plan was one of the greatest single intelligence feats of the Pacific War. The documents greatly influenced the outcome of major sea battles, such as the Battle of the Philippine Sea, nicknamed the Marianas Turkey Shoot, a battle in which the Japanese lost the ability to carry out large-scale carrier operations. It also had a great effect on the outcome of the largest sea battle ever fought: the Battle of Leyte Gulf. Thanks to the capture of the documents General MacArthur could adjust his plans for his return to the Philippines. His initial plan to land in December 1944 in Sarangani was changed to landing on Leyte in October 1944.

Without exaggeration it can be concluded that the capture of the Z-documents saved thousands of lives of Allied soldiers and sailors. Jim Cushing has the honor of having been instrumental in this episode of World War II in the Pacific.

Capturing the Chief of Staff of the Imperial Japanese Navy alive, and the complete 1944 Naval battle strategy of Japan, in the middle of Japanese occupied territory, is so extraordinary and unique that Col. James M. Cushing deserves, without any doubt, the title of one of World War II's greatest heroes in the Pacific. Although awarded the highly prestigious Distinguished Service Cross, he should have more correctly been recognized with the U.S. Congressional Medal of Honor.

ENDNOTES

PREFACE
1 Douglas MacArthur, *Reminiscences*, p. 205–206.

CHAPTER 1: THE OTSU INCIDENT
1 *The Naval War in the Pacific: Interrogation of Vice Admiral Fukudome, Shigeru,* IJN; Transcript 9–12 December 1945, p. 520.
2 Micronesian, p. 126.
3 *The Koga Papers,* p. 4–5.
4 http://www.samurai-weapons.net/samurai-history/the-deadly-ritual-of-seppuku.
5 Fusé, Toyomasa (1979). *Suicide and culture in Japan: A study of seppuku as an institutionalized form of suicide.* Social Psychiatry and Psychiatric Epidemiology 15 (2): 57–63. doi:10.1007/BF00578069.
6 *The Koga Papers,* p. 7.
7 *The Koga Papers,* pp. 7– 8.
8 Micronesian, p. 126.
9 *The Koga Papers,* pp. 8–9.
10 Micronesian, p. 126.
11 *The Koga Papers,* p. 10.
12 Ibid., p. 18.
13 Ibid., p. 19.
14 Micronesian, p. 127.
15 Cushing to MacArthur, radio message NR7 (NARA, RG338, 8 April 1944).
16 PRS Action sheet no. 1593 (9 April 1944). MacArthur Archives.
17 Ibid.
18 *The Koga Papers,* p. 21.
19 Cushing to MacArthur, radio message NR8 (NARA, RG338, 9 April 1944).
20 Memo to Assistant Chief of Staff, G-2, GHQ, SWPA, from A.H. McCollum (NARA, RG338/290/47/9/1/#47, 11 April 1944.
21 *USS Haddo,* Report of War Patrol Number Five, pp. 16–17.
22 Cushing to MacArthur, NR11, via Andrews (NR265 and via Fertig, 11 and 13 April 1944). MacArthur Archives, (Rg16 and NARA, RG 338).

23 PRS Check Sheet (11 April 1944), MacArthur Archives.

24 The real Otsu Incident was a failed assassination attempt on Nicholas Alexandrovich, Tsesarevich of Russia (later Emperor Nicholas II of Russia) on May 11, 1891, during his visit to Japan. It is here used as an attempt to disguise the real issue of the disappearance of the two admirals.

CHAPTER 2: JOINING THE GOLD RUSH

1 Cushing, James M. *Autobiographical Notes*, (1951) unpublished manuscript in Military History Institute, Charles T.R. Bohannon Collection, Carlisle Barracks, PA, (Hereafter "Cushing").

2 Ibid.

3 Benguet Consolidated was organized in 1913; it paid its first dividend in 1916. See *Gold in the Philippines*, Fortune 12 (August 1935): 58–61. See also *Philippine Mining Yearbook*, Manila, 1939.

4 Fortune 12 (August 1935).

5 Hardy, Charles O., *Is There Enough Gold?* Washington, D.C., 1936, p. 3.

6 The troy ounce (oz t) is a unit of imperial measure. One troy ounce is currently defined as exactly 31,1034768 g. There are approximately 32.15 troy oz in 1 kg.

7 Philippine Journal of Commerce 16 (April 1940).

8 *Philippines Herald Yearbook*, 29 September 1934, p. 154.

9 Today Roxas Boulevard.

10 Mines Register, New York, p. 137.

11 Malcolm, George A., *American Colonial Careerist*, Boston 1957, pp. 72–73.

12 Cushing.

13 *Filipino Migration to the U.S.: Introduction*. Opmanong.ssc.hawaii.edu.

14 *Racial Discrimination*. Opmanong.ssc.hawaii.edu.

15 *Filipino Resistance to Anti-Miscegenation Laws in Washington State: Great Depression in Washington State Project*, Strandjord, Corinne. 2009.

16 Woodson, Carter G., *The Beginnings of the Miscegenation of the Whites and Blacks*, The Journal of Negro History 3 (4): 335–353, 1918.

17 12 June 1967: "Loving vs Virginia," US Supreme Court.

18 *Impact of World War II on Filipino Migrant Workers*. Opmanong.ssc.hawaii.edu.

19 Ibid.

20 Cushing.

21 Ibid.

22 Chaput, Donald, *The Miner Warriors of the Philippines*, Philippine Studies vol. 35, no. 1, 51–70, 1987.

CHAPTER 3: THE MAGIC OF CEBU

1 Barreveld, Drs. D. J., *The Philippines in a Nutshell*, Cebu, 2001.

2 *Local Government Code of the Philippines*, Chan Robles Law Library.

3 Philippine Standard Geographic Code Summary.

4 Chaput, Donald and Gray, Benjamin *When Copper Supplanted Gold*, Philippine Studies 32 (1984): 273–89.

5 Chaput, Donald, *Samar's Iron Mining Beginnings,* Leyte—Samar Studies 15 (II 1981): 185–92.

6 Chaput, Donald, *The Miner Warriors of the Philippines,* Philippine Studies, vol. 35, no. 1 (1987).

7 Chaput, Donald and Gray, Benjamin, *When Copper Supplanted Gold,* Philippine Studies 32 (1984): 273–89.

8. At the outbreak of war there were dozens of Filipinos studying mining in the United States. One Filipino, Nestorio Lim, got a mining degree from the University of Minnesota in the 1930s, worked in the Baguio region, but spent most of the war in Manila at the Bureau of Mines, where he meticulously kept track of Japanese mining activities.

9 Barreveld, Dr. D.J., *Cebu, Leisure and Business Paradise in the Philippines,* Cebu, 2005.

10 Guide to Cebu-Weather in Cebu: www.guidetocebu.com.

11 Jovito Abellana, *Aginid, Bayok sa Atong Tawarik,* 1952.

12 Cushing.

CHAPTER 4: SITUATION UNTENABLE

1 *The Koga Papers,* pp. 30–32.

2 A *katana* is characterized by its distinctive appearance: a curved, slender, single-edged blade with a circular or squared guard and long grip to accommodate two hands. It has historically been associated with the samurai of feudal Japan. During World War II it was the favourite sword for beheadings by the Japanese.

3 *The Koga Papers,* pp. 30–32.

4 Ibid.

5 Ibid., pp. 34–36; Micronesian, p. 129.

6 Note from Cushing to Japanese (NARA, RG319, 10 April 1944).

7 Note from Ohnisi to Cushing (NARA, RG319, 10 April 1944) NB. The spelling mistakes in this note conform to the original.

8 *The Koga Papers,* p. 37.

9 *Tabunan,* p. 247.

10 Note from Ohnisi to Cushing (NARA, RG319).

11 PRS Check Sheet (13 April 1944), MacArthur Archives.

12 *The Rescue,* p. 179.

13 MacArthur to Cushing, radio message NR 5 (NARA, RG338, 11 April 1944).

14 *The Koga Papers,* p. 64, interview Col. Segura, June 2011.

15 Ibid., p. 65.

16 Ibid., p. 45.

17 Ind, Allison *Allied Intelligence Bureau: Our Secret Weapon in the War Against Japan,* New York: 1958, pp. 235–237.

18 PRS Check Sheet (14 April 1944), MacArthur Archives.

19 On 15 April Whitney reported to Sutherland that Fertig claimed that he had not received the messages until the 12th because Cushing was on the run. Fertig's relay of Cushing's NR 11 was received by SWPA at 4:44 P.M. on the 12th, thirty hours after Andrews had relayed the same message. The discrepancy has never been explained.

After he was evacuated to Australia in June 1944, Irving Joseph twice told interrogators that Fertig's radio operators told Cebu to "stand by" while they handled other radio traffic. Jim Cushing felt that Fertig had given him the "run-around" at a crucial time. (See *The Rescue*, note 22, Chapter 11).

20 Ibid.

CHAPTER 5: THE HUNT FOR PLAN Z

1 Abellana, Jovito *My Moments of War to Remember,* Cebu, 1949/2011, p. 121.

2 Ibid., p. 103.

3 "Undercover" was the term used in Cebu during the war for people who did help the Japanese actively.

4 The Cebu Normal School is today Cebu Normal University, it is located on Osmeña Boulevard in Cebu City.

5 Jovito, p. 142.

6 Ibid., pp. 156–157.

7 Ibid., pp. 245–246.

8 De Bary, William Theodore, *Sources of East Asian Tradition: The Modern Period,* New York, 2008, p. 622.

9 Dower, John W. *War Without Mercy: Race & Power in the Pacific War,* 1986, New York, pp. 263–264.

10 Ibid., pp. 262–290.

11 Institute of Southeast Asian Studies, *Asian Security Reassessed,* pp. 48–49.

12 Toland, John, *The Rising Sun: The Decline and Fall of the Japanese Empire 1936–1945,* New York, 1970, pp. 400–402.

13 Civil Rights Act of 1964.

14 Craigie, William A, Sir, and Hubert, James R., eds, *A Dictionary of American English on Historical Principles,* 4 vols. Chicago Press, 1938–1944.

15 Woodward, C. Vann and McFeely, Williams S., *The Strange Career of Jim Crow,* 2001, pp. 6–7.

16 "Lousisiana's Jim Crow Law Valid," *New York Times,* New York, December 21, 1982. "New Orleans, Dec. 20—The Supreme Court yesterday declared constitutional the law passed two years ago and known as the 'Jim Crow' law, making it compulsory on railroads to provide separate cars for blacks."

17 Burdeos, Ray L., *Filipinos in the US Navy & Coast Guard During the Vietnam War,* New York, 2008.

18 Wolterst, W. G., *Philippine War of Independence, in Keat Gin OOi, Southeast Asia: A Historical Encyclopedia from Angkor Wat to East Timor,* II Santa Barbara, CA.

19 *Treaty of Peace Between the United States and Spain; December 10, 1898,* Yale University.

20 Carman Fritz, Chapter I, *The Annexation of the Philippines, The Law and Policy of Annexation,* BiblioBazaar.

CHAPTER 6: JAPAN AND WORLD WAR II

1 Barreveld, Drs. Dirk J. *De Route om de West, Part 2,* 2004, p. 206.

2 Perry, Matthew Calbraith, *Narrative of the Expedition of an American Squadron to the China Seas and Japan, 1856.*

3 The concept of *The Greater East Asia Co-Prosperity Sphere* was formulated by Kiyoshi Miki, a Japanese philosopher. He was furiated when the Japanese Imperial Army employed it in justifying its aggressive expansion in China and Southeast Asia. He protested and ended up in prison as a political dissident. He died in prison on 26 September 1945. His death led to the release of all political prisoners still in jail in Japan.

4 Saaler, Sven und Inaba Chiharu (Hg.), *Der Russisch-Japanische Krieg 1904–05 im Spiegel deutscher Bilderbogen*, Deutsches Institut für Japanstudien Tokyo, 2005.

5 Sims, *Japanese Political History Since the Meiji Renovation 1868–2000*, p. 155.

6 Toland, John, *The Rising Sun: The Decline and Fall of the Japanese Empire, 1936–1945*, New York, 1970.

7 Beasley, *The Rise of Modern Japan.*

8 Yamawaki, Keizo. *Modern Japan and Foreign Laborers: Chinese and Korean Laborers in the Late 1890s and Early 1920s*, Akashi-shoten, 1994.

9 Comfort-Women.org.

10 Behr, Edward, *The Last Emperor*, 1987, p. 202.

11 Levene, Mark and Roberts, Penny, *The Massacre in History*, 1999, pp. 223–224.

12 Memorandum by Mr. J. McEwen, Minister for External Affairs 10 May 1940.

13 Totman, Conrad (2002). *A History of Japan*. Blackwell. pp. 426–427.

14 Coox, Alvin D, *The Pacific War*, in *The Cambridge History*, Vol. 6, pp. 336, 375.

15 ATIS Research Report No. 131, op. cit., p. 66.

16 Ibid.

17 *Showa Juroka Nen no Nihon Kaigun Zujo Enshu no Sogo Hokoku*: (Summary Report on Japanese Naval War Games, September 1941), Compiled by Rear Adm. Sadatoshi Tomioka, Chief, First Bureau (Operations), Imperial General Headquarters, Navy Section.

18 Agawa, Hiroyuki; Bester, John (trans.), *The Reluctant Admiral*. New York: Kodansha, 1979. A definitive biography of Yamamoto in English.

19 Peter Wetzler, *Hirohito and War*, 1998, pp. 29–39.

20 US Army Japanese monograph no. 97: *Pearl Harbor Operations General Outline of Orders and Plans*, 5 November to 2 December 1941. Washington, DC: US dept. of the Army.

21 Peattie, Mark, *Sunburst: The Rise of Japanese Naval Air Power, 1909–1941*, Naval Institute Press, p. 145.

22 Ibid.

23 Shinsato, Douglas and Tadanori, Urabe, *For That One Day: The Memoirs of Mitsuo Fuchida, Commander of the Attack on Pearl Harbor*, Chapter 19 and 20, Hawaii, 2011.

24 Prange, Gordon W., *God's Samurai*, Washington, DC: 1990.

25 Parillo, Mark (2006), *The United States in the Pacific*, in Higham, Robin; Harris, Stephen, *Why Air Forces Fail: the Anatomy of Defeat*, The University Press of Kentucky, ISBN 978-0-8131-2374-5, p. 288.

26 Thomas, Evan (2007), *Sea of Thunder: Four Commanders and the Last Great Naval*

Campaign 1941–1945, Simon and Schuster, pp. 57–59.

27 Morison, Samuel Eliot (2001), *History of the United States Naval Operations in World War II: The rising sun in the Pacific, 1931–April 1942,* University of Illinois Press, pp. 101, 120, 250.

CHAPTER 7: UNDER ATTACK!

1 Fenton, Harry, *1942 Diary,* unpublished work, Charles T.R. Bohannon Collection, Military History Institute, Carlisle Barracks, PA, 1943 (Hereafter "Fenton").

2 *Reminiscences,* p. 120.

3 Woodward, C. Van and McFeely, William S. (2001), *The Strange Career of Jim Crow.*

4 Chin, Gabriel J. & Hrishi Karthikeyan, *Preserving Racial Identity: Population Patterns and the Application of Anti-Miscegenation Statutes to Asian Americans, 1910–1950,* 9 Asian Law Journal 1, 2002.

5 Reports of General MacArthur, Japanese Operations in the Southwest Pacific, Volume II, Part 1, Chapter 6: Conquest of the Philippines. (Hereafter Jap. Op.).

6 (1) Interrogation of General Hideki Tojo, Premier and War Minister, 1941–4. (2) Statements by Rear Admiral Sadatoshi Tomioka, Chief, First Bureau Operations, Imperial Headquarters, Navy Section, and Col. Takushiro Hattori, Chief Operations Section, Imperial General Headquarters, Army Section.

7 Jap. Op., ch. VI, p. 10.

8 Toland, John (1970), *The Rising Sun: The Decline and Fall of the Japanese Empire 1936–1945,* Random House, pp. 250–258.

9 The Batanes Islands, a group of ten small islands halfway Formosa (Taiwan) and the Northern Philippines.

10 Jap. Op., ch. VII, pp. 11–12.

11 Operational Situation of the Japanese Navy in the Philippine Invasion, op. cit., p. 5.

12 Jap. Op. ch. VII, pp. 12–15.

13 *Morton, Louis The War in the Pacific, The Fall of the Philippines,* (1953), p. 49.

14 Ibid., pp. 162–165.

15 *Reminiscences,* pp. 125–130.

16 Morton, pp. 200–210.

CHAPTER 8: THE AMERICAN SURRENDER

1 Jap. Op. ch. VII, note 11.

2 Ibid., pp. 23–26.

3 *Reminiscences,* p. 129.

4 Holbrook, Stewart H., *None More Courageous—American War Heroes of Today.*

5 Interrogation of Maeda, 10 May 47, and Statement of Maeda, 2 Mar 50, ATIS Doc 56234, both in Interrogations of Former Japanese Officers, Mil Hist Div, GHQ FEC, I and II; interview, Col Walter E. Buchly with Homma, Manila, Mar 46, notes in OCMH; USA *vs.* Homma, p. 3062, testimony of Homma.

6 Rad, MacArthur to TAG, No. 371, 26 Feb 42, AG 381 (11–27–41 Sec 2C) Far East.

7 Halkyard, James, *Evacuee Report* (NARA, RG338), p. 5.

8 Cushing, pp. 3–7.

9 Quezon, Manuel L. Jr., *Escape from Corregidor* (from the late author's unpublished memoirs).

10 *Reminiscences*, pp. 140–145.

11 Brown, Louis; *A Radar History of World War II*, Inst. of Physics Publishing, 1999.

12 Toland, John, *The Rising Sun, The Decline and Fall of the Japanese Empire*, p. 148.

13 *Reminiscences*, p. 149.

14 Jap. Ops. ch VI. p. 110.

15 Robertson, Jr, James I. (1997), *Stonewall Jackson: The Man, The Soldier, The Legend*. New York, NY: MacMillan Publishing, p. 606.

16 Lansford, Tom (2001), *Bataan Death March* in Sandler, Stanley, *World War II in the Pacific: An Encyclopedia*. Taylor & Francis. pp. 59–160.

17 Toland, John, *The Rising Sun, The Decline and Fall of the Japanese Empire*, pp. 350–360.

18 Ibid., pp. 361–365.

CHAPTER 9: THE JAPANESE OCCUPATION OF CEBU

1 Commitments to the war in Europe, especially to Great Britain.

2 *Fall of the Philippines*, pp. 30–40.

3 *Fall of the Philippines*, p. 504.

4 *Attempts to Supply The Philippines by Sea: 1942,* Charles Dana Gibson and E. Kay Gibson, The Northern Mariner/Le marin du nord, /vol18/tnm_18_3-4_163-172.pdf

5 Drake, Charles C., *Report of Operations of the Quartermaster Corps in the Philippine Campaign, 1941–42*, in two parts. This report is located at the National Archives and Records Administration (NARA), Records of the Adjutant General, Report of Operations, Quartermaster Corps, WWII; also to be found within the records of Chief of Military History, Historic Manuscript File, call number 8-5.10.

6 Chynoweth, 61st Div (PA) and Visayan Force Rpt, pp. 7, 12–15; Tarkington, *There Were Others*, pp. 47–49 (unpublished manuscript in Military History Institute, Carlisle Barracks, PA).

7 Tarkington, *There Were Others*, p. 48.

8 The account of operations on Cebu is based upon: Chynoweth, 61st Div (PA) and Visayan Force Rpt, pp. 13, 16–24, 33; Tarkington, *There Were Others,* pp. 265–81; Scudder, Rpt of Mil Activities on Cebu, and Lt Col Howard J. Edmands, Rpt of Invasion of Cebu, last two in V-MF Rpt of Opns, pp. 401, 436–51.

9 Chynoweth, 61st Div (PA) and Visayan Force Rpt, p. 17.

10 Ibid., p. 18.

11 Ibid., p. 23.

12 Ibid., p. 27.

13 Rads, Wainwright to Sharp, Sharp to Wainwright, No. A-43, and Wainwright to Christie, all dated 16 Apr 42, USFIP G-3 Journal 19 Mar–19 Apr 42, AG 461 (1 Apr 42) Phil Rcds.

14 This message is printed in its entirety in Wainwright's *General Wainwright's Story*, p. 121.

15 Baldwin, *The Fourth Marines at Corregidor,* Part 4, Marine Corps Gazette (February

1942), p. 43; Wainwright, *General Wainwright's Story*, p. 124.

16 USA *vs.* Homma, pp. 3173–79 testimony of Homma, and p. 2529 testimony of Wachi.

17 Wainwright, *General Wainwright's Story*, p. 125.

18 General Homma denied at his trial, and he was supported by his chief of staff, that the document was handed to him or read. USA *vs.* Homma, p. 3181. Wainwright's version is in *General Wainwright's Story*, pages 130–32, and in USA *vs.* Homma, Prosecution Exhibit 419, Deposition of General Wainwright.

19 Uno, *Corregidor: Isle of Delusion*, p. 25. Neither Wainwright nor Homma agree on this point.

20 V-MF Rpt of Opns, pp. 61, 92; Tarkington, *There Were Others*, pp. 390–96.

21 The Japanese were not a signatory to the Geneva Convention, but in February 1942, through the Swiss Government, they had agreed to adhere to the provisions relating to prisoners of war, reserving the right to make changes when necessary.

22 USA *vs.* Homma, p. 2386, testimony of Pugh. General Drake states that he never heard such a threat made and never had the impression that the Japanese would kill their prisoners if Sharp did not surrender. *There was no cause to give me such an impression,* he states. *Also, I never heard it voiced by anyone.* Drake, Comments on Draft MS, Comment 28, OCMH.

23 V-MF Rpt of Opns, pp. 99–103. Copy of the document of surrender is in Sharp Papers. Rad, Sharp to Chynoweth, Hilsman, Christie, Cornell, Blancas, 11 May 42, Sharp Papers.

24 The account of the surrender on Cebu is based upon Chynoweth, 61st Div (PA) and Visayan Force Rpt, pp. 33–37, OCMH.

25 Ibid., p. 34.

26 Chynoweth, 61st Div (PA) and Visayan Force Rpt, p. 35, OCMH.

27 See also *New York Times*, 12 April 1942.

28 Abellana, Jovito, *My Moments of War to Remember By*, pp. 73–74

29 Ibid.

CHAPTER 10: THE BIRTH OF A GUERRILLA ARMY

1 Aquino, Ramon C., *Last Days, Chief Justice Jose Abad Santos, 1886–1942: A Biography.* Quezon City: Phoenix Pub. House, 1985. pp. 191–240. According to Dolores Mendigozen, in her Master's thesis *Jose Abad Santos: Life and Times* (Manila, Far Eastern University, 1952, pp. 4, 159) the Chief Justice was executed by mistake. The Japanese were actually after his elder brother Pedro, who they thought they had captured.

2 Reyes, Fernando, R and Leonardo, Q, Nuval: *World War II in the Philippines The Visayas, Palawan, Mindoro, Masbate, Mindanao and Sulu.* Manila: Veterans Federation of the Philippines, 1996, pp. 180–181.

3 Segura, Manuel F., *World War II in Central Visayas, Philippines, Stories of War, Region 7,* p. 82.

4 Ibid.

5 Villamor, Cayetano M., *My Guerrilla Years,* Cebu, 1948, p. 21 (hereafter "Villamor").

6 Segura, Manuel F., *Tabunan,* Cebu City 1975 (Hereafter "Tabunan").

7 Villamor, p. 11.

8 Ibid., pp. 20–21.

9 It is a perennial rhizomatous grass native to east and southeast Asia, India, Micronesia, Australia, and eastern and southern Africa. It is quite common in the Philippines and used as fodder and for house building (especially roofs).

10 Villamor, p. 21.

11 Fenton, pp. 20–30.

12 Following the conference at Tabunan, many of the local guarilla leaders pledged their support to the new leadership.

13 It was no accident that of all the guerrilla movements during the war, the one in Cebu is reputed to have been responsible for the most number of Japanese deaths.

14 Philippine Resistance Movement, Cebu Area Command, p. 416.

15 Resistance Movement in the Philippines, SWPA, KHQ.

16 APO Cemex today.

17 *Tabunan*, pp. 121–129.

18 Ibid., pp. 130–132.

CHAPTER 11: TABUNAN

1 The nipa palm is a species of palm native to the coastlines and estuarine habitats of the Indian and Pacific Oceans.

2 Duhat (Lamboy) or Jambul (Syzygium cumini) is an evergreen tropical tree in the flowering plant family Myrtaceae.

3 There are some 180 different snakes in the Philippines; according to the World Wild Life Guide, 19 of these snakes are venomous, of these the Philippine Cobra is the most dangerous. This snake is considered to be the world's third most venomous snake.

4 Watt G, Padre L, Tuazon M.L, Hayes, *Bites by the Philippine Cobra* (Naja naja philippinensis): an important cause of death among rice farmers. U.S. Naval Medical Research Unit No. 2, San Francisco 96528–5000.

5 When the U.S. entered the First World War, the British P14 was modified and standardized by the U.S. Ordnance Department and went into production at the same factories as had produced the P14, production of that rifle having ceased, as the Model of 1917. Sometimes called the M1917 Enfield, it was chambered for the standard US 30-06 cartridge and enjoyed some success as a complement for the Springfield M1903 rifles which were America's official standard issue, soon far surpassing the Springfield in total production and breadth of issue.

6 *Paltik* is a Filipino term for a homemade gun. Center of the *paltik industry* is Danao in Cebu.

7 A bolo is a large cutting tool of Filipino origin similar to the machete, used particularly in the sugar fields. The bolo is called an *iták* or *undáng* in Tagalog.

8 Indigenous healers (hilot), *Tabunan*, pp. 61–77.

9 *Tabunan*, p. 70.

10 Ibid., p. 66.

11 Ibid., p. 76.

12 Ibid., p. 77.

CHAPTER 12: JAPANESE COUNTERATTACKS

1 Segura, Col. Manuel F., *World War II in Central Visayas, Philippines*, pp. 81–83.

2 http://www.awf.or.jp/e1/philippine-00.html.

3 Today's APO cement plant in Naga.

4 UP: University of the Philippines.

5 *Tabunan*, p. 141.

6 Nakata & Nelson, *Imperial Japanese Army and Navy Uniforms & Equipment, New Revised Edition*, p. 31.

7 This was most probably a Type 90 Cal. 75 mm Field Gun with a range of 15 km.

8 Club Filipino is a golf club that used to be situated in the northern outskirts of Cebu City. For a canon the distance from Club Filipino to Babag is approximately 10 km.

9 The Aichi D3A, (Allied reporting name "Val") was a World War II carrier-borne dive bomber of the Imperial Japanese Navy (IJN). It was the primary dive bomber in the Imperial Japanese Navy, and participated in almost all actions, including Pearl Harbor.

10 The Type 92 Battalion Gun was a light howitzer used by the Imperial Japanese Army during the Second Sino-Japanese War and World War II. Each infantry battalion included two Type 92 guns; therefore, the Type 92 was referred to as "Battalion Artillery."

11 *Tabunan*, pp. 142–145.

12 Segura, Manuel F, *World War II in Central Visayas, Stories of World War II*, pp. 88–91 (hereafter "Stories").

13 Villamor, various pages.

14 Horse drawn carriages, the taxis of that time.

15 Cushing, p. 9.

16 *Stories*, pp. 91–94.

17 This term came from the Japanese cry *Tenno Heika Banzai* ("Long lives the Emperor"), shortened to banzai, and it specifically refers to a tactic used by Japanese soldiers during the Pacific War.

18 Cushing, p. 10.

CHAPTER 13: GUERRILLA WARFARE IN THE PHILIPPINES

1 Willoughby, Maj. Gen. Charles A., *The Guerrilla Resistance Movement in the Philippines: 1941–1945*, Vantage Press, New York, 1972, p. 39 (hereafter "Guerrilla").

2 Whitney, Courtney, *MacArthur: His Rendezvous With History* (NY: Knopf, 1956), p. 128. See also Douglas MacArthur, *Reminiscences* (NY: McGraw Hill, 1964), pp. 202–204.

3 Farolan, Ramon, *Message from Nakar*, Philippine Daily Inquirer, October 1, 2012.

4 Gause, Capt. Damon J., *The War Journal of Major Damon 'Rocky' Gause*. New York, 2000.

5 *Guerrilla*, p. 40.

6 *Guerrilla*, p. 41.

7 Pinoy (Watchdog).com, 18 Dec. 2012.

8 Ibid.

9 Ibid.

10 Ibid.

11 Ibid.

12 Ibid.

13 Long, Gavin (1963), *Appendix 4: Allied Intelligence Bureau* (PDF). Australia in the War of 1939–1945. Series 1—Army. Volume VII—The Final Campaigns (1st ed.). Canberra, Australia: Australian War Memorial. pp. 617–622.

14 *Jesus A. Villamor.* Hall of Valor, Military Times. Gannett Government Media Corporation.

15 Karsten, Peter (1998), *The Training and Socializing of Military Personnel,* Taylor & Francis, pp. 112–113.

16 Ostlund, Mike (2006), *Find 'Em, Chase 'Em, Sink 'em: The Mysterious Loss of the WWII Submarine USS* Gudgeon. Globe Pequot, pp. 391.

17 *Intelligence Activities in the Philippines During the Japanese Occupation,* Volume II, Intelligence Series, pp. 10–14.

18 Ibid., pp. 11–12.

19 Ibid., p. 12.

20 Mills, Scott A., *Stranded in the Philippines,* Annapolis: 2009, various pages.

21 Ibid., various pages.

22 See Vol. I: Intelligence Series, *The Guerrilla Resistance Movement in the Philippines,* Chap. VIII, pp. 69–77.

23 *Intelligence Activities in the Philippines During the Japanese Occupation,* Volume II, Intelligence Series, p. 11.

24 Ingham, Travis (1945), *Rendezvous by Submarine: The Story of Charles Parsons and the Guerrilla-Soldiers in the Philippines.* Doubleday, Doran and Company.

25 *Intelligence Activities in the Philippines during the Japanese Occupation,* Volume II, Intelligence Series, p. 14.

26 Ibid., p. 15.

27 In this period, the various guerrilla leaders adopted a somewhat exaggerated classification of their improvised units, viz., Corps, Divisions, Brigades, etc. GHQ attempted to discreetly "lower these estimates" without embarrassing the ambitious commanders. The delineation of pre-war Military Districts was a step toward normal standards.

28 *Intelligence Activities in the Philippines During the Japanese Occupation,* Volume II, Intelligence Series, p. 18.

29 Reports of General MacArthur, *The Campaigns of MacArthur in the Pacific,* Volume I, pp. 319–325.

30 Colonel Kobayashi, G-3, Fourteenth Area Army, paid tribute to Major (later Colonel) Anderson in the following words: "About the middle of October 1944, we attempted to extirpate the guerrilla movement in Luzon. Unfortunately for us, however, Colonel Anderson was too good a leader and the American guerrillas continued to function. ... In recalling the final stage of the war in the Philippines ... I remember how famous Colonel Anderson became among us." Interrogation Files, G-2 Historical Section, GHQ, FEC.

31 Reports of General MacArthur, *The Campaigns of MacArthur in the Pacific,* Volume I, pp. 319–325.

32 Ibid., Major Volckmann was promoted to the rank of Lieutenant Colonel on 9 October 1944.

CHAPTER 14: THE BATTLE FOR TABUNAN

1 *Stories*, p. 101.
2 *Stories*, pp. 96–101.
3 Cushing, p. 12.
4 *Tabunan*, pp. 160–170.
5 *Stories*, pp. 101–105.
6 Segura, Manuel F., *The Koga Papers*, p. 238.
7 Villamor, p. 29.

CHAPTER 15: THE STRUGGLE FOR RECOGNITION

1 *Tabunan*, p. 148.
2 Ibid., p. 149.
3 *Tabunan*, 192.
4 Scott A. Mills, *Stranded in the Philippines*, Annapolis: 2009, p. 112.
5 *Tabunan*, p. 190.
6 Ibid., p. 150.
7 Ibid.
8 Ibid.
9 Ibid.
10 Scott A. Mills, *Stranded in the Philippines*, Annapolis: 2009, Chapter 16.
11 Ibid.
12 Ibid., pp. 108, 110.
13 Ibid., pp. 111–112.
14 Villamor, p. 30.
15 *Tabunan*, p. 181.
16 *Manila Tribune*, 13 March, 1943. Willoughby, *Guerrilla Resistance*, p. 418; Philippine Studies, Donald Chaput, *The Miner Warriors of the Philippines*, Ateneo de Manila University, 1987.
17 Segura, Manuel F., *The Koga Papers*, Cebu City, 1992, pp. 223–224.
18 Ibid.
19 Villamor, p. 31.
20 *Tabunan*, p. 184.
21 Joseph, Irving Victor, *Philippine Evacuee Report 336* (7 August 1944), MacArthur Archives, RG16, p. 14 (Hereafter Joseph).
22 GHQ Far East Command, *Report Major Jesus A. Villamor*, Brisbane 1943, p. 26.
23 Ibid., p. 268.
24 Ibid., pp. 270–272.
25 Intelligence Activities in the Philippines During the Japanese Occupation, Volume II, Intelligence Series, p. 57.
26 Snell, Jay Russell, *Philippine Evacuee Report 294*, NARA, RG319, 13 June 1944 (Hereafter Snell).
27 Joseph.
28 Trent Smith, Steven, *The Rescue*, New York, 2001, pp. 106, 107.
29 Ibid., p. 118.

30 Villamor, Jesus A. and Snyder, Gerald S., *They Never Surrendered: A True Story of Resistance in World War II* (Manila: Vera-Ryes, 1982), pp. 195–200.

31 Trent Smith, Steven *The Rescue*, New York, 2001, p. 120.

32 Willoughby, Charles A. ed. *Guerrilla Resistance Movements in the Philippines*, Brisbane: GHQ, SWPA, NARA, RG338, 31 March 1945.

33 *Tabunan*, pp. 188–189.

34 *Tabunan*, pp. 192–193.

35 Youth and Student Movement in the Philippines, Anakbayan, LA.

36 Sounds of New Hope (trailer), December 2012.

37 Guerero, Amado, *Philippine Society and Revolution,* International Association of Filipino Books, pp. 78, 98, 215.

38 *Participating Organizations.* Fourth Assembly of the ILPS. International League of Peoples Struggles.

39 Villamor, pp. 196, 197.

40 Segura, Manuel F., *World War II in Central Visayas,* Cebu City, 2011. pp. 116–129.

41 Ibid.

42 *Tabunan*, p. 195.

43 Cayetano, p. 31.

44 *Tabunan*, pp. 197–201.

45 In his book *Tabunan* Segura states that the execution took place on 1 September 1943; according to the Office of the Judge Advocate Service HCAC, USFIP trial and execution took place on 16 September 1943.

46 *Tabunan*, pp. 210–214.

47 The *Guerrilla Resistance Movement in the Philippines,* Vol. I, Intelligence series, p. 37.

48 *Tabunan*, pp. 203–204.

49 Trent Smith, Steven, *The Rescue*, New York, 2001, p. 120.

50 US Army Recognition Program of Philipine Guerrillas, pp. 60–64.

51 The *Guerrilla Resistance Movement in the Philippines*, Vol. I, Intelligence series, p. 38.

52 *Tabunan*, pp. 85–90.

CHAPTER 16: THE CODE BREAKERS

1 Smith, Michael, *The Emperor's Codes: Bletchley Park and the Breaking of Japan's Secret Ciphers,* 2000, Bantam London.

2 Langer, Howard (1999), *World War II: An Encyclopedia of Quotations.* Greenwood Publishing Group. p.198.

3 Kahn, David (1996), *The Codebreakers: The Comprehensive History of Secret Communication from Ancient Times to the Internet.* Scribner. Text from excerpt [dead link] of first chapter on WNYC website.

4 *Red and Purple: A Story Retold NSA Analysts' Modern-Day Attempt to Duplicate Solving the Red and Purple Ciphers.* Cryptologic Quarterly Article (NSA), Fall/Winter 1984–1985, Vol. 3, Nos. 3–4 (last accessed: 2 April 2013).

5 Clark, R.W. (1977), *The Man Who Broke Purple.* London: Weidenfeld and Nicolson, pp. 103–112.

6 Herbert P. Bix, *Hirohito and the Making of Modern Japan*, p. 421.

7 Parker, Frederick D., *A Priceless Advantage: U.S. Navy Communications Intelligence and the Battles of Coral Sea, Midway, and the Aleutians,* National Security Agency, Central Security Service.

8 Holmes, W.J. (1979), *Double-Edged Secrets: U.S. Naval Intelligence Operations in the Pacific During World War II,* Annapolis: Blue Jacket Books/Naval Institute Press.

9 Gilmore, Allison (2004), *The Allied Translator and Interpreter Section: The Critical Role of Allied Linguists in the Process of Propaganda Creation, 1943–1944* (PDF). In Dennis, Peter and Grey, Jeffrey. *The Foundations of Victory: The Pacific War 1943–1944,* Proceedings of the 2003 Chief of Army's Military History Conference. Canberra: Army History Unit, p. 2.

10 http://www.ozatwar.com/sigint/atis.htm.

11 Marshal-Admiral (gensui kaigun-taishō) was the highest rank in the prewar Imperial Japanese Navy.

12 The original message, NTF131755, addressed to the commanders of Base Unit No. 1, the 11th Air Flotilla, and the 26th Air Flotilla.

13 Prados, John (1995), *Combined Fleet Decoded: The Secret History of American Intelligence and the Japanese Navy in World War II,* New York: Random House.

14 Davis, Donald A. (2005), *Lightning Strike: The Secret Mission to Kill Admiral Yamamoto and Avenge Pearl Harbor,* New York: St. Martin's Press, p. 232–233.

15 Toland, John, *The Rising Sun, The Decline and Fall of the Japanese Empire,* New York: 1970, p. 544.

16 Chen, Peter, *Shiguru Fukudome,* http://www.ww2db.com World War II Database .

CHAPTER 17: DOCUMENTS THAT CHANGED THE WAR IN THE PACIFIC

1 Bradsher, Greg, "The 'Z Plan' Story: Japan's 1944 Naval Battle Strategy Drifts into U.S. Hands," *Prologue Magazine,* Fall 2005, Vol. 37, No. 3.

2 *The Naval War in the Pacific: Interrogation of Vice Admiral Fukudome, Shigeru,* IJN; Transcript 9–12 December 1945, p. 511, 512.

3 Ibid., p. 516.

4 Bradsher.

5 Ibid.

6 Ibid.

7 Ibid.

8 *The Naval War in the Pacific: Interrogation of Vice Admiral Fukudome, Shigeru,* IJN; Transcript 9–12 December 1945, p. 519.

9 Ibid., p. 520.

10 *The Koga Papers,* pp. 10–14.

11 Ibid.

12 Ibid.

13 Cushing to MacArthur, NR13 (NARA, RG338, 14 April 1944).

14 *The Koga Papers,* p. 50.

15 PRS Check Sheet, 14 April 1944, MacArthur archives.

16 *The Koga Papers,* Tabunan, Snell, Dyer, Bradshaw.

17 *The Koga Papers,* p. 57.

18 Fertig to MacArhur (NARA, RG338, 25 April 1944).
19 *The Koga Papers,* pp. 310–313.
20 Ibid., p. 320.
21 Ibid., 321.
22 Jovito, p. 252.
23 PRS Check Sheet (NARA, RG338, 26 April 1944).
24 Bradshaw, Part 2.
25 Cushing to MacArthur, NR26 (NARA, RG338, 2 May 1944).
26 Bradshaw, Part 2.
27 Ibid.
28 Crane, Koga (May 3, 1944) 1200.
29 Bradshaw, Part 2.
30 MacArthur to Abcede, NR69 (NARA, RG407, 7 May 1944).
31 Bradshaw, Part 2.
32 MacArthur to Abcede, NR70 (NARA, RG407, 7 May 1944).
33 MacArthur to Abcede, NR72 (NARA, RG407, 10 May 1944).
34 MacArthur to Abcede, SVC15 (NARA, RG407, 11 May 1944).

CHAPTER 18: PLAN Z IN AMERICAN HANDS

1 Dissette, Edward and Adamson, Hans Christian, *Guerrilla Submarines,* New York: 1980, Chapter 7.
2 Report War Patrol-3, USS *Crevalle,* (RWP-3) p. 1.
3 Ships of the US Navy, 1940–1945, www.ibiblio.org/hyperwar/USN/ships/SS/SS-291 _Crevalle.html.
4 RWP-3, p. 11, 31.
5 Smith, Steven Trent: *The Rescue,* New York: 2001.
6 Ibid., p. 198–199.
7 RWP-3, Special Mission Report.
8 Russell L. Forsythe, Philippine Evacuee Report 303 (NARA, RG338, 13 June 1944).
9 Bradshaw, Part 2.
10 RWP-3, pp. 33–38.
11 Ibid.
12 Bradshaw, Part 2.
13 RWP-3, p. 41.
14 *The Rescue,* pp. 235–236.
15 Ibid., p. 237.
16 Bradshaw, Part 2.
17 *The Rescue,* pp. 240–241.
18 Records of General Headquarters, Far East Command, Supreme Commander Allied Powers, and United Nations Command, RG 554.
19 *Tabunan,* p. 250.
20 Prados, John, *Combined Fleet Decoded: The Secret History of American Intelligence and the Japanese Navy in World War II,* New York: 1995, p. 551.
21 Bradshaw, Part 2.

22 *The Rescue*, p. 245.

23 Bradshaw, Part 2.

24 *Tabunan*, p. 251.

25 *The Koga Papers*, p. 59.

26 Whitney to Cushing (NARA, RG338, 23 May 1944).

27 MacArthur to Abcede, NR59 (NARA, RG338, 31 May 1944).

28 Bradshaw, Part 2.

29 Ibid.

30 Ibid.

31 Shores, Christopher, *Duel for the Sky: Ten Crucial Battles of World War II*, Grub Street, London: 1985, p. 205.

32 Smith, Robert Ross, *The War in the Pacific: Triumph in the Philippines* (Washington, DC). Department of the Army, Office of the Chief of Military History, 1963, pp. 607, 608.

33 Advanced Allied Translator and Interpreter Section, South West Pacific Area, No. 45, 24 January 45, p. 1, 2, 3.

CHAPTER 19: GENERAL DOUGLAS MACARTHUR AND THE PHILIPPINES

1 Home page, McArthur Museum of Arkansas.

2 Leary, William, M (2001), *MacArthur and the American Century: A Reader*, University of Nebraska Press.

3 MacArthur, *Reminiscences*, p. 29.

4 Ibid.

5 Ibid., pp. 103–104.

6 Ibid., p. 106.

7 *Reminiscences*, p. 113.

8 *The Fall of the Philippines—US Army in World War II*, p. 499. The two divisions used as reserves, the 71st and 91st, were not from Luzon but from the Visayas, and each had only two regiments.

9 Ibid., p. 499.

10 Strength and Composition of U.S. Army Troops in Philippine Islands, 30 November 1941.

11 *Reminiscences*, p. 114.

12 The Advertiser (Adelaide, SA: 1931–1954).

13 Gailey, Harry A. (2004), *MacArthur's Victory: The War in New Guinea, 1943–1944*, New York (Hereafter Gailey), p. 7.

14 Manchester, William, *American Caesar*, New York: 1950 (Hereafter Caesar), p. 327.

15 Drea, Edward; Bradsher, Greg; Hanyok, Robert; Lide, James; Petersen, Michael; Yang, Daqing (2006), *Researching Japanese War Crimes Records*. Washington, D.C.: pp. 18–19.

16 Alexander, Joseph H. (2000), *Edson's Raiders: The 1st Marine Raider Battalion in World War II*, Naval Institute Press, p. 72; Frank, Richard (1990), *Guadalcanal: The Definitive Account of the Landmark Battle*, New York: Random House, p. 240; *Guadalcanal*, New York, p. 5; Lundstrom, John B. (2005 New edition), *The First Team and the*

Guadalcanal Campaign: Naval Fighter Combat from August to November 1942, p. 39.

17 Edwin P. Hoyt, *Japan's War*, p 305–6.

18 Frank, Richard, *Guadalcanal: The Definitive Account of the Landmark Battle*, New York, 1990, p. 247–252, 293, 417–420, 430–431, 521–522, 529.

19 Ibid.

20 Ibid., p. 156–157, 164.

21 Ibid., p. 589–597.

22 Ibid., p. 589–59729 American Caesar, p. 378.

23 Hough, Frank O.; Ludwig, Verle E., and Shaw, Henry I., Jr. (Unknown date). *Pearl Harbor to Guadalcanal.* History of U.S. Marine Corps Operations in World War II, p. 372.

24 Samuel Eliot Morison, *History of United States Naval Operations in World War II.* Vol. 3.

25 Willmott, H. P., *Barrier and the Javelin* (Annapolis: Naval Institute Press, 1983).

26 Toland, John, *The Rising Sun: The Decline and Fall of the Japanese Empire 1936–1945*, New York, 1970, p. 368–371; 376–392.

27 Parshall, Jonathan; Tully, Anthony (2005). *Shattered Sword: The Untold Story of the Battle of Midway.* Potomac Books. pp.19–38.

28 Reports of General MacArthur, *The Campaigns of MacArthur in the Pacific*, Vol. 1., p. 132.

29 United States Strategic bombing Survey, *The Allied Campaign Against Rabaul.* p. 24.

30 Reports of General MacArthur, *The Campaigns of MacArthur in the Pacific*, Vol. 1., p. 133.

31 Parillo, Mark P., *Japanese Merchant Marine in World War II,* United States Naval Institute Press, 1993.

32 Reports of General MacArthur, *The Campaigns of MacArthur in the Pacific*, Vol. 1., Ch. VI.

33 Ibid., Ch. VI.

34 Evans, David C & Peattie, Mark R, *Kaigun: Strategy, Tactics, and Technology in the Imperial Japanese Navy, 1887–1941*, Annapolis: 1997.

35 Keegan, John, *The American Civil War*, New York: Knopf, 2009. p. 272.

36 Mahan, Alfred Thayer, *The Influence of Sea Power upon History, 1660–1783* (1890) online edition.

37 Ibid.

38 Peattie, Mark & Evans, David, *Kaigun*, U.S. Naval Institute Press, 1997.

39 Mahan, Proceedings article 1906.

40 Goldstein, Donald & Dillon, Katherine *The Pearl Harbor Papers*, Brassey's, 1993.

41 Crowl, Philip A., *Alfred Thayer Mahan: The Naval Historian in Makers of Modern Strategy from Machiavelli to the Nuclear Age*, Peter Paret, ed., Oxford: Clarendon Press, 1986.

42 Reports of General MacArthur, *The Campaigns of MacArthur in the Pacific*, Vol. 1., p. 134.

43 CINCSWPA Radio No. C-1217 to WARCOS, 2 Feb 44, WD CIS, JCS and CCS Papers No. 2, G-3, GHQ Exec Files (S).

CHAPTER 20: PLANNING THE RETURN

1 Interrogation Files, G-2 Historical Section, GHQ, FEC.
2 Reports of General MacArthur, *The Campaigns of MacArthur in the Pacific*, Vol. 1, p. 170–172.
3 G-2, GHQ, SWPA, *Philippine Monthly Combined Situation Report*, 15 Jun 44. Japanese reinforcement in the Philippines continued throughout the summer and autumn of 1944. G-2, GHQ, SWPA, *Philippine Monthly Combined Situation Report*, 15 Jul and 15 Aug, 44. See also G-2, GHQ, SWPA, *Monthly Summary of Enemy Dispositions*, 30 Sep 4.
4 COM3rdFLT Radio to CINCPOA, CINCSWPA, COMINCH, 13 Sep 44, G-3, GHQ, Admin 385 (TS).
5 CINCPOA Radio to COM3rdFLT, 13 Sep 44, CIS, GHQ, SOPAC NO. 522(S).
6 CINCSWPA Radio No. C-17744 to JCS, CINCPOA, 14 Sep 44, G-3, GHQ, Admin 385 (TS).
7 *Biennial Report of the Chief of Staff of the United States Army to the Secretary of War, July 1, 1943 to June 30, 1945.*
8 Ibid.
9 Reports of General MacArthur, *The Campaigns of MacArthur in the Pacific*, Vol. I, p. 197.
10 *Tabunan*, p. 80.
11 Ibid., p. 81.
12 Abellana, Jovito, *My Moments of War to Remember By*, Cebu City: 2011, pp. 253, 254.
13 Report War Patrol-12 USS *Nautilus*.
14 Ibid., p. 4.
15 Ibid.
16 Japanese soldiers had short hair, Filipino guerrillas had long hair.
17 RWP-12, p. 6.
18 *The Koga Papers,* p. 334.
19 Ibid., p. 335–336.
20 Ibid., p. 337–341.
21 RWP-12, p. 6.
22 Running on command from starboard to port and back.
23 RWP-12, p. 7.
24 Ibid.
25 Ibid.
26 Ibid.
27 *Tabunan*, p. 80.

CHAPTER 21: "I HAVE RETURNED"

1 Reports of General MacArthur, *The Campaigns of MacArthur in the Pacific*, Vol. I, p. 195.
2 Ibid., p. 196.
3 10th Information and Historical Service, HQ Eighth Army, *Staff Study of Operations of the Japanese 35th Army on Leyte,* Part I (R).

4 General MacArthur's radio broadcast, 20 October 1944.

5 Interrogation Files, G-2 Historical Section, GHQ, FEC.

6 Reports of General MacArthur, *The Campaigns of MacArthur in the Pacific*, Vol. I, p. 204.

7 USSBS, *The Campaigns of the Pacific War*, p. 281.

8 The strength of the Japanese Fleet was estimated at 4–5 BB, II CA, 2 CL, 22 DD, plus 2 XCV-BB, 2 CV, 4 CVL." COM7thFLT Report Serial No. 000107 to CINCSWPA, 10 Jan 45.

9 Reports of General MacArthur, *The Campaigns of MacArthur in the Pacific*, Vol. I, p. 204.

10 Parkinson, Roger (1977), *Encyclopedia of Modern War*, p. 132.

11 Woodward, C. Vann (1947), *The Battle for Leyte Gulf*, New York: Macmillan.

12 Fuller, John F. C. (1956), *The Decisive Battles of the Western World III*. London: Eyre & Spottiswoode.

13 COM7thFLT Report to COMINCH US Fleet: *Report of Operation for the Capture of Leyte Island including Action Report of Engagements in Surigao Strait and off Samar Island on 25 October 1944 (King Two Operation)*, p. 37. Hereinafter cited as COM7th FLT Report.

14 Reports of General MacArthur, *The Campaigns of MacArthur in the Pacific*, Vol. I.

15 COM7thFLT Report, p. 37.

16 Admiral Kurita's formidable force was consistently underestimated in the early sightings. It was composed of the battleships, *Yamato, Musashi, Nagato, Kongo,* and *Haruna;* 10 heavy cruisers, the *Atago, Maya, Takao, Chokai, Myoko, Haguro, Kumano, Suzuya, Tone,* and *Chikuma;* 2 light cruisers, the *Noshiro* and *Yahagi;* and 15 destroyers.

17 COM7thFLT Report, p. 37.

18 The Southern Force at this time comprised 2 battleships, the *Yamashiro* and *Fuso,* the heavy cruiser *Mogami,* and 4 destroyers, the *Michishio, Asagumo, Yamagumo,* and *Shigure.*

19 Reports of General MacArthur, *The Campaigns of MacArthur in the Pacific*, Vol. I, p. 209.

20 Ibid., Ch. VIII.

21 Morison, Samuel E. (1956), *Leyte, June 1944–January 1945,* History of United States Naval Operations in World War II XII. Boston: Little & Brown.

22 Hackett, Bob & Kingsepp, Sander (2012), *IJN Battleship Musashi: Tabular Record of Movement.*

23 Lacroix, Eric & Wells, Linton (1997), *Japanese Cruisers of the Pacific War.* Annapolis, Maryland: Naval Institute Press. I, p. 347.

24 The battleship *Fuso* suffered minor damage in this attack which took place at 0800 on 24 October.

25 Admiral Oldendorf's fleet comprised 6 battleships, 8 cruisers, 26 destroyers, and several squadrons of torpedo boats. The battleships included some veterans of the Pearl Harbor disaster. The more modern battleships were with Admiral Halsey.

26 COM7thFLT Report p. 28.

27 Ibid., pp. 19-20.

28 Morison, Samuel E. (1956), *Leyte, June 1944–January 1945.* History of United States

Naval Operations in World War II, XII, Boston: Little & Brown.

29 COM7thFLT Report p. 14.

30 Morison, Samuel E. (1956), *Leyte, June 1944–January 1945* History of the United Naval Operations in World War II, XII. Boston: Little & Brown.

31 *Reminiscences*, p. 226.

32 Halsey and Bryan, op. Cit., pp. 216–217.

33 Reports of General MacArthur, *The Campaigns of MacArthur in the Pacific*, Vol. I, p. 218.

34 USSBS, *Interrogation of Japanese Officials*, Vol. I, pp. 151–152.

35 Morison, Samuel E. (1956), *Leyte, June 1944–January 1945*. History of United States Naval Operations in World War II, XII. Boston: Little & Brown.

36 Interrogation Files, G-2 Historical Section, GHQ, FEC.

37 Eighth Army, *Staff Study, Leyte*.

38 Interrogation of Col. Junkichi Okabayashi, Chief of Staff, Japanese 1st Division. Eighth Army, *Staff Study, Leyte*.

39 Ibid., pp. 235–236.

40 Reports of General MacArthur, *The Campaigns of MacArthur in the Pacific*, Vol. I, pp. 235–238.

CHAPTER 22: THE LIBERATION OF CEBU

1 GHQ, SWPA, *MUSKETEER III, Basic Outline Plan for Revised Philippine Operations*, 26 Sep 44. (Hereinafter cited as: MUSKETEER III.)

2 Ibid.

3 *Tabunan*, p. 254–257.

4 A History of Marine Fighter Attack Squadron 115 (https://www.mcu.usmc.mil/history division/Pages/StaffPublication20PGFs/A20HistoryOf20Marine20Fighter20Attack 20Squadron20115.pdf

5 Ibid.

6 *Tabunan*, p. 263.

7 A History of Marine Fighter Attack Squadron 115 (www.mcu. usmc.mil/ historydivision/Pages/ Staff/Publication20PDFs/A20History20Of20Marine20Fighter20Attack 20Squadron20115.pdf.

8 Ibid.

9 Ibid.

10 Ibid.

11 Ibid.

12 Ibid.

13 Ibid.

14 Ibid.

15 *Tabunan*, p. 280.

16 Lofgren, Stephen (1996), *Southern Philippines: The U.S. Army Campaigns of World War II*. Washington, DC: U.S. Army Center of Military History, p. 7.

17 Chant, Christopher (1986), *The Encyclopedia of Codenames of World War II*, Routledge, p. 322.

18 GHQ AFPAC, Staff Studies OLYMPIC and CORONET, 28 Mar and 15 Aug 45.
19 The Japanese side of the Cebu story comes from: Narrative of Maj Gen Yoshiharu Tomochika (CofS *35th Army*) and narrative of Col Junkichi Okabayashi (CofS *1st Div*), 10th I&H Staff Study.
20 *Triumph*, p. 610.
21 *Tabunan*, pp. 290–291.
22 *Cebu: Hostile Beach 1945*. Company G, 182d Infantry Regiment: Fighting the War in the Pacific. (http://www.182ndinfantery.org/history/exhibits/show/182nd/pacific/cebu). (Hereafter "Hostile.")
23 *Triumph*, p. 611.
24 Ibid., p. 612.
25 Manuel F. Segura, *World War II in Central Visayas*, Philippines, p. 156.
26 Hostile.
27 Ibid.
28 Ibid.
29 *Triumph*, p. 612.
30 Hostile.
31 Lofgren, p. 20.
32 http://en.wikipedia.org/wiki/Battle_for_Cebu_City.
33 *Triumph*, p. 613.
34 Rottman, p. 311.
35 *Triumph*, p. 613.
36 Ibid., p. 614.
37 Ibid.
38 Ibid.
39 Ibid., p. 615.
40 *Tabunan*, p. 223, 224.
41 Ibid., p. 326.
42 *Triumph*, p. 615.
43 Some of these 8,500 undoubtedly included a few late escapees from Leyte, for a tiny trickle of Japanese continued to make their way to Cebu from Leyte even after 26 March.
44 Eighth Army Report Panay-Negros and Cebu Operations, pp. 163–64. General Arnold, in his comments on this MS dated 26 December 1956 took exception to the part about relaxed discipline in the medical report.

CHAPTER 23: THE END OF WORLD WAR II

1 *Triumph*.
2 *Creating Military Power: The Sources of Military Effectiveness*. Risa Brooks, Stanley, Elizabeth A., 2007, Stanford University Press. p.41.
3 White, Matthew, *Death Tolls for the Man-made Megadeaths of the 20th Century*.
4 O'Reilly, Charles T. (2001), *Forgotten Battles: Italy's War of Liberation, 1943–1945*, Lanham, MD: Lexington Books, p. 244.
5 Glantz, David M. (1998), *When Titans Clashed: How the Red Army Stopped Hitler*, Uni-

versity Press of Kansas, p. 24.

6 Powers, D. (2011), *Japan: No Surrender in World War,* Two BBC History, 17 February 2011.

7 Dear, I.C.B & Foot, M.R.D. (2005), *Blitz: The Oxford Companion to World War II,* Oxford: Oxford University Press. pp. 108–109.

8 Overy, Richard & Wheatcroft, Andrew (1999), *The Road to War* (2nd ed.), New York: p. 328–30.

9 Cantril, Hadley (1940), "America Faces the War: A Study in Public Opinion," *Public Opinion Quarterly* 4(3): 387–407.JSTOR 2745078, p. 390.

10 Clancey, Patrick, *The Voice of the Crane: The Imperial Rescript of 15 Aug 45,* University of North Carolina at Chapel Hill; retrieved 27 September 2012.

11 "The Emperor's Speech: 67 Years Ago, Hirohito Transformed Japan Forever," *The Atlantic,* 15 August 201.

12 *Triumph,* p. 650.

13 Ibid., p. 651.

14 Ibid., p. 656.

15 Ibid., p. 658.

16 Treaty of General Relations Between the United States of America and the Republic of the Philippines. Signed At Manila on 4 July 1946 (pdf), United Nations.

17 Schirmer, Daniel B & Shalom, Stephen Rosskamm (1987), *The Philippines Reader: A History of Colonialism, Neocolonialism, Dictatorship, and Resistance,* South End Press, p. 88.

18 Drogin, Bob, "After 89 Years, U.S. Lowers Flag at Clark Air Base." *Los Angeles Times,* November 27, 1991.

CHAPTER 24: THE OTSU INCIDENT IN HINDSIGHT

1 USSBS, Interrogations of Japanese Officials, V.Ad. Fukudome, Interrogation NAV NO 115, USSBS NO 503, 9–12 December 1945, p. 519–522.

2 Pacific War Online Encyclopedia.

3 http://wcsc.berkeley.edu/wp-content/uploads/Japan/singapore/ Trials/Fukudome.htm# top.

4 Pacific War Online Encyclopedia.

5 Crane Files,NARA, RG38/370/05/16, 1602.

6 Cramoisi, George, *Air Crash Investigations: Lost Over the Atlantic, the Crash of Air France Flight 447,* 2013.

CHAPTER 25: COLONEL JAMES M. CUSHING

1 Toland, John, *The Rising Sun, The Decline and Fall of the Japanese Empire,* New York: 1971, p. 547.

2 *Manila Times,* 29 August 1963.

3 *New York Times,* 29 August 1963.

BIBLIOGRAPHY

BOOKS

Abellana, Jovito, *Aginid, Bayok sa Atong Tawarik*, 1952.

Abellana, Jovito, *My Moments of War to Remember By*, Cebu, 1949/2011.

Agawa, Hiroyuki (Bester, John, trans.), *The Reluctant Admiral*, New York: Kodansha, 1979.

Alexander, Joseph H., *Edson's Raiders: The 1st Marine Raider Battalion in World War II*, Annapolis, MD: Naval Institute Press, 2000.

Ancheta, Celedonio, ed., *The Wainwright Papers, Vol. I*, Quezon City, Phil.: New Day Publishers, 1980.

Aquino, Ramon C., *Last Days, Chief Justice Jose Abad Santos, 1886–1942: A Biography*, Quezon City: Phoenix Publishing House, 1985.

Baclagon, Uldarico S., *They Chose to Fight*, Quezon City: Capitol Publihing House, 1962.

Barreveld, Drs. Dirk J., *De Liefde's Tragiek en Triomf*, Epe, 2001.

Barreveld, Drs. Dirk J., *The Philippines in a Nutshell*, Cebu, 2001.

Barreveld, Drs. Dirk J., *Cebu, Leisure and Business Paradise in the Philippines*, Cebu, 2005.

Beasley, W. G,. *The Rise of Modern Japan*, 2000.

Behr, Edward, *The Last Emperor*, 1987.

Bix, Herbert P. *Hirohito and the Making of Modern Japan*, 2001.

Bleakley, Jack, *The Eavesdroppers*. Canberra: AGPS (Australian Government Publishing Service), 1991.

Bradsher, Dr. Greg, *Japanese War Crimes and Related Topics: A Guide to Records at the US National Archives*.

Brown, Louis, *A Radar History of World War II*, Inst. of Physics Publishing, 1999.

Burdeos, Ray L., *Filipinos in the US Navy & Coast Guard During the Vietnam*

War, New York, 2008.

Cayetano M. Villamor, *My Guerrilla Years,* Cebu City, 1955.

Chant, Christopher, *The Encyclopedia of Codenames of World War II,* New York Routledge, 1986.

Clark, R.W., *The Man Who Broke Purple,* London: Weidenfeld and Nicolson, 1977.

Coronel, Chua, Rimban, & Cruz, *The Rulemakers,* Philippine Center for Investigative Journalism, 2007.

Craigie, William A., & Hubert, James R., eds., *A Dictionary of American English on Historical Principles,* 4 vols., Univ. of Chicago Press, 1938–1944.

Crowl, Philip A., *Alfred Thayer Mahan: The Naval Historian in Makers of Modern Strategy from Machiavelli to the Nuclear Age,* Oxford: Clarendon Press, 1986.

Davis, Burke, *Get Yamamoto,* New York: Random House, 1969.

Davis, Donald A., *Lightning Strike: The Secret Mission to Kill Admiral Yamamoto and Avenge Pearl Harbor,* New York: St. Martin's Press, 2005.

deBary, William Theodore, *Sources of East Asian Tradition: The Modern Period,* New York: Columbia University Press, 2008.

Dennis, Peter, & Grey, Jeffrey, *The Foundations of Victory: The Pacific War 1943–1944.* Proceedings of the 2003 Chief of Army's Military History Conference, Canberra: Army History Unit.

Dissette, Edward, & Adamson, Hans Christian, *Guerrilla Submarines,* New York: Bantam Books, 1980.

Dower, John W., *War Without Mercy: Race & Power in the Pacific War,* New York: Pantheon, 1986.

Drea, Edward J., *In the Service of the Emperor: Essays on the Imperial Japanese Army.* Lincoln: University of Nebraska Press, 1998.

Dull, Paul S., *A Battle History of the Imperial Japanese Navy, 1941–1945,* Annapolis, MD: Naval Institute Press, 1978.

Evans, David C., & Peattie, Mark R., *Kaigun: Strategy, Tactics, and Technology in the Imperial Japanese Navy, 1887–1941,* Annapolis, MD: Naval Institute Press, 1997.

Ezrow, Natasha M., & Franz, Erica, *Dictators and Dictatorships: Understanding Authoritarian Regimes and Their Leaders,* London: Continuum Publishing, 2011.

Frank, Richard, *Guadalcanal: The Definitive Account of the Landmark Battle,* New York: Penguin, 1990.

Fuller, John F. C., *The Decisive Battles of the Western World, Vol. III,* London: Eyre & Spottiswoode, 1956.

Fusé, Toyomasa, *Suicide and culture in Japan: A study of seppuku as an institutionalized form of suicide,* Jnl. of Social Psychiatry and Psychiatric Epidemiology 15(2), 1979.

Gailey, Harry A., *MacArthur's Victory: The War in New Guinea, 1943–1944,* Novato, CA: Presidio Press, 2004.

Gause, Capt. Damon J., *The War Journal of Major Damon 'Rocky' Gause,* New York: Hachette, 2000.

Gilmore, Allison, *The Allied Translator and Interpreter Section: The critical role of allied linguists in the process of propaganda creation, 1943–1944,* 2004.

Glines, Carroll V. *Attack on Yamamoto,* Atglen, PA: Schiffer, 1990.

Goldstein, Donald, & Dillon, Katherine, *The Pearl Harbor Papers* (Brassey's, 1993).

Griffith, Samuel B., *The Battle for Guadalcanal,* Champaign: University of Illinois Press, 1963.

Guardia, Mike, *American Guerrilla: The Forgotten Heroics of Russell W. Volckmann, the Man Who Escaped Bataan, Raised a Filipino Army against the Japanese, and Became the True "Father" of Army Special Forces,* Havertown, PA: Casemate, 2010.

Guerero, Amado, *Philippine Society and Revolution,* International Association of Filipino Books (n.d.).

Hall, Cargill R., *Lightning Over Bougainville,* Washington, D.C.: Smithsonian Institution Press, 1991.

Hammel, Eric, *Carrier Clash: The Invasion of Guadalcanal & The Battle of the Eastern Solomons, August 1942,* St. Paul, MN: Pacifica Military History, 1999.

Hardy, Charles O., *Is There Enough Gold?* Washington, D.C.: The Brookings Institution, 1936.

Hayashi, Saburo, *Kogun: The Japanese Army in the Pacific War.* Marine Corps Association, 1959.

Henry, James S. & Bradley, Bill, *The Blood Bankers: Tales from the Global Underground Economy,* Basic Books, 2005.

Holbrook, Stewart H., *None More Courageous: American War Heroes of Today,* Macmillan & Co, 1942.

Holmes, Richard *The World Atlas of Warfare,* Viking Press, 1988.

Holmes, W. J., *Double-Edged Secrets: U.S. Naval Intelligence Operations in the*

Pacific During World War II. Annapolis, MD: Blue Jacket Books/Naval Institute Press, 1979.

Hough, Frank O., Ludwig, Verle E., & Shaw, Henry I., Jr., *Pearl Harbor to Guadalcanal: History of U.S. Marine Corps Operations in World War II, Volume 1,* The Battery Press, 1993.

Hoyt, Edwin P., *Japan's War: The Great Pacific Conflict,* Cooper Square Press, 2001.

Hoyt, Edwin P., *Yamamoto: The Man Who Planned Pearl Harbor.* New York: McGraw-Hill, 1990.

Ingham, Travis, *Rendezvous by Submarine: The Story of Charles Parsons and the Guerrilla-Soldiers in the Philippines.* Doubleday, Doran and Company, 1945.

Jersey, Stanley Coleman, *Hell's Islands: The Untold Story of Guadalcanal.* College Station, TX: Texas A&M University Press, 2008.

Kahn, David, *The Codebreakers: The Comprehensive History of Secret Communication from Ancient Times to the Internet,* Scribner, 1996.

Karsten, Peter, *The Training and Socializing of Military Personnel.* Taylor & Francis, 1998.

Keats, John, *They Fought Alone.* Pocket Books, 1965.

Keegan, John, *The American Civil War,* New York: Knopf, 2009.

Lacroix, Eric, & Wells, Linton, *Japanese Cruisers of the Pacific War,* Annapolis, MD: Naval Institute Press, 1997.

Langer, Howard J., *World War II: An Encyclopedia of Quotations,* Greenwood Publishing Group, 1999.

Leary, William M., *MacArthur and the American Century: A Reader,* University of Nebraska Press, 2001.

Levene, Mark & Roberts, Penny, *The Massacre in History,* Berghahn Books, 1999.

Liddell, Henry & Scott, Robert, *Scott's Greek-English Lexicon.* Oxford University Press, 1984.

Lide, James; Drea, Edwin; Bradsher, Greg, & Hanyok, Robert, *Researching Japanese War Crimes Records,* CreateSpace Independent, 2015.

Lofgren, Stephen, *Southern Philippines: The U.S. Army Campaigns of World War II.* Washington, DC: U.S. Army Center of Military History, 1996.

Lundstrom, John B., *The First Team and the Guadalcanal Campaign: Naval Fighter Combat from August to November 1942,* Naval Institute Press, 1993.

MacArthur, Douglas, *Reminiscences,* New York: McGraw-Hill, 1964.

Mahan, Alfred T., *The Influence of Sea Power Upon History, 1660–1783,* Pelican Publishing, 2003.

Malcolm, George A., *American Colonial Careerist,* Literary Licensing, 2012.

Manchester, William, *American Caesar: Douglas MacArthur 1880–1964,* New York: Little, Brown and Company, 1978.

Miller, Thomas G., *Cactus Air Force,* New York: Harper & Row, 1969.

Mills, Scott A., *Stranded in the Philippines: Professor Bell's Private War Against the Japanese,* Annapolis: Naval Institute Press, 2009

Molina, Antonio, *The Philippines: Through the Centuries,* Manila: University of Sto. Tomas Cooperative, 1961.

Morison, Samuel E., *History of United States Naval Operations in World War II.* Boston: Little, Brown, 1961.

Murray, Williamson & Millett, Allan R., *A War To Be Won: Fighting the Second World War,* Belknap Press, 2001.

Nakata & Nelson, *Imperial Japanese Army and Navy Uniforms & Equipment,* Ironside Intl Publishers, 2009.

Ostlund, Mike, *Find 'Em, Sink 'Em: The Mystrious Loss of the WWII Submarine USS* Gudgeon. Globe Pequot, 2006.

O'Reilly, Charles T., *Forgotten Battles: Italy's War of Liberation, 1943–1945,* Lanham, MD: Lexington Books, 2001.

Overy, Richard & Wheatcroft, Andrew, *The Road to War* (2nd ed.), New York: Vintage Books, 2009.

Parillo, Mark, *The United States in the Pacific,* in Higham, Robin; Harris, Stephen, *Why Air Forces Fail: the Anatomy of Defeat,* The University Press of Kentucky, 2006.

Parillo, Mark P., *Japanese Merchant Marine in World War II,* Naval Institute Press, 1993.

Parker, Frederick D., *A Priceless Advantage: U.S. Navy Communications Intelligence and the Battles of Coral Sea, Midway, and the Aleutians,* National Security Agency, Central Security Service.

Parkinson, Roger, *Encyclopedia of modern war,* Stein & Day, 1979.

Parshall, Jonathan & Tully, Anthony, *Shattered Sword: The Untold Story of the Battle of Midway,* Potomac Books, 2005.

Peattie, Mark, *Sunburst: The Rise of Japanese Naval Air Power, 1909–1941,* Naval Institute Press,

Peattie, Mark & Evans, David, *Kaigun,* U.S. Naval Institute Press, 1997.

Perry, Matthew C., *Narrative of the Expedition of an American Squadron to the Chinese Sea and Japan*, Nabu Press, 2010.

Petillo, Carol M., *Douglas MacArthur and Manuel Quezon: A Note on an Imperial Bond, Volume 48*, University of California Press, 1979.

Piccigallo, Philip, *The Japanese on Trial*, Austin: University of Texas Press, 1978.

Powers, D., *Japan: No Surrender in World War Two*, BBC History, 2011.

Prados, John, *Combined Fleet Decoded: The Secret History of American Intelligence and the Japanese Navy in World War II*. New York: Random House, 1995.

Prange, Gordon W., *At Dawn We Slept: The Untold Story of Pearl Harbor*, New York: Penguin Group/Viking Studio, 1981.

Prange, Gordon W., *God's Samurai: Lead Pilot at Pearl Harbor*, Brassey's (UK) Ltd, 1990.

Rees, Lawrence, *Horror in the East: Japan and the Atrocities of World War II*, Da Capo Press, 2002.

Reyes, Fernando R. & Nuval, Leonardo, Q., *World War II in the Philippines: The Visayas, Palawan, Mindoro, Masbate, Mindanao and Sulu*. Manila: Veterans Federation of the Philippines, 1996.

Rin-siyo, Siyun-zai, *Annales des empereurs du Japon, (1834)*, Nabu Press, 2011

Rivest, Ronald L., *Cryptology*, in Leeuwen, J. Van (ed.) *Handbook of Theoretical Computer Science*, Elsevier, 1990.

Robertson, James I., Jr., *Stonewall Jackson: The Man, The Soldier, The Legend*, New York: MacMillan Publishing, 1997.

Rummel, Rudolf, J., *Statistics of Democide: Genocide and Mass Murder since 1900*, LIT Verlag, 1998.

Saaler, Sven & Inaba Chiharu (Hg.), *Der Russisch-Japanische Krieg 1904/05 im Spiegel deutscher Bilderbogen*, Deutsches Institut für Japanstudien Tokyo, 2005.

Sauer, Howard, *The Last Big-Gun Naval Battle: The Battle of Surigao Strait*. Glencannon Press, 1999.

Schirmer, Daniel B. & Shalom, Stephen R., *The Philippines Reader: A History of Colonialism, Neocolonialism, Dictatorship, and Resistance*, South End Press, 1987.

Schultz, Duane, *Hero of Bataan: The Story of General Jonathan M. Wainwright*, St Martin's Press, 1981.

Segura, Manuel F., *Tabunan: The Untold Exploits of the Famed Cebu Guerrillas in World War II,* Cebu City: MF Segura Publications, 1975.

Segura, Manuel F., *The Koga Papers: Stories of World War II in Cebu, Philippines,* Cebu City: MF Segura Publications, 1992.

Shaw, Henry I., *First Offensive: The Marine Campaign For Guadalcanal,* Marines in World War II Commemorative Series, Project Gutenberg, 1992.

Shinsato, Douglas & Tadanori, Urabe, *For That One Day: The Memoirs of Mitsuo Fuchida, Commander of the Attack on Pearl Harbor,* Hawaii: eXperience, inc., 2011.

Shores, Christopher, *Duel for the Sky: Ten Crucial Battles of World War II,* Grub Street, London 1985.

Sides, Hampton, "The Trial of General Homma," *American Heritage,* February/March 2007.

Sims, Richard, *Japanese Political History Since the Meiji Renovation 1868–2000,* Palgrave Macmillan, 2001.

Smith, Michael, *The Emperor's Codes: Bletchley Park and the Breaking of Japan's Secret Ciphers,* Bantam London, 2000.

Smith, Robert R., *Triumph in the Philippines: The War in the Pacific,* University Press of the Pacific, 2005.

Smith, Steven, T., *The Rescue: A True Story of Courage and Survival in World War II,* NY: Wiley, 2003.

Stanley, Elizabeth A. & Brooks, Risa (Ed), *Creating Military Power: The Sources of Military Effectiveness,* Stanford University Press, 2007.

Tanaka, Yuki, *Hidden Horrors, Japanese War Crimes in World War II,* Boulder, CO: Westview Press, 1997.

Thomas, Evan, *Sea of Thunder: Four Commanders and the Last Great Naval Campaign 1941–1945,* Simon and Schuster, 2007.

Toland, John, *The Rising Sun: The Decline and Fall of the Japanese Empire, 1936–1945,* NY: Modern Library (Reprint), 2003.

Totman, Conrad, *A History of Japan,* Wiley-Blackwell (2nd ed.), 2005.

Uno, Kazumaro, *Corregidor: Isle of Delusion,* Shanghai: The Mercury Press, 1942.

Villamor, Cayetano M., *My Guerrilla Years: Experiences and Observations During the Japanese Occupation in the Province of Cebu,* Villamor Pub. House, 1955.

Villamor, Jesus A. & Snyder, Gerald S., *They Never Surrendered: A True Story of Resistance in World War II,* Manila: Vera-Ryes, 1982.

Wainwright, Jonathan M, *General Wainwright's Story: The Account of Four Years of Humiliating Defeat, Surrender, and Captivity*, Doubleday & Co, 1946.

Wetzler, Peter, *Hirohito and War: Imperial Tradition and Military Decision Making in Pre-War Japan*, University of Hawaii Press, 1998.

Whitney, Courtney, *MacArthur: His Rendezvous With History*, NY: Knopf, 1956.

Willmott, H.P., *Barrier and the Javelin*. Annapolis: Naval Institute Press, 1983.

Woodward, C. Van & McFeely, William S., *The Strange Career of Jim Crow*, Oxford University Press, 2001.

Woodward, C. Vann, *The Battle for Leyte Gulf*, NY: Macmillan, 1947.

Willoughby, Maj. Gen. Charles A., *The Guerrilla Resistance Movement in the Philippines: 1941–1945*, NY: Vantage Press, 1972.

Yamawaki, Keizo, *Modern Japan and Foreign Laborers: Chinese and Korean Laborers in the late 1890s and early 1920s*, Akashi-shoten, 1994.

Zimmerman, John L., *The Guadalcanal Campaign*, Marines in World War II Historical Monograph, 1949.

U.S. MILITARY PUBLICATIONS
Reports of General MacArthur: Volume 1—The Campaigns of MacArthur in the Pacific; Volume II Part I—Japanese Operations in the Southwest Pacific Area; Part II—Japanese Operations in the Southwest Pacific Area

US ARMY IN WORLD WAR II: THE WAR IN THE PACIFIC
(US ARMY GREEN BOOK)
- Louis Morton: *Strategy and Command: The First Two Years*
- Louis Morton: *The Fall of the Philippines*
- John Miller Jr.: *Guadalcanal: The First Offensive*
- Samuel Milner: *Victory in Papua*
- John Miller Jr.: *The Reduction of Rabaul*
- Philip A. Crowl & Edmund G. Love: *Seizure of the Gilberts and the Marshalls*
- Philip A. Crowl: *Campaign in the Marianas*
- Robert Ross Smith: *Approach to the Philippines*
- M. Hamlin Cannon: *Leyte: The Return to the Philippines*
- Robert Ross Smith: *Triumph in the Philippines*

- Roy A. Appleman, James M. Burns, Russel A. Gugeler John Stevens: *Okinawa: The Last Battle*
- United States Strategic Bombing Survey [Pacific] Naval Analysis Division
- Interrogations of Japanese Officials OPNAV-P-03-100
- The Guerrilla Resistance Movement in the Philippines: Volume I, Intelligence Series
- Intelligence Activities in the Philippines During the Japanese Occupation, documentary
- Appendices Volume II Intelligence Series
- Combat Lessons Gained From Overseas Observers, Part I, II and III
- Far Eastern Survey Report
- Japanese Land Operations 08 Dec. 1941 to 08 June 1942—Campaign Study I, II

ARCHIVAL SOURCES
- Military History Institute, Carlisle Barracks, Pennsylvania
- MacArthur Memorial Archives, Norfolk, Virginia
- National Archives II, Modern Military Records, College Park, Maryland: RG24, RG38, RG85, RG319, RG338, RG360, RG407
- U.S. Naval Institute, Annapolis, Maryland
- Naval Historical Center
- Reports War Patrols USS *Crevalle,* USS *Nautilus,* USS *Narwhal,* USS *Haddo,* USS *Dudgeon*
- Dr. Greg Bradsher: *Japanese War Crimes and Related Topics: A Guide to Records at the National Archives*
- Various ATIS Reports
- Various Evacuation Reports

Messages to and from Cushing and related memorandums are contained in GHQ Messages in the Guerrilla Resistance Movement in the Philippines, Cushing to MacArthur and GHQ Messages in the Guerrilla Resistance Movement in the Philippines, MacArthur to Cushing, Records of General Headquarters, Southwest Pacific Area and United States Army Forces, Pacific (Record Group 496). Other related correspondence can be found in the Records of the Assistant Chief of Staff, G-2, Military Intelligence Section and the records of G-2, Philippine Section, both in Record Group 496.

UNPUBLISHED SOURCES

Fenton, Harry, *1942 Diary,* Charles T. R. Bohannon Collection, Military History Institute, Carlisle Barracks, PA, 1943.

Cushing, James M., *Autobiographical Notes*, unpublished manuscript in Military History Institute, Charles T.R. Bohannon Collection, Carlisle Barracks, PA, 1951.

Quezon, Manuel L., Jr., *Escape from Corregidor* (from the late author's unpublished memoirs).